Manufacturing Consent

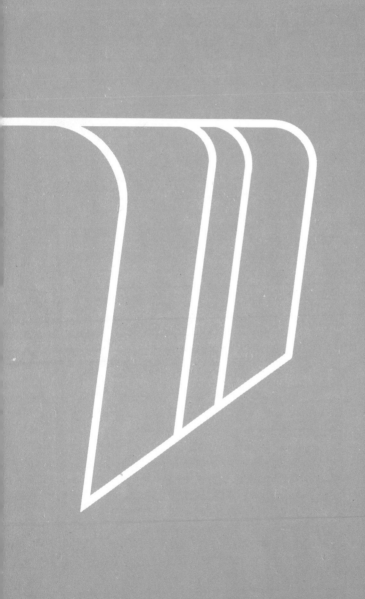

Michael Burawoy

Manufacturing Consent

Changes in the
Labor Process under
Monopoly Capitalism

The University of
Chicago Press
Chicago and London

Michael Burawoy is Assistant Professor of
Sociology at the University of California at
Berkeley. His previous publications include
The Colour of Class on the Copper Mines
(Manchester University Press, 1972).

The University of Chicago Press, Chicago, 60637
The University of Chicago Press, Ltd., London

Library of Congress Cataloging in Publication Data

Burawoy, Michael
    Manufacturing consent.

    Bibliography: p.
    Includes index.
    1. Industrial sociology—Case studies.
2. Industrial relations—Case studies.   3. Labor
and laboring classes—Case studies.   I. Title.
HD6955.B85   301.5'5   79-10188
ISBN 0-226-08037-4

To my mother and to the
memory of my father

Contents

vii

Preface

On 2 July 1974 I began work as a miscellaneous machine operator at the engine division of Allied Corporation—a multinational that produced, among other things, a wide range of agricultural equipment. The piecework machine shop of the small-parts department reminded me of Donald Roy's famous accounts of output restriction. After rereading those articles, I was struck by the similarities between his observations and my own at Allied. But this was nothing unusual. I knew that machine operators in Britain responded to piecework in just the same way that Roy described, by goldbricking, quota restriction, and by establishing informal ties with auxiliary workers. I therefore turned to Roy's 546-page Ph.D. dissertation, crammed full of vivid details relating his experiences between 1944 and 1945 in a shop that produced railway jacks. In the opening chapters I discovered that the layout of the machines—the drills, mills, lathes, etc.—was quite similar to the layout in my own shop, and I drew the reasonable conclusion that machine shops are generally organized in similar ways. Moving further into his dissertation each day, I eventually came upon a reference to the Illinois Central

Railroad, which Roy, like myself, rode from the University of
Chicago to where he worked. And then I encountered a reference to
the town where his company, which he called Geer, was situated. It
happened to be the same place where I was working and living. But
this was not surprising; after all, there were many machine shops in
the area. Then I caught a reference to a four-story building. Lo and
behold, according to my fellow workers, Allied had once been
located in a four-story building. Indeed, the building stood abandoned next to the Illinois Central Railroad tracks about a mile away
from the present site. Yes, a few of the old-timers could remember a
jack shop. The clincher came toward the end of the dissertation,
where Roy let drop the number of his union local. It was the same as
my own. I had indeed fortuitously stumbled on the very factory that
Roy had studied thirty years before. Even though Geer had been
taken over by Allied, Roy's Jack Shop and the small-parts department in which I worked bore a remarkably close resemblance to
each other. To discover what had remained the same on the shop
floor and what had changed in the thirty years separating Roy's
experience and mine inevitably became one of the central tasks of
my study.

Donald Roy's dissertation provided the empirical context. But the
analysis of the shop floor required a framework as well as a focus for
assessing changes over time. Roy's theoretical concerns were deeply
embedded in the tradition of industrial sociology and revolved
around "restriction of output." In attributing the source of this
"problem" to the rational response of workers to managerial irrationality, Roy successfully upended the gospel according to Elton
Mayo, which accounted for restriction of output in terms of
workers' nonlogical system of beliefs and their failure to comprehend managerial logic. The debate that threads through the industrial-sociology literature is caught up in the same problematic—why
workers don't work harder. The difference between radical and
conservative accounts lies in the assumptions they make. Radicals
point to restriction of output as an expression of class consciousness,
of the structural and inevitable conflict between capital and labor,
or of the alienating nature of work. Conservatives, on the other
hand, working from assumptions of underlying harmony, attribute
restriction of output to the natural indolence of workers, poor

communication between workers and managers, inadequate attention to the human side of the worker, or the "false consciousness" of workers in not appreciating that their interests are identical with those of management. As I understood the issue, the conflict and consensus perspectives both seemed out of tune with what was actually taking place on the shop floor. Instead, the terrain of discourse should be transformed and the original question posed in different terms. As the Lynds put it in 1929: Why do workers work as hard as they do?

The actual narrative in Roy's dissertation suggests that this is the more reasonable question. Machine operators in Roy's Jack Shop worked at a hectic pace and could become furious if interrupted. To be sure, it was a piece-rate system, but, as Roy makes clear, operators were not "busting their asses" for a few extra cents. Nor did they launch into their work through any great love for the bosses. Indeed, throughout his dissertation Roy highlights their resentment at being treated like "yardbirds." Yet, paradoxically, he tried to measure and explain the time that workers "waste." He did not examine why they didn't waste more time, although answers can be found in his account. Between the observations he made and the questions he posed there seems to be a basic incongruity.

The intensity of work struck me as forcibly at Allied as it did in Roy's account of Geer. In the beginning, largely out of fear and ineptitude, I shifted between contempt and awe for what I thought was an excessive expenditure of effort and ingenuity. Why should workers push themselves to advance the interests of the company? Why cooperate with and sometimes even exceed the expectations of those "people upstairs" who "will do anything to squeeze another piece out of you"? But it wasn't long before I too was breaking my back to make out, to make the quota, to discover a new angle, and to run two jobs at once—risking life and limb for that extra piece. What was driving me to increase Allied's profits? Why was I actively participating in the intensification of my own exploitation and even losing my temper when I couldn't? That is the problem I pose.

For Karl Marx it was also a problem, and his solution was coercion. At the time he wrote, unbridled subordination of labor to capital could explain much that took place on the shop floor. The system of piecework was used to intensify work arbitrarily, since workers were unable to resist arbitrary price-cutting. Where there were time wages, the overseer could arbitrarily fire workers for failing to fulfill their quotas. But with the emergence of trade unions and the protection of certain minimal rights of employment, the threat of losing one's job or failing to obtain a subsistence wage was gradually unhinged from the application of effort at the workplace. Coercion alone could no longer explain what workers did once they arrived on the shop floor. As my day man, Bill, assured me, "No one pushes you around here; you've got to get on with the work yourself." An element of spontaneous consent combines with coercion to shape productive activities.

Within the Marxist tradition the most sophisticated and enlightening analysis of consent is to be found in the prison writings of Antonio Gramsci. However, he is more concerned with the organization of consent in the political arena than he is with the labor process. In developing theories of the state, the party, and the intellectuals, he incorporates and combines force and persuasion, coercion and consent, domination and hegemony. Only in one essay, "Americanism and Fordism," does he examine the labor process itself. There he considers the revolutionary changes in the labor process taking place in the United States before, during, and after World War I. Unhampered by the parasitic residues of previous systems of domination, in the United States the entire life of the nation revolves around production; "hegemony here is born in the factory." In this study I try to develop and elaborate this suggestive but elusive comment. In contrast to the conventional wisdom among both Marxists and non-Marxists, I propose to demonstrate how consent is produced at the point of production—independent of schooling, family life, mass media, the state, and so forth. In short, the book takes off with a critique of Marx only to return, with the instruments of Marxism, to his focal interest in the labor process.

Let me hasten to add that this is not an exercise in neo-Marxism, Marxist revisionism, or any other label social scientists may apply to the Marxism they may wish to take seriously. Rather, it is a Marxist study. That means at least three things. First, I am concerned with change and continuity in capitalism conceived of as a particular way of appropriating unpaid labor from direct producers. Second, I assume that capitalism is not the last type of society in history.

There is no reason that history should somehow stop with capitalism. Third, I take as a point of departure the possibility and desirability of a fundamentally different form of society—call it communism, if you will—in which men and women, freed from the pressures of scarcity and from the insecurity of everyday existence under capitalism, shape their own lives. Collectively they decide who, how, when, and what shall be produced. It is in terms of this possibility, although not necessarily its inevitability, that Marxists interpret the present and the past. Sociology, on the other hand, treats this possibility as either utopian or with us already. It therefore looks upon the future as ironing out the imperfections of the present, and upon the present as the natural and inevitable culmination of the past.

Just as sociology has borrowed much from Marx and emerged in part through a debate with him, so Marxism cannot afford to dismiss sociology. Instead, it must selectively incorporate sociology's partial truths. Indeed, the most outstanding Marxist theoreticians of the twentieth century—Georg Lukács, Antonio Gramsci, Theodor Adorno, Herbert Marcuse, Louis Althusser, and Galvana Della Volpe—have all freely borrowed from liberal and conservative social theory and philosophy. Marx himself established the pattern by taking Hegel, Smith, and Ricardo, among others, as points of departure and transforming their insights into the basic elements of his own theories. In my endeavors to build a theory of the capitalist labor process, I shall take the dominant perspectives of industrial sociology as my point of departure and reintegrate its many insights into a Marxist framework.

Accordingly, the main dialogue that flows through these pages is with sociology. For reasons of space and ease of reading I have avoided entering into debates with alternative Marxisms. But it should not be inferred that there are no other Marxist approaches to the labor process. The most prominent and comprehensive of these is Harry Braverman's *Labor and Monopoly Capital,* which appeared while I was struggling to make out at Allied. No one writing on the labor process in 1978, particularly those writing in a Marxist tradition, can be uninfluenced by this creative rehabilitation of Marx's own theory of the labor process. As I have elaborated at length elsewhere, the approach I adopt here has been largely shaped in opposition to many of the dominant themes of *Labor and Monopoly Capital.*[1]

Limitations of space have imposed other constraints on the contents of this book. Although it would have brought more life to the account, for the sake of excursions into theorizing I decided to sacrifice some of the rich ethnographic data I had collected. Also dropped are fourteen graphs that statistically document some of the conclusions I draw, chiefly in chapter 8, where I discuss changes in the labor process that resulted from the recession of 1974–75. All the graphs can be found in my dissertation, "Making Out on the Shop Floor" (University of Chicago, 1976). A third omission is the ritual methodological appendix that sociologists, unlike anthropologists, for whom participant observation is their trade, feel compelled to include. The special problems of a study made over a period of time, in which the observations of one participant observer are compared with those of another, would perhaps make such an appendix more necessary. One particular problem I confronted in evaluating the differences between Roy's and my own observations lay in distinguishing actual changes in the labor process from differences in our perspectives and situations. Since we were in almost identical positions in the labor process, and since the experiences we recorded were largely a function of those positions, I am confident that the changes I present are "true" changes and not artifacts of any different orientation. As I suggested earlier, Roy's concern with restriction of output in no way restricted his vision and portrayal of the totality as it appeared to a machine operator. To help readers judge for themselves as to the validity of the comparison, I have quoted extensively from Roy's dissertation.

No doubt some will raise their eyebrows at the sweeping conclusions I draw from a single case study. What relevance, one may ask, does a study of a relatively insignificant piecework machine shop in the Midwest have for understanding the basic production technologies of modern industry—the assembly line, the continuous-flow technology, office work, and so forth? Such skepticism is frequently voiced by those steeped in the methodology of statistics, that is, of generalizing from a sample to a population. But there are ways of understanding the relationship of the part to the whole other than through statistical extrapolation. First, there is the position that regards the part as an expression of the totality, that is, each part contains within it the essential principles of the whole. By studying Allied in comparison with Geer, I can extract essential attributes of the labor process under advanced capitalism—for example, the construction of consent through the internal labor market and the internal state. Second, there is the complementary notion of the totality as composed of mutually interdependent parts. By understanding the relationship of Allied to other institutions, such as the family, the school, the state, the trade union, other corporations, and so on, we can begin to construct a picture of the entire society. This is generalization by extension from the part to the whole.

Yet my main endeavor has been to use the case study to illustrate and develop a theoretical framework for understanding and posing questions about the capitalist labor process. If the conclusions I draw provoke readers to deny their validity, I shall be more than satisfied that my efforts have not been in vain.

Field workers have numerous debts to record and tributes to pay. These acknowledgments are made somewhat difficult in the present case because, as a condition of my research as a participant observer, I had to assure Allied personnel, both management and workers, that I would preserve their personal anonymity and that of the company as well. For this reason I have also omitted all dates of publication when citing newspaper and journal articles about Allied Corporation.

My first acknowledgment is to my fellow workers. If it is nothing else, this study is about their lives on the shop floor, and its completion depended on their willingness to include me in their community. Although I frequently explained why I was there, they regarded my enterprise with a mixture of disbelief and amusement. Some couldn't understand why there wasn't an easier way of obtaining a degree than by working in a factory for a year. Others assured me that if I ever got my dissertation published, and if they were mentioned, it would surely be a best-seller. From time to time people would come up to me with a juicy story and say, "You, put that in your book." Their good humor and willingness to respond to some very strange inquiries made my task much more pleasant.

Particular thanks must go to my day man—Bill—who taught me how to get by and make out. He tolerated my incompetence and tempered the rougher sides of working life with his sense of the absurd. Even such characters as Morris (the trucker), Ed (the rate-buster), and Jim (the union president), although they frequently aroused the ire of their fellow workers, nevertheless added drama to the shop floor.

I should also like to thank trade-union officials and management for providing me with data and interviews. The personnel department was always helpful in supplying me with information. I was also able to trace, to places as far apart as Springfield, Illinois, and Southern California, a number of management officials associated with the old Geer Company. I am grateful to them for granting me interviews.

Intellectually, my debts are widespread. My interest in the organization of work was first cultivated in Zambia, where I undertook a number of studies of the copper industry between 1968 and 1972. During this period, Jaap van Velsen gave me an intensive training in social anthropology of the "Manchester School" variety. His teaching is deeply embedded in the way I orient myself to theory and research, and it pervades the analysis in this book. My debts to Bill Wilson, who chaired my dissertation committee at Chicago, are too numerous to record. From the beginning of my first year in graduate school he has given me unswerving moral support and constructive criticism in all my intellectual endeavors. Without his courage and his confidence in his own judgment that what I was doing could indeed be regarded as sociology—a position he held in opposition to a number of his colleagues—the dissertation, and now this book, would never have been written. My debt to Adam Przeworski can be expressed quite simply. His seminar on Marxist theories of the state in 1973–74 turned out to be a transformative intellectual experience. It had all the exhilaration of a puberty rite. Both Bill and Adam devoted a great deal of time and energy to guiding the dissertation through its various stages.

They were aided and abetted by Charles Bidwell, Raymond Smith, Richard Taub, and Arthur Stinchcombe, whose healthy skepticism and critical commentary forced me to reconsider and reformulate many parts of the study. Special mention must be made of Donald Roy, who enthusiastically supported my return to Geer.

His comments on an early paper were particularly important in confirming my interpretation of changes that had occurred over the past thirty years. Had I deliberately planned to undertake a "revisit," I doubt that I could have chosen a more astute and perceptive field worker or a richer account of shop-floor life.

Since arriving in Berkeley, I have been forced to shift my intellectual orientation somewhat. Both Margaret Cerullo and Tom Long have persuaded me of the dangers of competing with sociology on its own terrain in the production of a Marxist "science." They have convinced me that Marxism without critique is as dangerous as the history of Marxist "science" is ignominious. Their influence can be found in a number of places in the book. As friends who share my interests and with whom I share my work, both Erik Wright and Bill Friedland have been important in their encouragement and criticism of the completed dissertation. As a referee, Maurice Zeitlin went far beyond the call of duty in providing twenty-five pages of relentless criticism. The very substantial rewriting of the original manuscript is largely a response to the many weaknesses he drew to my attention. For their comments and advice at various stages I would like to thank José de Alencar, Paul Attewell, Robert Blauner, David Brody, Mitchell Fein, Bob Fitzgerald, Gretchen Franklin, Robert Jackson, Randy Martin, Lynne Pettler, David Plotke, and Ida Susser, and I owe thanks to Olivia Inaba for her expert typing and for catching many errors in the manuscript.

In adapting to, or resisting, the processes of mortification that characterize graduate life in the Department of Sociology at the University of Chicago, I depended on a number of friends for moral and intellectual support. I thank them all, but in particular Terence Halliday and Kathleen Schwartzman.

1

From Sociology to Marxism

One

The Demise of Industrial Sociology

An account of the demise of industrial sociology must examine trends in sociology and their relationship to changes in capitalism. The rise of "the end of ideology" through the 1950s led Daniel Bell, Clark Kerr, Seymour Martin Lipset, Talcott Parsons, Edward Shils, and others to claim that the major problems of capitalism had been overcome. All that remained was to perfect modern society. Among the accomplishments of United States capitalism they counted the incorporation of industrial workers and the institutionalization of industrial conflict. Strikes were "withering away," and those that continued to break out affected the marginal sectors of the labor force—those not yet integrated into the wider society.[1] The industrial worker was no more an agent of revolution than the burgeoning middle classes. Rather, workers were portrayed as "authoritarian" rather than radical; "capitalist" rather than "socialist."[2] A kind of euphoria had descended on the cold-war sociologists. In particular, blue-collar workers were no longer perceived as a "potential problem," and so they receded from the sociological focus.[3]

The shift of interest away from the industrial laborer was

accompanied by mounting criticism of the early studies of industrial behavior for their supposed myopia. These commentaries frequently took the seminal Western Electric studies of "restriction of output" as a point of departure. Plant sociology, as Clark Kerr and Lloyd Fisher referred to it, paid little attention to the environment. It ignored the constraints of technology and paid too much attention to "human relations." It ignored external orientations to work. It tended to downplay the economic rationality of the worker. It ignored class conflict and presented only managerial perspectives.[4] Without doubt, the various critiques were long overdue and provided important correctives. Yet they also overlooked the real if partial truths embedded in the early studies. In this work I shall try to rescue the rational kernel of plant sociology by thematizing these partial truths within a Marxist framework. Thus, rather than highlight the absurdity of isolating the factory from its environment, I shall try to pin down the precise nature of its isolation or relative autonomy—an autonomy that allowed the early researchers to make so many contributions to the understanding of industrial organizations. Rather than argue that conflict between management and worker is endemic or "structural," I shall show how both conflict and consent are organized on the shop floor. Rather than continually harp on the manipulativeness and inefficacy of the human-relations attempt to elicit greater cooperation from workers, I shall stress its essential truth, namely, that activities on the shop floor cannot be understood outside the political and ideological realms of the organization of production. While the view that workers are somehow irrational in their responses to work is an untenable position, the notion that they lean toward economic rationality is equally unsatisfactory. In this study I shall show how rationality is a product of the specific organization of production and is part and parcel of the factory "culture." In short, rather than dismiss the findings of industrial sociology, I shall move beyond them by placing and sometimes incorporating them into a broader perspective.

The Emergence of Organization Theory

The new studies that emerged to replace plant sociology shifted the focus of investigation to organizations in general—to hospitals, voluntary associations, trade unions, political parties, and so on. General theories, conceptual schemes, and focal problems were constructed to encompass behavior in all types of organizations. Three themes appeared to dominate the literature. First, there were the studies of bureaucracy—the functions and dysfunctions of rules.[5] These sprang from Max Weber's speculations on the relationship between bureaucracy and efficiency. A second set of studies developed a behavioralist framework that looked at organizations from the point of view of the individual as a decision-maker.[6] The psychological emphasis of these theorists can be seen as deriving from the human-relations perspectives on industrial work. Finally, a number of students began to develop frameworks for understanding the relationship between organizations and their environment. Some concentrated on the influence of socialization, community, etc., on industrial behavior, while others dwelt on the dependence of the organization on environments characterized by different degrees of uncertainty. Still others began to combine these two approaches in an attempt to understand the conditions of industrial development.[7]

Whatever their shortcomings, about which I shall have more to say below, all these developments represented important departures from the earlier studies. The questions they raise, as well the questions from which they arise, appear and reappear throughout the body of this work. The importance of rules will be central to my interpretation of shop-floor politics, although their implications will be understood in terms of domination rather than efficiency. The fact that even the most oppressed worker is faced with making decisions that appear to be significant is something no study of work can avoid. However, the importance of these choices for the production of consent, and the link between such "indeterminacy" at the individual or micro level and the more limited variation at the macro level, will be the focus of my discussion. Finally, I shall spell out the relationship between the organization and its environment in terms of both markets and the processes of socialization, and in the appendix I shall address these issues in terms of industrial development in Zambia. As in earlier industrial-sociology studies, advances made by organization theory will be incorporated into a Marxist framework.

With the subsumption of industrial sociology under organization theory, the distinctiveness of the profit-seeking capitalist enterprise is lost. At the same time, the development of conceptual schemes and theories to encompass all forms of organizations and associations expresses a very real truth, namely, the penetration of bureaucratic patterns and commodity relations into all areas of society. However, being unreflective about its roots in capitalist society, organization analysis loses this truth by projecting it into general theories that conceal the historically specific features of capitalist and, in particular, advanced capitalist society. Thompson's concern with an organization's ability to control or contain uncertainty in its environment reflects the emergence of large corporations or government agencies that possess resources to engage in buffering, leveling, forecasting, rationing, and so forth. As I hope to suggest, later in this study, restoring Thompson's insights to their political and economic context sheds much light on changes occurring in contemporary society. In the same vein, criticisms of studies like the Western Electric experiments are often based on observations made in organizations in a different period, without due regard to changes in the historical context—a context that the studies themselves deemphasize. Would the bank wiring room look the same today as it did in 1932? What differences might one observe, and how might we explain them? These are the sorts of questions a theory sensitive to historical change might pose.

There have, of course, been attempts to explain change in organizations; the point is that these attempts have been of an ahistorical nature. Descriptions of changes are elevated into spurious explanations of change through the constitution of natural laws of development—the ineluctable processes of rationalization, bureaucratization, the pursuit of efficiency, and so on.[8] Others, with less grand visions, substitute the empiricism of shopping lists for the development of explanations.[9] Where explanations are attempted, they tend to preserve the isolation of the organization from its environment, except in moments of transition. These are the theories of organizational persistence, which highlight efficiency, traditionalizing forces, vested interests, absence of competition, and so on.[10] But organizations do not simply "persist." Like any other enduring patterns of social relations, they have to be continually produced—that is, reproduced. While one of the unique features of the capitalist enterprise is its apparent ability to reproduce its own relations, it must be stressed that this autonomy is *only* apparent (relative). Theories of organizational persistence take for granted the conditions of persistence and ignore the tendencies toward the erosion of these conditions by the very reproduction of relations.

Once the question of reproduction is posed, one must go beyond the organization and examine the interrelationship of the different parts of society that guarantee its reproduction. But this involves, first, examining *what* different organizations produce and, second, recognizing not only that they produce useful things or "services" but that, directly or indirectly, they also produce profit. It involves the construction of a concrete totality that represents capitalist or advanced capitalist society—in fact, the construction of a theory of advanced capitalism. Not only would it go beyond organization theory; it would deny the latter its right to exist as a distinctive enterprise. It would restore the timeless generalities of organization theory to their specific historical context. And, by the same token, it would unmask appearances, link the part to the whole, the past to the future, and thereby shatter the appearance of naturalness and inevitability in the present order of things.

The Paradox of Organization Theory

In the development of its general and abstract concepts, organization theory has missed the particular and concrete products of organizations. It has substituted formal rationality for substantive rationality and has underplayed the essential feature of the capitalist labor process—the transformation of nature or raw materials into useful things, on the one hand, and into profit, on the other. Instead, the ahistorical formulations are upheld by dwelling on universal aspects of social relations and by thrusting aside concrete action, practices, the doing and making of things. And it is precisely out of this one-sided picture that a fundamental paradox emerges. These studies, both the early and the late ones, rest on one or the other, or on some combination, of two divergent premises, namely, *the assumption of underlying harmony* and *the necessity of social control.* Taken together, these premises appear contradictory; for if there is underlying harmony and consensus is not problematical, then why is social control important or necessary? And, conversely, if social control is so important, then how can we take consensus as given?

The paradox has remained latent in part because the two themes have in general been developed separately, by authors drawing on the different sociological traditions originating with Emile Durkheim, on the one hand, and Max Weber, on the other. In this way the contradictory assumptions have been kept apart. Moreover, writers in the two traditions have not always pursued the implications of their respective positions. Thus, where social control has been a focal concern, no theory of conflict has been developed to establish the necessity of social control. When the emphasis has been on harmony, harmony is assumed rather than explained, and conflict is looked on as pathological or even accidental. I will deal with each theme in turn.

The assumptions of the social-control literature have been formulated by Arnold Tannenbaum:

> Organization implies control. A social organization is an ordered arrangement of individual human interactions. Control processes help circumscribe idiosyncratic behaviors and keep them conformant to the rational plan of organization. Organizations require a certain amount of conformity as well as integration of diverse activities. It is the function of control to bring about conformance to organizational requirements and achievement of the ultimate purposes of the organization. The coordination and order created out of the diverse interests and potentially diffuse behaviors of members is largely a function of control. [11]

But what are these "idiosyncratic" behaviors, "diverse" interests, etc., that have to be controlled? Can one study control in organizations without a theory of what is to be controlled? Tannenbaum manages to do so by asking general questions of the type, "In general how much say or influence does the manager of your station have on what the following groups do in the company?" [12] So, without reference to the activities being controlled or to the resources wielded to exercise that control, let alone to the "deviant" tendencies against which control is directed, Tannenbaum is able to characterize organizations by their total amount of control and its distribution. This purely formal mode of measuring control (is he in fact measuring control at all?) enables him to compare very different types of organizations and to construct typologies of "control." But what "control" is all about—why it is there in the first place and the possibility that it has to be understood, at least in part, in terms of its function—is totally lost from sight.

Amitai Etzioni's synthesis does recognize that the underlying impetus to social control cannot be ignored.[13] Etzioni stands in the Weberian tradition of organization theory and creates typologies based on the type of power (resources) mobilized to elicit conformity (compliance) and the types of "involvement" of participants. Although he acknowledges that conflict is endemic in organizations, Etzioni fails to present a basis or source for particular patterns of conflict. While he does advance beyond Weber in positing different orientations of participants, he provides no theory to account for these orientations or to explain how they generate conflict. At best he provides ad hoc hypotheses, which tend to lose historical specificity under the pressure to develop more general formulations.

In the other tradition, which postulates an underlying harmony among members of the industrial organization, the focal concern is the very presence of conflict. Those who have been concerned with efficiency and productivity have frequently located the source of conflict in workers' adherence to a "lower social code" and their failure to comprehend the "economic logic" of management.[14] From a different perspective, the same observations signify an embryonic form of class consciousness.

Others have suggested that conflict stems from the lack of integration of worker and organization. New patterns of management, including employee-centered supervision and granting greater responsibility to the work group, are proposed for reintegrating individual and organization.[15] Another perspective attributes lack of cooperation to the agencies of industrial work and suggests minor restructuring of the organization of production. "Job enlargement," "job enrichment," "job rotation," and so on, are part of the everyday vernacular of management consultants. Less concerned with social engineering, Robert Blauner has tried to establish a curvilinear relationship between the level of "alienation" and the type of "technology," suggesting that automation will usher in a less oppressive regime of labor.[16] The approach of the sociotechnical systems associated with the Tavistock Institute emphasize a lack of congruence between the technical and social systems as the source of inefficiency and conflict.[17]

In combating the literature on "restriction of ouput," which portrays workers as compulsive soldierers, a number of studies document the ways in which management is responsible for lapses in the translation of effort into output. In other words, the responsibility for "restriction of output" is placed at the feet of management.[18] A related analysis attributes conflict to uncertainty in the process of production or in the environment.[19] Here, as in all the above cases, it is implied that, in principle, the source of conflict can be removed. That is, conflict is not inherent or inevitable but reflects some irrationality—human, technical, or environmental—that is not a necessary feature of capitalism.

Finally, mention must be made of those who, while retaining the assumption of an underlying harmony of interests, nevertheless regard conflict as endemic to the industrial organization. The "unitary" framework of industrial relations is replaced by a "pluralist" framework, which conceives of the workplace as an arena for a number of competing groups.[20] The pluralism of the factory is a sibling of the pluralism of the political realm, in which groups compete for "values" through a shared framework of norms and rules. Undoubtedly, I am doing some injustice to these studies by forcing them into the mold of the "harmony" or "social-control" perspectives. Undoubtedly, many of them combine features of both perspectives. But none of them resolves the paradox, because they all miss the specifically capitalist aspects of the labor process—the very features that provide the focus of my study.

A False Resolution of the Paradox

It is necessary to consider one possible resolution of the paradox that has gained some currency. It emerges from what is sometimes referred to as "the conflict" perspective. An underlying, ever-present, and structured conflict is postulated, so that, to the extent that harmony prevails, social control must also be ubiquitous and systematic. Moreover, the outbreak of conflict signifies not some irrationality but rather a lapse of, or inadequate, social control. I shall take as representative of this rather diffuse school of thought the important work of William Baldamus, who views "the entire system of industrial production...as a system of administrative controls which regulate quantity, quality and distribution of human effort."[21]

> We shall assume from the start that employer-employee relations present a structure of differentiated power that reflects unequally distributed advantages and disadvantages. Consequently the emphasis will be on the causes of conflict and disorganization. This will have the advantage of obtaining a more consistent explanation of the relevant observations than has so far been possible. But some unexpected difficulties will also arise. Once the assumption of a harmonious and self-regulating system is removed, we are faced with the vastly complicated jungle of industrial administration that would seem to be without any system at all. If conflict is basic and unavoidable, how do we account for the apparent stability of employer-employee relations when there are no strikes, no grievances, no dissatisfactions? In other words, it is now the ordinary pursuit of work, the daily run of routine activities, that has to be explained.[22]

But this framework is never coherently elaborated, because, as with the social-control literature, we are still not treated to a systematic analysis of the patterns of underlying conflict, of the "structure of differentiated power that reflects unequally distributed advantages and disadvantages."

Baldamus successfully sidesteps the issue by arguing that the day-to-day expenditure of labor on the shop floor is governed by a normative relationship between effort and reward. That Baldamus is not able to make a convincing argument for the existence of a norm rather than an average is less significant than his location of the source of the norm, the content of a "fair day's work," in socialization processes outside the factory.[23] In this way the application of effort is detached from the postulated underlying conflict, which then becomes irrelevant in Baldamus's framework. What has to be explained—the normative relationship between reward and effort, and the underlying conflict—is taken as given. Why should reward be based on effort in the first place? Why do workers act as though this is a principle that regulates their lives when capitalism blatantly refutes its validity every moment of its existence? These are questions a framework that takes capitalism for granted cannot even pose, let alone answer.

Conclusion

All these theories are unsatisfactory. Insofar as they stress social control, they tend at best to introduce some typologies but miss their historical roots. Moreover, if such theories acknowledge the existence of some underlying conflict, they fail to pin down its form and origin. The harmony theories, on the other hand, have difficulty, as we have seen, in accounting for the outbreak of conflict and the empirical existence of punitive or coercive controls. Industrial sociology and organization theory proceed from the facts of consensus or social control. They do not explain them. It is necessary, therefore, to break with the transhistorical generalities and partial perspectives of industrial sociology and organization theory and to dispense with metaphysical assumptions about underlying conflict or harmony. Conflict and consent are neither latent nor underlying but refer to directly observable activities that must be grasped in terms of the organization of the labor process under capitalism. Conflict and consent are not primordial conditions but products of the particular organization of work. We must avoid being trapped in the various debates between "consensus theory" and "conflict theory" and move the discourse onto an entirely different terrain. To do this we must restore historical context to the discussion. Our first task, therefore, is to comprehend the specificity of the capitalist labor process as one that is distinct from both precapitalist and postcapitalist labor processes.

Two

Toward a Theory of the Capitalist Labor Process

The political implications of sociology stem from the adoption of a particular philosophy of history in which the future is the perfection of the present, and the present is the inevitable culmination of the past. From this all else follows. By taking the particular experiences of capitalist society and shaping them into universal experiences, sociology becomes incapable of conceiving of a fundamentally different type of society in the future; history is endowed with a teleology whose realization is the present. The sociological imagination is riveted in the present. What exists is natural, inevitable, and unavoidable.

In order to conceive of, to anticipate, something "new," one must begin with different premises, which regard history as discontinuous and capitalist societies as fundamentally different from precapitalist and postcapitalist societies. But differences can be grasped only in relationship to one another. A basis for comparison is necessary—a set of general concepts of universal applicability. But, their applicability must rest on their "particularization." General concepts can be specified in order to develop theories of particular societies. There are no general theories, only *general concepts and particular theories.* History is received neither as a succession of "facts" nor as the teleological emergence of the present; rather, it is constituted as a discontinuous succession of particular societies. A distinction is drawn between history as the dynamics of a given society, which is nothing less than a theory of that society, and history as the transition from one society to another. Only this dual conception of history can comprehend a future at odds with the present without being utopian.[1]

In this chapter I will present some general concepts—mode of production, relations of production, labor process, relations in production, reproduction, politics, ideology, interests, and so on—and will then indicate how they can be particularized to enable us to understand different societies. I shall outline the rudiments of a theory of feudalism and a theory of capitalism in order to grasp the specificity of the capitalist labor process.

Premises and Concepts

We must begin at the beginning

> by stating the first premise of all human existence, and therefore, of all history, the premise, namely, that men must be in a position to live in order to be able to "make history." But life involves before everything else eating and drinking, a habitation, clothing and many other things. The first historical act is thus the production of the means to satisfy these needs, the production of material life itself.[2]

In order to make history, men and women must survive, and, in order to survive, they must transform nature into useful things. Such activities we call economic activities. A society comes into being when men and women enter into social relations with one another as they transform nature. The particular relations so produced and reproduced define the character of economic activities, that is, the manner or *mode of production.* History is constituted out of different modes of production, that is, different patterns of social relations into which men and women enter as they transform nature. In other words, history is periodized into a succession of dominant modes of production.

The defining set of social relations in a class society is between those who produce the necessities of life and those who live off the product of others; between those who produce surplus and those who expropriate surplus; between those who are exploited and those who exploit; between peasant and lord; between worker and capitalist. Class societies can be distinguished from one another by the particular manner in which surplus labor is expropriated from the direct or immediate producers, that is, by the *relations of production.*

A mode of production is not simply a set of relations that define a particular way of distributing and appropriating labor time and its product. It is also a particular manner of appropriating nature, or producing useful things.[3] Thus, the relations of production are always combined with a corresponding set of relations into which men and women enter as they confront nature, as they transform raw materials into objects of their imagination. This is the *labor process.* It has two analytically distinct but concretely inseparable components—a relational and a practical aspect.[4] I refer to the relational aspect of the labor process as the *relations in production* or *production relations.* They are, for example, the relations of the shop floor into which workers enter, both with one another and with management. In its practical aspect the labor process is a set of activities that transform raw materials into useful objects or fractions of useful objects with the assistance of instruments of production. This involves labor, the expenditure of effort, the translation of the capacity to work into actual work, of labor power into labor. It is in this practical activity that the human species exhibits its potential for creativity, while the relational aspect expresses the potential for an ethical community of freely associated producers. The relations of production shape the form and development of the labor process, and the labor process in turn sets limits on the transformation of the mode of production.

The particular mode of expropriation of surplus labor defines a set of conditions that must be met if the mode of production is to persist, that is, if its characteristic social relations of production are to be *reproduced.* In other words, as a condition for the existence of a given mode of production, there must be a set of mechanisms that guarantee the reproduction of the relations of production. By definition, these mechanisms are *political* structures. Political activities concern the reproduction (or transformation) of social relations.[5] A particular mode of production, therefore, defines a corresponding mode of politics:

> The specific economic form, in which unpaid surplus-labour is pumped out of direct producers, determines the relationship of rulers to ruled, as it grows directly out of production itself and, in turn, reacts upon it as a determining element. Upon this, however, is founded the entire formation of the economic community which grows up out of the production relations themselves, thereby simultaneously its specific political form. It is always the direct relationship of the owners of the means of production to the direct producers—a relation always naturally corresponding to a definite stage in the development of the methods of labour and thereby its social productivity—which reveals the innermost secret, the hidden basis of the entire social structure, and with it the political form of the relation of sovereignty and dependence, in short, the corresponding specific form of state.[6]

It is in this sense that we can speak of "determination in the last instance by the economic"; that is, we can say that the social structure as a whole is to be understood in terms of the conditions of existence of the economic, of the reproduction of the relations of production. When we turn to specific modes of production, we shall see how this works itself out concretely.

The production of things is simultaneously not only the production and reproduction of social relations but also the production of an *experience* of those relations. As men and women engage in production, they generate a world of appearances, "... not the relation between them and their conditions of existence, but *the way* they live the relation between them and their conditions of existence: this presupposes both a real relation and an '*imaginary*,' '*lived*' relation."[7] Thus, in his discussion of the fetishism of commodities, Marx writes, "it is a definite social relation between men, that assumes, in their eyes, the fantastic form of a relation between things."[8] That is, in a commodity-producing society, the social nature of production is expressed only through the market, in which "isolated" producers or groups of producers exchange their goods.

It is there that they discover that the value of their goods is determined by the embodied labor. What they can exchange for their own goods is determined by the labor embodied in the produce of others, something beyond their control. That is, relations among producers appear as a relationship among things. In this way the social nature of labor is stamped on things, which turn on their producers like an alien power over them. As a lived experience, the "commodification" of social relations (and, the opposite side of the coin, the personification of things) detaches itself from the conditions that produced it; it thus assumes an autonomy of its own and appears to be natural and inevitable.

No amount of *knowledge* (theory, science, etc.) of the inseparable connection between the structure of the relations of production and the lived experience of those relations can alter that experience, just as no amount of science can affect the fact that the sun appears to move around the earth or that a stick appears to bend when it is placed in water. "The recent discovery, that the products of labour, so far as they are values, are but material expressions of the human labour spent in their production. . .by no means dissipates the mist through which the social character of labour appears to us to be an objective character of the products themselves."[9] Lived experience presents what is socially produced as "natural" and beyond human control. It is unaffected by knowledge and the consciousness individuals carry. It makes no difference whether the occupant of a place in production be Karl Marx, John Rockefeller, or Joe Hill, the fetishism of commodities will be equally real to all.

What is the relationship between this world of appearances and *ideology?* Within Marxist literature there is tension over the autonomy of ideology with respect to lived experience, a tension to be found in Marx's own writings.[10] Clearly, this relationship is historically determined, but here I will lean toward emphasizing lived experience and the constraints it imposes on ideology. Ideology is, therefore, not something manipulated at will by agencies of socialization—schools, family, church, and so on—in the interests of a dominant class. On the contrary, these institutions elaborate and systematize lived experience and only in this way become centers of ideological dissemination.[11] Moreover, dominant classes are shaped by ideology more than they shape it. To the extent that they engage in active deception, they disseminate propaganda, not ideology. As a first approximation, it is lived experience that produces ideology, not the other way around. Ideology is rooted in and expresses the activities out of which it emerges. As Althusser writes, citing Pascal, "Kneel down, move your lips in prayer, and you will believe."[12]

People do not carry ideologies around in their heads. They carry theories, knowledge, attitudes in the form of consciousness. These become an ideology, "a material force once it has gripped the masses."[13] Ideology is neither "a cold utopia" nor "learned theorizing" but a "creation of concrete phantasy which acts on the dispersed and shattered people to arouse and organize its collective will."[14] Ideology acts as a cement for social relations; it binds individuals to one another; it connects immediate experiences to each other, to the past, and to the future. Thus, Marxism as a theory of how capitalism works *can* become an ideology—a political force—during certain periods or among certain sectors of the working class. It *may* be more likely to grip people outside the workplace in political activities rather than in the workplace, where it has traditionally been thought to have "made most sense." During periods of crisis or struggle, when the "naturalness" of lived experience is shaken, a wider range of theories can become a political force. At such times competition between ideologies may be more important. But it is clear that teaching theories in school is not the same as producing an ideology. Making Marxism the official "thought" of a country does not necessarily affect the way people behave at work.

What is the significance of ideology? In what sense is it a material force? Since ideology expresses the way people experience relations, so is it through ideology that "men become conscious of...conflict and fight it out."[15] Eugene Genovese shows how struggles between slaves and slave-owners were shaped by paternalism—an ideology that expressed the "humanity" of slaves in the context of a mode of production that did not recognize slaves as other than objects.[16] When slaves rejected slavery, they embraced or rejected paternalism according to the form of religious ideology. According to Genovese, religion was a critical factor in the accommodation of slaves to paternalism in the South and in their rebellions elsewhere. When struggle takes place on the terrain of ideology, the consequences of struggle must be understood through an examination of the actual relations behind ideology. To take a relatively clear example, in South Africa struggles among classes take place on the terrain of racism, but the consequences can be grasped only by analyzing the reproduction of the relations that both shape racism and are obscured by racism.

But what are these struggles if they are not struggles over the realization of *interests?* And where do interests come from? From what has been said so far, they clearly emerge out of ideology. However, this is not the most generally accepted view. As we saw in chapter 1, much of sociology takes interests as given. It is here that we encounter the problem of rationality and irrationality, logical and nonlogical behavior, and interests real and false, short- and long-term, immediate and fundamental, arising out of some discrepancy between actual and postulated behavior. Where interests are taken as given, ideology becomes a resource that people manipulate to advance their "interests" or a cement that contains conflict or minimizes strain.[17] On the other hand, where interests are not imputed, they are empirically discovered or constructed in a tautological fashion after the event. A particular group voted thus because its interests are so and so. Why are its interests so and so? Because it voted thus. But why, for example, do workers sometimes fight for their racial interests and sometimes for their class interests? The problem is to explain interests in any given situation, not to describe them empirically. Rather than postulate interests either metaphysically or empirically, we must develop a theory of interests, a theory of how they are constituted out of ideology.

It is clear that, as we have defined them, interests cannot be understood outside the particular spontaneous consciousness of social relations, that is, outside a theory of those relations themselves. The interests in material gain, in quantity rather than quality, in competition in a commodity-producing society, are inscribed in the "fetishism of commodities" analyzed by Marx as the consequence of a particular form of production. This is the same as the problem of rationality.

> ...we can see the rationality of the economic behaviour of individuals as one aspect of a wider, social rationality, based upon the internal relationship between economic and non-economic structures in the different types of society.... It can then be

understood that, without a scientific knowledge of the internal
relations of the social structures, the economist cannot acquire
more than a statistical knowledge of individual preferences,
which necessarily appear to him as matters of taste, in relation to
which the question of rationality does not arise. [18]

But if interests are wholly of, and born in, a given society, how do
we talk about struggles leading beyond that society? How do we
conceive of a society with an alternative "rationality," a society in
which history is made consciously and collectively, not unwittingly, a
society in which there is no discrepancy between appearances and
reality, between experience and the object of appearance—in short, a
society in which there is no ideology and in which there are therefore
no "interests"? Indeed, as Agnes Heller has persuasively argued, the
very concept of interest reflects the standpoint of capitalist society,
in which individuals become slaves to motives beyond their control.
The concept of interest expresses the reduction of needs to greed.
Instead of "fundamental interests" or "class interests" she speaks
of *"radical needs."* " 'Class interest' cannot be the motive of a class
struggle that goes beyond capitalist society: the true motive, free
from fetishism, is represented by the 'radical needs' of the working
class." [19] But does capitalism tolerate such radical needs? Does it
generate them, as Marx asserted, as a condition for its own development? If so, then how, where, and why? And under what conditions
might such radical needs be realized in a new society? What circumstances might become the basis for turning a potentiality into an
actuality?

From Feudalism to Capitalism

Having developed some general concepts, we can now particularize
them to illuminate the capitalist labor process. But in order to
highlight the features of the capitalist labor process and establish its
distinctiveness, it is necessary to compare it with a noncapitalist
labor process. What comparison should we adopt? It is tempting to
use socialism, in order simultaneously to engage in a critique of
capitalism. However, there is little indication that the labor process
in so-called socialist countries is all that different, and the comparison would therefore shed little light on the capitalist labor
process. Alternatively, we could construct an ideal type of socialist

labor process; but such idealizations are normally constructed through an inversion of selected features of capitalism and therefore presuppose an understanding of the capitalist labor process. A contrast with precapitalist modes of production is more appropriate. It is possible to draw a contrast between capitalism and *all* precapitalist modes of production based on the "extraeconomic" elements necessary for the appropriation of surplus labor in the latter and absent in the former. But the variation among precapitalist modes of production is so great and what they share is so minimal that a comparison of this kind promises limited dividends. I shall therefore pick one precapitalist mode of production—feudalism—about which a great deal has been written and which has existed historically in forms untouched by capitalism.

Within the Marxist literature there have been numerous debates over the nature of feudalism, usually in connection with the transition to capitalism.[20] However, we are not directly concerned here with the nature of feudalism itself or with the transition to capitalism; we are using it only as a contrast to capitalism. Therefore, it is not necessary to enter into the controversies over the nature of the feudal dynamic, the dissolution of feudalism, the role of class struggle in this dissolution and in the genesis of capitalism, the relationship between town and country, the role of the market in all of these, and so forth. Rather, our conceptualization of feudalism will be directed to throwing the form of its labor process into relief. Moreover, our conceptualization does not correspond to any historically concrete feudalism, for this would present a more complex and variegated picture than the one I am about to offer. In fact, I am going to confine myself to a discussion of one particular form of feudalism, the one that Jairus Banaji refers to as its pure, classical, or crystallized form, namely, the one based on labor services.[21] Ultimately, the proof of this feudal pudding rests in what it will reveal about capitalism.

A defining characteristic of feudal relations of production is appropriation of surplus labor in the form of rent. Serfs, in order to maintain themselves on the land they hold at the will of the lord, are compelled to render a rent in kind, money, labor services, or, more commonly, in some combination of these. I shall restrict myself here to rent in the form of labor services that serfs perform on the land of their lord—the lord's demesne. The cycle of production in its simplest form is then as follows: serfs work on the lord's demesne for so many days each week, and during the remaining days they cultivate their "own" land for the means of survival. The former is fixed and surplus labor; the latter is necessary labor.

Five features of this pure form of feudalism should be stressed. First, necessary and surplus labor are separated in both time and place. Serfs work on the demesne in "exchange" for the right to cultivate a plot or strip of land, to gain access to common fields, and so on. Second, the serfs are in immediate possession of the means of their subsistence, that is, they consume the crops that they themselves grow. Third, serfs are able to set the instruments of production in motion independently of the lord. To be sure, they cooperate in ploughing, harvesting, and so forth, particularly under an open-field system of crop rotation, but they possess their own tools and can use these without the intervention of the lord.[22] Fourth, although serfs organize the labor process on their own land largely independently of the lord, production on the demesne is supervised and coordinated by his agents—the reeve or bailiff. Actual work obligations are laid down in minute detail in the manorial custumals and enforced in the manorial courts by representatives of the lord.[23] That is, the productive activities that constitute surplus labor are specified and secured through political-legal institutions. Finally, the lord's right to exclude serfs from the land they cultivate for their own use, a right protected by regional apparatuses of the state, renders labor services inescapable. At the same time, ideologies of fair exchange and military protection present the system of exploitation as natural and inevitable.

Under the feudal mode of production, surplus labor is transparent. It is produced neither automatically nor simultaneously with subsistence production. Rather, serfs can produce the means of existence independently of working for the lord, and surplus labor therefore has to be extracted through extraeconomic means. In short, because surplus labor is separated from necessary labor, the appropriation of surplus is directly intertwined with the political, legal, and ideological realms. Is this true for capitalism? Do direct producers spend a certain amount of time working for capitalists and a certain amount for themselves? Are workers in possession of the means of subsistence as a product of their own activities? Are workers able to set the instruments of production into motion themselves, independently of the capitalist? Does the appropriation of surplus labor depend on the intervention of extraeconomic means in the cycle of production? The answer to all these questions is no.

Under capitalism workers cannot by themselves transform nature and autonomously provide their own livelihood. They are dispossessed of access to their own means of production—raw materials as well as instruments of production. In order to survive, direct producers have no alternative but to sell their capacity to labor—their labor power—to the capitalist in return for a wage, which they then turn into the means of existence. In working for a capitalist, they turn their labor power into labor; their wage appears as compensation for the entire period they are at work. In reality they are paid only the equivalent, in monetary terms, of the value they produce in part of the working day, say five out of eight hours. The five hours constitute necessary labor (necessary for the reproduction of labor power), while the remaining three hours constitute surplus or unpaid labor. Just as workers are dependent on a market for selling their labor power for a wage, so capitalists are dependent on a market for selling their commodities. Surplus labor produces not only useful things but commodities that can be bought and sold, that is, things with exchange value. In other words, under capitalism, surplus labor takes the form of *surplus value*, which is realized as profit in the market.

Five points of contrast with feudalism should be stressed. First, there is no separation in either time or space between necessary and surplus labor. This distinction, upon which a Marxist theory of the labor process rests, does not appear as such at the phenomenal level. The entire product of labor is appropriated by the capitalist. In normal times necessary and surplus labor are experienced only through their effects: the daily appearance of the worker at the factory gates or office doors and, on the other side, the continued existence of the capitalist and his agents, who keep the gates and doors open, replace worn-out machines, pay out wages, and realize a profit in the market. Only in crisis situations is it possible for the workings of capitalism to be laid bare and for the existence of necessary and surplus labor to assume an unmediated force of its own.

Second, workers cannot live off what they produce on the shop floor. Serfs can live off the land, but laborers cannot live off pins, let alone pin heads. The only way that laborers gain access to the means of existence (except, of course, through poor relief, unemployment compensation, etc.) is through the market—through the sale of their labor power in return for a wage, which is then converted into consumption goods. Equally, capitalists, if they are to remain capitalists, are dependent on selling their products and purchasing labor power and other necessaries in a market. The existence of a market as a *necessary* feature of capitalism, upon which all agents of production depend, sets capitalism apart from feudalism. Although markets are by no means incompatible with feudalism, they are not necessary to it.

Third, workers neither possess the means of production nor can they set them in motion by themselves. They are subordinate to, rather than in control of, the labor process through their subjugation to the agents of capital—the managers who direct the labor process. At the same time, and this is the fourth point, this direction of the labor process is very different from the supervision and coordination exercised by the agents of the lord in demesne production. Under feudalism, productive activities are largely fixed outside the labor process, in the manorial courts. The functions of controlling and coordinating the labor process are separated in time and place. Under capitalism, the direct producers render labor power, not labor services. There is no prior specification of the productive activities; instead, management attempts to extract as much labor from workers as possible. That is, management exists not merely to coordinate, as under demesne production, but also to control. The functions of control and coordination, separate under feudalism, become two aspects of the same process under capitalism.[24] Accordingly, struggles over productive activities take place on the shop floor, whereas struggles over labor services take place outside the labor process in the political-legal arena of the manorial courts.[25]

Finally, just as extraeconomic elements shape the expenditure of labor in the feudal labor process but not in the capitalist labor process, so the same contrast carries over into the reproduction of the relations of production. The relationship between lord and serf is guaranteed through the lord's right to exclude the serf from the land, a right defined and protected in political and legal institutions, whereas the relationship between worker and capitalist is based on their *economic* interdependence. Under capitalism, the production of commodities is simultaneously the production of the laborer on the one side (through necessary labor—the wage equivalent) and of the capitalist on the other side (through surplus labor and its realization in the form of profit); that is, the production of commodities is, simultaneously, the reproduction of the relations of production, whereas, under feudalism, production for the lord is connected to production for the serf through political and legal mechanisms.

The political, legal, and ideological institutions of capitalism guarantee the external conditions of production. In contrast, their feudal counterparts directly intervened in the cycle of production to ensure its continuity and to determine its content, that is, to reproduce the relations of production and the relations in production. Therefore, the political, legal, and ideological institutions of feudalism recognized agents of production for what they were—villeins, cotters, franklins, reeves, lords, and so on—whereas, under capitalism, these institutions mystify the productive status of workers, capitalists, managers, etc. Thus, the political, legal, and ideological apparatuses of the capitalist state transform relations among agents of production into relations among citizens, sexes, races, and so on. Moreover, the capitalist state, because it is relatively independent of the economic in a way that the feudal state is not, can assume a variety of forms—dictatorship, fascism, parliamentary democracy, apartheid, etc. Even such a cursory examination of feudalism and capitalism suggests how the conditions of existence (reproduction) of a mode of production shape a corresponding set of political and ideological structures.

The Essence of the Capitalist Labor Process

Having established certain distinctive features of the capitalist mode of production by contrasting it with a particular idealized variant of the feudal mode of production, we can focus more closely on the generic character of the capitalist labor process. A worker is employed by a capitalist—a firm. At the end of the week the worker is paid a wage, based on either an hourly rate or a piece rate that is fixed before the worker enters the factory gates, that is, before the expenditure of effort. Furthermore, the worker receives the wage long before the capitalist has had the opportunity to realize the value of the product of that labor. How is it, then, that, per unit of product, a capitalist can commit himself to a wage that will be no higher than what he can obtain for that unit of product and no lower than what is necessary to attract workers and to maintain their families? More specifically, how is the labor process organized so as to guarantee the production of surplus value?

To claim that capitalism would collapse if there were no surplus value is not to explain its existence. If class struggles can force the price of labor power (the wage) above its value, that is, above the labor time socially necessary for its reproduction, then what places a limit on the rising wage level? How can the capitalist know beforehand at what level the wage per unit of product will exceed the price it can fetch? In talking about the tendency for the rate of profit to fall, Marx assumed, among other things, that workers continue to produce surplus value in ever increasing amounts but that the number of workers (variable capital) and therefore total surplus value shrink relative to the expansion of total capital. That is, Marx's analysis of the demise of capitalism is premised on workers producing more than their wage.

We can see why the production of surplus value is a problem when we compare the position of the capitalist to that of the lord. Under feudalism it is surplus labor in the form of rent that is fixed ahead of time, whereas under capitalism it is the wage that is predetermined. Just as serfs have to fend for themselves in the time remaining for their own production, so capitalists or their managerial agents have to organize the labor process so as to ensure the extraction of unpaid labor.

Marx, of course, had a great deal to say about the mechanisms of securing surplus value in the labor process. Thus, he described how, prior to the Factory Acts in England, capitalists could prolong the working day. When restrictions on working hours were legislated, capitalists resorted to intensification of the labor process through speedups, introduction of piece wages, and mechanization. But these gave only temporary competitive advantages to individual capitalists, since, eventually, the pace of work was stepped up by their competitors. Reducing the amount of necessary labor (that is, cheapening the costs) in the reproduction of labor power by increasing productivity in the subsistence-goods sector was the only lasting way to increase the rate of surplus value.

All these mechanisms, and Marx's analysis of the labor process in general, rest on the assumption that the expenditure of effort is decided by coercion. For their economic survival, workers are presumed to be totally at the mercy of the capitalist or his agent, the overseer, who can arbitrarily intensify the work, provided that his demands are compatible with the reappearance of the worker the next day (and sometimes not even then) and that they remain within certain broad and often unenforced legal limits. In other words, Marx had no place in his theory of the labor process for the organization of consent, for the necessity to elicit a willingness to cooperate in the translation of labor power into labor. The omission, if not legitimate, is perhaps understandable in the context of nineteenth-century capitalism, where the arena of consent was small. With the passage of time, as the result of working-class struggles, the wage becomes increasingly independent of the individual expenditure of effort. Accordingly, coercion must be supplemented by the organization of consent. Unlike legitimacy, which is a subjective state of mind that individuals carry around with them, consent is expressed through, and is the result of, the organization of activities. It is to be distinguished from the specific consciousness or subjective attributes of the individual who engages in those activities. Within the labor process the basis of consent lies in the organization of activities as though they presented the worker with real choices, however narrowly confined those choices might be. It is participation in choosing that generates consent. As long as the application of force is restricted to transgressions of the narrow but specific and recognized limits of choice, it too can become the object of consent.[26] The securing of surplus value must therefore be understood as the result of different combinations of force and consent.

But *securing* unpaid labor is not the same as *realizing* surplus value, and it is their separation that presents further problems for the capitalist. Under feudalism, not only is surplus labor fixed but it also assumes a directly visible and usually directly consumable form. Under capitalism, surplus labor is neither visible nor consumable. The origins of profit in unpaid labor are therefore concealed in a number of ways. First, capitalists commonly increase profits most by introducing new techniques and, in particular, new machinery—that is, through capital investment. Thus, capital appears as a power unto itself—the power to generate profit. From the point of view of the capitalist, varying the intensity of labor contributes only to variations in the rate of profit around some average profit. That is, from the standpoint of those who direct the process of production, the source of profit is capital, not labor.

Second, surplus value is realized in the form of profit only through the sale of commodities in the market. The price fetched by a particular commodity is usually beyond the control of the individual capitalist. The size of the profit therefore appears to be determined by the market forces of supply and demand, not by the amount of embodied unpaid labor time. Although there is a relationship between price and the labor time embodied in a commodity, it is complicated and obscure to the individual capitalist. Therefore, profit is not only realized in the market; it also appears to originate there. In short, the defining dilemma of the capitalist lies in securing surplus value that is also invisible.[27]

The obscuring of surplus value presents itself as a problem of securing and realizing surplus value for the capitalist, but it is at the same time a necessary feature of capitalism as far as subordination of the workers is concerned. If the existence of unpaid labor becomes transparent, we find ourselves in the realm of a precapitalist mode of production, requiring the intervention of extraeconomic elements for the renewal of the production cycle. How, then, is unpaid labor mystified to the worker under capitalism? We have already seen that necessary and surplus labor time are not distinguished within the labor process and also how the wage conceals such a distinction. Workers have no sense of producing the wage equivalent or the means of subsistence, since what they produce is but a fraction of a useful object that they may never even see. Nevertheless, the process of production appears to workers as a labor process, that is, as the production of things—use value— rather than the production of exchange value. This is enhanced by the institutional separation of ownership and control—that is, by the separation of the relations of production from the relations in production. In the labor process, workers experience managers as agents of domination, to be sure, but also as sellers of labor power who, by virtue of their training and expertise, receive greater compensation than the workers themselves. That managers also receive part of the surplus value is not apparent in the labor process.

Although surplus value is mystified to both worker and capitalist, Marx claimed that there were tendencies immanent in capitalism that would reveal to workers the movement behind appearances. Through the emergence of the collective worker, through the development of interdependence and the homogenization of work, and, above all, through class struggle, the proletariat would come to recognize the antagonism between its interests and those of capital, which are rooted in the appropriation of unpaid labor. History has shown that Marx's prognosis was inadequate. In general, workers do not attribute to their own labor the difference between what they produce and what they receive.[28] The notions of exploitation and unpaid labor are even more removed from everyday life on the shop floor today than they were in Marx's time.

If workers do not regard their own labor as the source of profit, to what theories of profit do they subscribe? The most frequently held view that I encountered on the shop floor was that profit is some form of earned reward for past sacrifices or for the risk of capital investment. Others argued that profit is generated in the market, particularly as a result of the manipulation of prices. This convergence of worker and capitalist theories of profit reflects a convergence rather than divergence of interests as these are organized under advanced capitalism. To the degree that workers come to regard their future livelihood as contingent on the survival and expansion of their capitalist employer, they will also come to accept theories of profit that reflect the experiences of the capitalist seeking profit through the sale of commodities.[29]

How is it that surplus value continues to be obscure to workers? How is it that the evolution of the labor process and class struggle has not demystified the source of profit? How is it that workers do not constitute themselves as a class whose interests are irreconcilable with those of capital? Twentieth-century Marxism offers many

answers to these questions—answers that take us beyond the labor
process into the state, the school, the family, and the culture industry or that rely on the construction of a Marxist psychology. In this
study I will selectively appropriate the insights of these developments but will relocate them within the labor process. I will return to
Marx's focal concern, but with the ammunition of Marxism.

Conclusion

The defining essence of the capitalist labor process is the simultaneous obscuring and securing of surplus value. How does the
capitalist assure himself of surplus value when its production is
invisible? Marxist theories of the labor process have frequently
referred to fragmentation and atomization of the working class at
the point of production—essential features of the obscuring of
surplus value—but these theories do not explain how surplus value is
secured.[30] Obscuring surplus value is a necessary but not sufficient
condition for securing surplus value. In other words, it is necessary
to explain not only why workers do not act according to an imputed
set of interests but also why they attempt to realize a different set of
interests. The labor process, therefore, must be understood in terms
of the specific combinations of force and consent that elicit cooperation in the pursuit of profit.

By examining changes in the labor process at one particular
factory over a period of thirty years I hope to illuminate the mechanisms of organizing consent on the shop floor, of constituting workers
as individuals rather than members of a class, of coordinating the
interests of labor and capital as well as those of workers and managers, and of redistributing conflict and competition. In short, I
shall discuss the mechanisms through which surplus value is simultaneously obscured and secured, in addition to those outlined above;
this is the subject of parts 2 and 3. In part 4 I shall show how
variations in markets and imported consciousness have effects only
within limits defined by the labor process, and in part 5 I shall
explain the source of those changes in the labor process that enhance its capacity to obscure and secure surplus value.

2

Changes in the Labor Process

Three

From Geer Company to Allied Corporation

The particular plant in which I worked for ten months as a miscellaneous machine operator between July 1974 and May 1975 and which constitutes the empirical context of my inquiry is the engine division of a multinational corporation, referred to here as Allied Corporation. For eleven months, between October 1944 and August 1945, Donald Roy worked in the same plant as a radial-drill operator. It was then part of what he called Geer Company. On the basis of his observations, Roy wrote a series of seminal studies on restriction of output.[1] I shall liberally refer to his voluminous doctoral dissertation, which vividly portrays life on the shop floor at the end of World War II.

Roy was interested in why workers do not work harder, and at one point he even goes so far as to measure the time "wasted" on the shop floor.[2] Yet, in recording his observations, he continually refers to the authoritarian system into which he had been inserted and how management treats workers as "yardbirds." Thus, the concluding paragraph of his dissertation reads:

The hunch here is that somewhere in the continual reciprocal interplay between the hostile communication of mutually threatening "bosses" and "Yardbirds" and the divergence of the norms of their respective groups lies an explanation for restriction that can point to procedures for its substantial reduction. Administrative adjustments of the piecework incentive may effect some gains in worker output, but production cannot be expected to approach potentialities until major operations of reconstruction change basic group relationships. The institution of a participative social structure, in which Yardbird Man assumes first-class citizenship, may solve the problem.[3]

Beginning where Roy ends—that is, beginning with the "authoritarian system"—the logical question becomes: Why do workers work as hard as they do?

In the period when Roy undertook his research, the most natural and important work to respond to was Roethlisberger and Dickson's *Management and the Worker* and the writings of Elton Mayo. Roy's major contribution has been to cast doubt on the universal validity of the conclusions then being drawn from the Western Electric studies.[4] Nevertheless, his dissertation does provide many insights into the sources of cooperation as well as noncooperation. Unfortunately, the restricted framework in which he posed his questions went along with the "closed system" analysis that was then dominant in studies of industrial relations (particularly those influenced by the Chicago School).[5] The environment was generally ignored, and the study stopped at the factory gates. In addition, Roy's observations are entirely limited to what went on around him while he worked on second shift. What he could not gather from participant observation is not to be found in his work. We therefore learn virtually nothing about Geer Company, the union, other departments, the nature of various markets, and so on. His insistence on being a closed (secret) participant observer imposed serious limitations on the material he could collect. My own approach was very different. I took the job with the explicit consent and knowledge of management as to why I was there. They agreed to provide me with access to managerial records and data. In assessing changes since 1945, I have had to reconstruct the social and economic context of

Geer Company from interviews with management (particularly with retired managers) and workers, from odd comments in Roy's thesis, and from information available in business journals.

The task of this chapter will therefore be to place Geer Company and Allied Corporation in their different social and economic contexts. In the following chapters I will compare Roy's observations, supplemented by my reconstructions, with the organization of work as I found it in 1974–75.

Geer Company in 1944

Geer Company began operations in 1881 at a railroad junction in southern Illinois. It produced railroad supplies and moved to the Chicago area around the turn of the century. In the first few years it became involved in the manufacture of two-cylinder air-cooled engines and then, between 1910 and 1920, entered the booming business of automobile engines. It was one of the first companies to make an eight-cylinder engine. Competition in the automobile industry forced Geer into a new market—engines for trucks. It became one of the leading producers in the field. The railroad-supplies business dipped in the first quarter of the century, and Geer entered into the production of diesel engines in the late twenties. In 1933 it negotiated a contract with the Navy for the manufacture of diesel engines for lifeboats. After World War II began, demand for engines soared, and, like so many other companies in the defense industry, Geer rapidly expanded from a jobbing shop, with net sales of about $3.5 million and net profits of around $41,000 in 1939, to a relatively large concern, with net sales of $45.5 million and net profits of $907,000 (see table 1). In other words, there was a fifteen-fold increase in sales and a more than twenty-fold increase in profits. As regards the number of employees, before the war there were less than 1,000; at the end of the war there were almost 4,000.

At the beginning of the war Geer also got involved in the lift-truck business and in producing engines not only for cars, trucks, and lifeboats but for tanks and even airplanes. Just before he left in September 1945, Roy received the following V-J Day statement from the president of the company:

Table 1   **Annual Financial Position**
                                                of Geer Company

Year	Net sales (In millions)	Net profits (In thousands)	Earnings per Share of Common Stock	Number of Employees
1936	$ 3.7	$ 199.4	$8.86	880
1937	5.4	354.9	1.93	535
1938	3.5	156.3	0.84	n.a.*
1939	3.5	41.3	0.22	739
1940	4.3	113.6	0.62	1,278
1941	12.3	615.4	3.34	n.a.
1942	24.8	788.4	4.21	2,675
1943	36.7	900.1	4.81	3,780
1944	45.6	942.6	5.04	3,922
1945	45.4	906.9	4.85	2,694
1946	22.8	977.7	4.72	2,429
1947	30.5	1,832.9	4.43	2,500
1948	26.0	1,101.4	2.66	2,500
1949	22.4	707.6	1.71	1,450
1950	17.7	656.4	1.59	1,568
1951	29.2	1,127.6	2.72	n.a.
1952	40.5	1,075.6	2.60	n.a.

Source: *Moody's Industrials.*
*Not available.

The Geer Company is now 64 years old and has built up a world wide commercial trade in several important industrial fields where it expects to expand with the cessation of wartime demands.

Nearly all Geer products are readily adjustable to peacetime use, such as all types of gasoline and Diesel engines, railway maintenance products, earth drills, multiple gauge railway cars, industrial chore boys, and other leading lines.

In consequence, although Geer will be affected similarly to other companies, having gone "all out" for four years building products for the armed services and lend-lease, by cancellations and adjustments of present governmental products, we feel that this company has a vast future of peacetime activity immediately ahead and we are planning to successfully compete for this actual and prospective increased commercial business.

During 1945 Geer employment mounted to near the 5000 mark, and to date there have been virtually no layoffs. Geer now has effected reduction of the 48 hour week to 40 hours, working on a five day basis, and this will, of course, spread the work to take care of many employees. Geer has enjoyed excellent management-labor relations during the entire war.

During the adjustment period there is bound to be some cutback in employment, but Geer hopes to keep this as low as possible and to continue to increase its commercial production, including export trade. The fact that Geer products are so readily adaptable to commercial use and that Geer has a reputation all over the world makes us confident that Geer can soon show a peacetime advance that will compare favorably with any other company.[6]

Geer's wartime success is an example of the economic boom that lifted the entire economy. Thus, in the United States as whole, corporate profits rose from $9.3 billion before taxes in 1940 to $24.3 billion in 1944, or, after payment of taxes, from $6.4 billion in 1940 to $10.8 billion four years later.[7]

By contrast, labor was expected to exercise self-restraint during the war. The United Steelworkers of America established a local at Geer Company in 1937, and that was when the first contract was signed. During Roy's sojourn in the Jack Shop, he experienced only negative attitudes toward the union.[8] Here, again, Roy's observations must be seen, at least in part, as a reflection of wartime conditions.[9] As Joel Seidman remarks:

To too great an extent there was a tendency [during the war] to treat the wage dollar as inflationary, but to look upon the salary of the executive or the earnings of business as a necessary incentive to peak production and a proper reward for competent performance. The outcry by supporters of the Little Steel formula against Roosevelt's proposal to limit income after taxes to $25,000 a year suggests that many who examined the problems of consumer purchasing power suffered from a pronounced class astigmatism.[10]

After 1942, the Little Steel formula stabilized and in effect froze wages at their January 1941 level.[11] At Geer Company the minimum wage rose from 62.5 cents an hour in 1937 to 75 cents an hour in 1942 and to 80 cents in 1945. In addition, following Pearl Harbor there was a general freeze on labor mobility, and this reduced the bargaining power of management, since firing a worker was difficult.[12]

Owing to the general shortage of labor that existed at the time of the writer's employment in the Jack Shop, transferral, instead of firing, was used as an extreme disciplinary measure. Many workers would have welcomed being fired.

"No, they won't can you. A while back one of the tool grinders got sore, and tried to quit, but, they wouldn't release him. He tried to get canned by laying off three days at a time, coming in late, and sitting down on the job and refusing to grind a tool except when he felt like it. He did a couple of hours work a day. Finally he refused to grind a tool for the superintendent; but still he didn't get canned. They finally transferred him to day shift."[13]

At the same time, the labor freeze reduced the bargaining strength of workers, since they could not voluntarily quit:

If I could get another job without waiting sixty days for a WMC referral, I would have walked out of this place long ago. That sixty day wait gives a man plenty of food for thought, especially if he is supporting a family.[14]

As one of their contributions to the war commitment, union leaders in the A. F. of L. and CIO entered into a no-strike pledge with the government.[15] In return, union leadership was granted security of membership, which allowed unions to maintain, and in some instances to increase, membership. Management was encouraged to assist unions by implementing checkoff systems. One of the very few occasions on which Roy ever set eyes on a shop steward was soon after he had begun work, when the steward came round to ask him to sign a checkoff form. Overall union membership expanded during the war from 10.3 million workers to 14.8 million. By safeguarding union membership and, above all, the unions' financial status, the maintenance-of-membership clause dampened the militancy of union leaders and drove them apart from the rank and file. In many industries union-management relations were routinized during the war under enforced industrial peace. Collective bargaining and the institutionalization of the union function as an agent of enforcing worker discipline spread to many sectors of the economy.[16] Fringe benefits also increased in many industries as a substitute for wage increases.[17]

The combination of union cooperation with government imposed restraints on labor, backed up by military force where necessary, and the processing of unresolved grievances through the overworked War Labor Board left workers defenseless against managerial abuses. Bad working conditions, long hours, and the accumulation of unresolved grievances created widespread discontent.

> In prewar years the strike weapon often backstopped local grievance procedures and provided an incentive for management to resolve grievances at the lowest possible level. But with the adoption of the no-strike pledge this incentive evaporated and grievances left unresolved were dumped into the lap of a distant and cumbersome War Labor Board. Local unions found themselves "plagued by a malady of unsettled grievances" which undermined the solidarity and effectiveness of the union.[18]

The response from the rank and file was frequently militant action in the form of wildcat strikes, walkouts, or sitdowns. While 1942 was a quiet year for strikes, discontent mounted in succeeding years, and in 1944 the number of strikes reached an all-time high. Most of these were relatively short wildcat strikes, always staged in opposition to the union, except, of course, in the case of the United Mineworkers.[19] In Geer Company, Roy reported one walkout, prompted by the company's failure to fire an employee who refused to join the union, and one sitdown strike, which concerned the prices of piece-rate jobs and the lack of warm water for washing up.[20]

With the collapse of much of the government business after the war, Geer Company had to reorganize and reduce its volume of production, but it continued to operate most of its lines, consolidating the materials-handling department, where lift trucks were built, while allowing some of the railroad supplies to be phased out. Table 1 indicates the changing fortunes of Geer Company and its employees after the war.

The Decline of Allied Corporation

After the war, Geer Company began selling diesel engines to a construction-equipment company that was subsequently bought out by Allied Corporation. Allied Corporation had always been in the top 100 United States industrial corporations as measured by net sales. Before World War II, *Fortune* had referred to Allied as

America's Krupp: "Its enterprises were so numerous that it believes only one other company in the world—Krupp of Essen—is capable of producing a greater assortment of those primary tools with which man wrests goods and power from the earth." With annual sales of around $500 million, Allied Corporation was a giant compared to Geer, which had annual sales of $30 million.

Farm and construction equipment were Allied's biggest money-makers, even before the war, while their capital goods accounted for large net sales but made little profit. The main area of expansion has continued to be in agricultural and construction equipment, and a number of lines in the capital-goods business have been dropped. Whereas the immediate competitors of Allied's Tractor Division, as it was called then, built their own engines, Allied was still buying its engines from outside suppliers, such as General Motors. Having immediate access to and direct control over one's own supply of engines offered such competitive advantages that it was only a matter of time before Allied would develop its own engine division. Geer Company, which was now selling diesel engines to Allied, was an obvious candidate. Allied bought out Geer in 1953. From the point of view of the Geer shareholders—mainly confined to a single family, although a number of executives also held stock—the take-over was very lucrative. During the war the plant had been worked to its limit, and after the war management had allowed the plant to run down. It was in poor shape. There had been relatively little reinvestment of profits. Machinery needed replacement, and the factory building was in poor repair. I shall return later in this chapter to what became of the engine division. In the next few paragraphs I wish to describe the postwar fortunes of Allied Corporation as a whole.

Renowned for its paternalistic and conservative labor policies, Allied Corporation experienced an eleven-month strike at its major plant in 1946. In succeeding years it recovered, and until 1952 it was, according to *Forbes*, "the apple of Wall Street's eye due to its remarkable sales growth and intelligent diversification." However, in the two decades after 1952, Allied entered upon a course of setback, crisis, and decline. Earnings per share fell from $4.09 in 1951 (an all-time high) to 57 cents in 1961, when it experienced its first crisis, and then dropped further, to 47 cents in 1967. For reasons that I will briefly explain, in 1968 earnings showed a net loss

of $5.24 per common share. After hitting the low point of 42 cents
per share in 1971, earnings rose, reaching $1.77 per share in 1974.
To what can we attribute the decline of this powerful multinational
corporation?

When Harrington took over as chairman and chief executive
officer in 1951, he instituted a program of centralization, with the
following results, as reported by *Business Week:*

> Some executives were overloaded and unable to function
> effectively. For instance, when Geer Company was acquired in
> 1953, it became a separate third division, but its sales force re-
> ported to the general sales manager of the Tractor Division....
> To complicate things further, the Tractor Division had four dif-
> ferent businesses to oversee.... Says a Geer man: "The sales
> manager had 68 people reporting to him and was trying to oversee
> 16,000 altogether from his desk in a corner of Allied Corpora-
> tion's headquarters."

Also, according to *Forbes,* Harrington had so overbuilt the company
that in 1961, for example, it was operating at only 60 percent
capacity.

At a time when major corporations had long since passed from
centralized, functionally departmentalized divisions to decentralized, multifunctional divisions,[21] Allied Corporation was moving
in the opposite direction. Accordingly, when Crosland took over as
chief executive in 1955, he immediately reorganized. The two major
divisions were split into five. Geer remained separate. Nevertheless,
Allied Corporation retained an anachronistic organizational structure. It was only in 1962, following a further crisis, that Allied
Corporation brought in consultants. According to *Forbes:*

> It was apparent to both Crosland and to the outside consultants
> that Allied Corporation's old-fashioned corporate organization
> was hampering the company as much as were its manufacturing
> facilities. Allied had continued to group its men in departments
> by the jobs they performed: sales, engineering, production. It
> had never gotten around to grouping them by the more modern
> concept of the markets they served.

The general manager who took over the engine division in 1957
told me, "Yes, Allied has been in trouble, but that is because we
made the change to decentralized, autonomous divisions, each

responsible for showing profit, much too long after everyone else."

But the pattern of corporate organization was not the only problem. Originally the principle of industrial diversification was based on the logic that, if one line should suffer a decline in any one year, it was likely that another line would do well and compensate. The overall strength of the company would thus be maintained. *Forbes* commented in 1961 on Allied's failure compared with its competitor's success in this regard:

> . . . the very proposition on which Allied Corporation's diversification was based had gone sour. One capital goods cycle was supposed to balance another. Farm equipment with a rhythm of its own was to provide further balance. But all of the cycles went down at once.

But the most fatal drawback to the strategy of diversification was that, in each of the product lines in which it specialized, Allied Corporation was far weaker than its rivals, who were both less diversified and had bigger sales than the entire Allied Corporation and therefore operated on significantly higher profit margins. In 1969 *Forbes* noted, "In nearly every field Allied Corporation is too small, too old. Its competitors benefit from larger volume, newer plants, and widespread integrated manufacturing and marketing facilities." Summarizing Allied's disastrous performance in 1961, *Forbes* commented:

> . . . Allied Corporation [was left] with a net profit margin of less than one cent on the dollar, barely a quarter of what it was earning a few years ago. Of Allied's major rivals . . . no one was taking this kind of beating in 1961. Most, in fact, were at least holding their own and many were showing improved results.

Its problems were compounded by an expensive antitrust case, which cost the company $127,500 in court-imposed fines and more than $20 million to settle suits filed by customers.

Apart from reorganizing the corporate structure, Crosland cut back his labor force in 1962, and salaried employees took a pay cut. Allied Corporation also bowed out of a number of the capital-goods markets in which its reputation had originally been established.

There was a clear reluctance to take such steps, as *Fortune* reported in 1967:

> Crosland's view of management still remains largely passive. An associate once heard him compare Allied Corporation to a log floating down a stream, which is the economy, and its executives to ants trying to cling to that log. Even when things looked brightest, company statements attributed the bulk of sales and earnings growth to increased demand and gave almost no credit to management's actions.

The year 1967 was a trying one for the corporation and its new chairman, Hillary. Most of the year was spent fighting off suitors who were attempting to buy out Allied Corporation. Among those showing an interest were the Ling-Temco-Vought corporation, General Dynamics, Signal Oil and Gas, City Investment, and Gulf and Western. The most serious challenge came from Ling-Temco-Vought, but it backed down, for reasons that remain obscure, when the directors of Allied Corporation turned down their second offer. The most sustained effort, however, came in the following year, from White Consolidated. Allied resorted to creating a new block of shares, which it sold to a Rockefeller interest and a large European automobile company. Hillary also took Allied into the household-appliance market in order, it was speculated, to establish an anti-trust case against the proposed merger with White Consolidated. Eventually the latter withdrew.

Soon after assuming control, Hillary decided to write off in a single year the losses that were due to past mistakes. This raised a few eyebrows on Wall Street, but the Securities and Exchange Commission regarded it as legitimate. Accordingly, in 1968, Allied Corporation registered a $122 million deficit on its tax forms, though it presented this, by some intricate bookkeeping, as a loss of $54 million to its shareholders! Hillary set about streamlining the organization, cutting corporate staff from 1,510 to 138 and reducing employment by 3,400. After a few fateful years under his chairmanship, a boom in the farm-equipment business, together with the discontinuance of unprofitable products and the adoption of more successful ones, arrested the corporation's decline, at least for the moment.

The Fortunes of the
Engine Division

What happened to Geer Company when, in 1953, it became a division of Allied Corporation? Not much. The takeover agreement left Geer management intact for at least another three years. There are reports of continual friction during the period between Geer management and Allied headquarters over such matters as production priorities and sales. Geer management maintained a diversity of products and sometimes resisted the immediate demands of the larger corporation. Some lines were gradually discontinued. First to go were some of the railroad supplies. Roy's Jack Shop disappeared in 1956. In 1957 the old general manager left, and a new man—Wilson—took over. He had had experience in running other Allied plants, and his task was to reorganize the old Geer Company.

Before he arrived, there was much concern on all levels of management that many personnel would be dismissed and new ones brought in. Wilson, however, decided to make do with the old management and replaced none. But he did introduce a number of other changes. He brought new tooling to the plant and began to plan for the movement into a new building. In 1961 the materials-handling department split off and became an independent division in another town. The engine division became formally constituted as such and moved to a new plant about a mile from the old one. In line with changes taking place throughout the corporation at that time, Wilson initiated new relations with the other divisions of Allied Corporation. As part of corporate policy, each division was now placed on a profit-making basis, and, before it could buy engines, its purchasing department had to sign a contract indicating the size of the order and its duration. Each purchasing department, whether of the tractor, lift-truck, or construction-equipment division, would be held to the original contract or incur penalties for its violation, even though the agreement was between divisions within the corporation. In this way the engine division was able to finance tooling without risk to its profits. Nevertheless, the engine division was to remain a service division within the corporation. The prices at which engines were to be sold were negotiated each year and fixed in a way that left only the slimmest of profit margins for the engine division.[22]

Orders from within the corporation naturally took priority over any commercial venture the engine division could establish for itself outside Allied. Yet it was the outside business that was profitable and provided the basis for expansion. Accordingly, incentives for top management in the division were not based on commercial ventures, which frequently ran counter to the interests of the corporation as a whole, but on the fulfillment of annual plans, which established a range of targets for the year's production.

Conclusion

From this brief narrative history it is possible to isolate two sets of forces that shaped the changes that occurred in the organization of work at Geer and Allied between 1945 and 1975. The first is the secular changes in the labor process due to the consolidation of the new patterns of industrial relations that emerged during World War II. Superimposed on such "processual" change, which affected the entire organized sector of the economy, is the "situational" change experienced by Geer Company. In 1945 it supplied engines, railroad jacks, lift trucks, and other equipment to a number of companies as well as to the government. In 1975 the plant served as an engine division of a large multinational corporation. The effect of this movement from the competitive sector to the monopoly sector has to be disentangled from the independent effects of historical change affecting the United States over the past thirty years. I shall turn to this task in part 5, but first I must specify the nature of the change I am seeking to explain.

Four

Thirty Years of
Making Out

The study of changes in the labor process is one of the more neglected areas of industrial sociology. There are global theories, which speak generally of tendencies toward rationalization, bureaucratization, the movement from coercive to normative compliance, and so forth. There are the prescriptive theories of human relations, of job enrichment, job enlargement, worker participation, and so on, which do express underlying changes but in a form that conceals them. There are attempts to examine the implications of technological change for worker attitudes and behavior, but these do not examine the forces leading to technological change itself. There are also theories of organizational persistence, which stress the capacity of enterprises to resist change. The few attempts at concrete analysis of changes in the labor process have usually emerged from comparisons among different firms. Such causal analysis, based on cross-sectional data, is notoriously unsatisfactory under the best of conditions, but when samples are small and firms diverse, the conclusions drawn are at best suggestive. As far as I know, there have been no attempts to undertake a detailed study of the labor process of a single firm over an extended period of time. Thus, my revisit to Geer, thirty years after Roy, provides a unique opportunity to examine the forces leading to changes on the shop floor. In this chapter I am mainly concerned with documenting the nature of those changes, leaving their explanation to later chapters.

Technology

Whenever technology changes its character, it has a transformative impact on the organization of work. However, the study of techno-logical innovation and adoption is still in its primitive stages. Apart from the conventional models of neoclassical economics, which stress the cumulative role of science in the pursuit of ever greater efficiency, there have been few attempts to examine the political and social forces leading to technological change in advanced capi-talism. A notable exception is the recent work by David Noble, which suggests that capitalists choose among available technologies not only to increase productivity but, in addition, to gain control over the labor process and push smaller capitalists out of business.[1] A recent study of the mechanization of harvesting shows that growers develop new technologies but that adoption is contingent on the level of class struggle.[2]

Undoubtedly the examination of the forces leading to techno-logical change is important. However, if we are to understand the changes in the labor process that are brought about by social imperatives other than those introduced by new machines, we must keep technology constant, since it would be impossible to isolate its impact. Fortunately, machine-tool technology, in its principles at least, has remained relatively constant over the past century, with the exception of the recent development of computer-controlled machines. It therefore provides a useful basis for studying "non-technical" sources of change in the organization of work. Thus, the machine shops described in the writings of Frederick Winslow Taylor bear a remarkable resemblance to those of Geer and Allied.[3] The agglomeration of speed drills, radial drills, vertical and hori-zontal mills, chuck and turret lathes, grinders, etc., could be found in essentially the same forms in machine shops at the end of the nineteenth century as they are today. Even in the layout of its machines, the Jack Shop, where Roy worked, closely resembled the small-parts department where I worked. The organization of work and the incentive schemes, as well as the various forms of output restriction and the informal worker alliances, all described by Roy, are to be found today and can be traced back to the turn of the century.

However, outside the small-parts department there have been major changes in technology, in the direction of increased automation. The most impressive change at Allied came in the machining of rough cylinder-block castings. First introduced at a Ford plant in 1935, these monstrous integrated machine tools are programmed to perform several operations simultaneously (milling, tapping, boring, drilling, grinding, etc.) at each work station before the cylinder block is automatically transported to the next work station. Despite, or perhaps because of, its sophistication, this elaborate technology was out of order much of the time. In some departments one or two computer-controlled machines had been installed, but they, too, seemed to experience considerable downtime. Generally, the wide variety and relatively small volume of engines produced at Allied made it uneconomic to transform the technology of the entire plant, and, when new automated equipment was introduced, it frequently created more problems than it solved. As I shall suggest toward the end of this chapter, piecemeal technological innovation can easily become the focus of struggles on the shop floor.

Even in the small-parts department, by no means the most technologically sophisticated of the departments of the engine division, machines are now more reliable, flexible, precise, and so forth than they were in 1945. A very noticeable change from Geer is the absence of the huge belt lines that used to power the machine tools. Now each machine has its own source of power. In the remaining sections of this chapter I shall indicate how these small changes in technology have become part of, have facilitated, and have sometimes stimulated changes in productive activities and production relations.

The Piece-Rate System

In a machine shop, operators are defined by the machine they "run" and are remunerated according to an individual piece-rate incentive scheme. While machine operators comprise the majority of workers on the shop floor, there are also auxiliary workers, whose function it is to provide facilities and equipment as well as assistance for the "production" workers (operators). For each production operation the methods department establishes a level of effort, expressed in so many pieces per hour, which represents the "100 percent" benchmark. Below this benchmark, operators receive a base rate for the job, irrespective of the actual number of pieces they produce. Above this standard, workers receive not only the base rate for the job but, in addition, a bonus or incentive, corresponding to the number of pieces in excess of "100 percent." Thus, output at a rate of 125 percent is defined as the "anticipated rate," which—according to the contract—is the amount "a normal experienced operator working at incentive gait" is expected to produce and represents 25 percent more pieces than the base rate. Producing at "125 percent," an operator will earn himself or herself an incentive bonus that adds around 15 percent to the amount earned when producing at 100 percent or less. Earned income per hour is computed as follows:

Base earnings (determined by job's labor grade)
+ Base earnings × (% Rate - 100%) (if rate is greater than 100%)
+ Override (determined by job's labor grade)
+ Shift differential (25 cents for second and third shifts)
+ Cost-of-living allowance

In 1945 the computation of earnings was simpler. The system of remuneration was a straight piece-rate system with a guaranteed minimum. There were no extra benefits. Each operation had a *price* rather than a *rate*. Earnings were calculated by simply multiplying the number of pieces produced in an hour by the price. If the result was less than the guaranteed minimum, the operator received that guaranteed minimum, known as the day rate. If output was greater than that corresponding to the day rate, an increase of 25 percent in the number of pieces led to a 25 percent increase in earnings. How the day rate was determined was not always clear. It reflected not only the job but also the operator's skill. Thus Roy received a day rate of 85 cents per hour, but Al McCann, also working on a radial drill on second shift but a more experienced operator, received a day rate of $1.10. The day rate on first shift was 5 cents lower than on second shift, so that, to make 85 cents an hour, Joe Mucha, Roy's day man, had to work harder than Roy. The price for a given operation, however, was the same for all operators.

The two systems thus encourage different strategies for achieving increased earnings. In 1945 Geer operators might fight for higher day rates by bargaining individually with management, but this did not guarantee them increased earnings if they were regularly turning out more pieces than corresponded to the day rate. Furthermore, the very operators who might be eligible for higher day rates would also be the ones for whom a guaranteed minimum was not so important. So the way to drive up income was to increase prices, and this could be accomplished either by fighting for across-the-board-increases on all prices or by fighting with the time-study man for improved prices on particular jobs. Operators did in fact spend a great deal of time haggling with time-study men over prices. These ways of increasing earnings are now relatively insignificant compared to two alternative methods. The first is via increases in the base earnings for the job and the fringes that go along with each labor grade. These are all negotiated at three-year intervals between management and union. Under the present system, the methods department is not necessarily involved in changes in the *price* of an operation, since this varies with base earnings. Increases in fringes, such as override, are also independent of the piece-rate system. The second method is to transfer to another job with higher base earnings—that is, of higher labor grade—or with easier rates. Frequently, the higher the labor grade, the easier the rates; for to encourage workers to remain on the more skilled jobs, of the higher labor grades, and thereby avoid the cost of training new workers, the rates on those jobs tend to be looser. In 1945, when earnings were closely tied to experience and less associated with particular types of jobs, transfer to another job was frequently used as a disciplinary measure, since it was likely to lead to reduced earnings.[4]

The implications are not hard to foresee. Whereas in 1945 bargaining between management and worker over the distribution of the rewards of labor took place on the shop floor, in 1975 such bargaining had been largely transferred out of the shop and into the conference room and worker-management conflict on the shop floor had found a safety valve in the organization of job transfers on a plant-wide basis. As a consequence of changes in the system of remuneration, management-worker conflict has abated and individualism has increased.

Making Out—A Game
Workers Play

In this section I propose to treat the activities on the shop floor as a series of games in which operators attempt to achieve levels of production that earn incentive pay, in other words, anything over 100 percent. The precise target that each operator aims at is established on an individual basis, varying with job, machine, experience, and so on. Some are satisfied with 125 percent, while others are in a foul mood unless they achieve 140 percent—the ceiling imposed and recognized by all participants. This game of making out provides a framework for evaluating the productive activities and the social relations that arise out of the organization of work. We can look upon making out, therefore, as comprising a sequence of stages—of encounters between machine operators and the social or nonsocial objects that regulate the conditions of work. The rules of the game are experienced as a set of externally imposed relationships. The art of making out is to manipulate those relationships with the purpose of advancing as quickly as possible from one stage to the next.

At the beginning of the shift, operators assemble outside the time office on the shop floor to collect their production cards and punch in on the "setup" of their first task. If it has already been set up on the previous shift, the operator simply punches in on production. Usually operators know from talking to their counterpart, before the beginning of the shift, which task they are likely to receive. Knowing what is available on the floor for their machine, an operator is sometimes in a position to bargain with the scheduling man, who is responsible for distributing the tasks.

In 1945 the scheduling man's duties appeared to end with the distribution of work, but in 1975 he also assumed some responsibility for ensuring that the department turned out the requisite parts on time. Therefore, he is often found stalking the floor, checking up on progress and urging workers to get a move on. Because he has no formal authority over the operators, the scheduling man's only recourse is to his bargaining strength, based on the discretion he can exert in distributing jobs and fixing up an operator's time. Operators who hold strategic jobs, requiring a particular skill, for example, or who are frequently called upon to do "hot jobs" are in a strong bargaining position vis-à-vis the scheduling man. He knows this and is careful not to upset them.

By contrast, Roy complained that the scheduling man was never to be found when he needed him and, when he was around, showed little interest in his work.[5] This caused great annoyance when the time clerks were not sure which job Roy had to punch in on next. Equally significant was the relative absence of hot jobs in 1945.[6] In sum, the department takes its responsibility to get jobs finished on time more seriously, but, so long as operators are making out, this responsibility falls on the shoulders of the scheduling man rather than on the foreman or superintendent.[7] The change is possibly a result of heightened departmental autonomy and responsibility, reflected in departmental profit-and-loss statements and in the penalties incurred by the company when engines are delivered late to the customer.[8]

After receiving their first task, operators have to find the blueprint and tooling for the operation. These are usually in the crib, although they may be already out on the floor. The crib attendant is therefore a strategic person whose cooperation an operator must secure. If the crib attendant chooses to be uncooperative in dispensing towels, blueprints, fixtures, etc., and, particularly, in the grinding of tools, operators can be held up for considerable lengths of time. Occasionally, operators who have managed to gain the confidence of the crib attendant will enter the crib themselves and expedite the process. Since, unlike the scheduling man, the crib attendant has no real interest in whether the operator makes out, his cooperation has to be elicited by other means. For the first five months of my employment my relations with the crib attendant on second shift were very poor, but at Christmas things changed dramatically. Every year the local union distributes a Christmas ham to all its members. I told Harry that I couldn't be bothered picking mine up from the union hall and that he could have it for himself. He was delighted, and after that I received good service in the crib.

Many of Roy's troubles also originated in the crib. As in 1975, so in 1945: there were not enough crib attendants. Roy dramatically shows how the attendant who tries to serve operators conscientiously becomes a nervous wreck and soon transfers off the job. Problems may have been more acute under Geer, in Roy's time, since tools and fixtures were then located in the crib according to size and type rather than assembled in pans according to job, as in 1975. On the other hand, there were always at least two crib attendants when Roy was working at Geer, whereas in 1975 there was never more than one on second shift.

While I was able to secure the cooperation of the crib attendant, I was not so fortunate with the truck drivers. When I was being broken in on the miscellaneous job, I was told repeatedly that the first thing I must do was to befriend the truck driver. He or she was reponsible for bringing the stock from the aisles, where it was kept in tubs, to the machine. Particularly at the beginning of the shift, when everyone is seeking their assistance, truck drivers can hold you up for a considerable period. While some treated everyone alike, others discriminated among operators, frustrating those without power, assisting those who were powerful. Working on the miscellaneous job meant that I was continually requiring the truck driver's services, and, when Morris was in the seat, he used to delight in frustrating me by making me wait. There was nothing I could do about it unless I was on a hot job; then the foreman or scheduling man might intervene. To complain to the foreman on any other occasion would only have brought me more travail, since Morris could easily retaliate later on. It was better just to sit tight and wait. Like the crib attendants, truckers have no stake in the operator's making out, and they are, at the same time, acutely conscious of their power in the shop. All they want is for you to get off their backs so that they can rest, light up, chat with their friends, or have a cup of coffee—in other words, enjoy the marginal freedoms of the machine operator. As one of the graffiti in the men's toilet put it, "Fuck the company, fuck the union, but most of all fuck the truckers because they fuck us all." Operators who become impatient may, if they know how, hop into an idle truck and move their own stock. But this may have unfortunate consequences, for other operators may ask them to get their stock too.

While it is difficult to generalize, it does appear that under Geer the service of the truck drivers—or stock chasers, as they were called—was more efficient. For one thing, there were two truckers in 1945 but only one in 1975 to serve roughly the same number of operators. For another, as the setup man told me from his own experience,

> "In the old days everyone knew everyone else. It was a big
> family, and so truck drivers would always try and help, bringing
> up stock early and so on. In those days operators might not
> even have to tell the truck driver to get the next load. Now every-
> one moves around from job to job. People don't get to know
> each other so well, and so there's less cooperation."

As they wait for the stock to arrive, each operator sets up his machine, if it is not already set up. This can take anything from a few minutes to two shifts, but normally it takes less than an hour. Since every setup has a standard time for completion, operators try to make out here, too. When a setup is unusually rapid, an operator may even be able to make time so that, when he punches in on production, he has already turned out a few pieces. A setup man is available for assistance. Particularly for the inexperienced, his help is crucial, but, as with the other auxiliary personnel, his cooperation must be sought and possibly bargained for. He, too, has no obvious stake in your making out, though the quicker he is through with you, the freer he is. Once the machine is set up and the stock has arrived, the operator can begin the first piece, and the setup man is no longer required unless the setup turns out to be unsatisfactory.

The quality and concern of setup men vary enormously. For example, on day shift the setup man was not known for his cooperative spirit. When I asked Bill, my day man, who the setup man was on day shift, he replied, "Oh, he died some years ago." This was a reference to the fact that the present one was useless as far as he was concerned. On second shift, by contrast, the setup man went about his job with enthusiasm and friendliness. When he was in a position to help, he most certainly did his best, and everyone liked and respected him. Yet even he did not know all the jobs in the shop. Indeed, he knew hardly any of my machines and so was of little use to me. Roy experienced similar differences among setup men.

Johnny, for example, was not a great deal of help, but when Al McCann came along, Roy's life on the shop floor was transformed.[9] Al McCann had been a radial-drill operator of long experience and showed Roy all the angles on making out.

In 1945 there were more setup men than in 1975; this was due in part to wartime manpower policies but also to a greater need for setup men. Fixtures and machines have improved and become more standardized over the past thirty years, and the skill required in setting up has therefore declined. Moreover, under Geer, there was greater diversity in the operations that any one machine could perform, and it therefore took operators much longer to master all the jobs that they would have to run. On the other hand, it appears that mobility between different machines is now greater and average experience therefore less than at the end of the war. Roy also reports that, according to his fellow workers, the setup function was itself relatively new; this suggests again how recent was the specialization of the functions that earlier were performed by a single person—the foreman.

The assigned task may be to drill a set of holes in a plate, pipe, casting, or whatever; to mill the surface of some elbow; to turn an internal diameter on a lathe; to shave the teeth on a gear; and so on. The first piece completed has to be checked by the inspector against the blueprint. Between inspector and operator there is an irrevocable conflict of interest because the former is concerned with quality while the operator is concerned with quantity. Time spent when an operation just won't come right—when piece after piece fails, according to the inspector, to meet the specifications of the blueprint—represents lost time to the operator. Yet the inspector wants to OK the piece as quickly as possible and doesn't want to be bothered with checking further pieces until the required tolerances are met.

When a piece is on the margin, some inspectors will let it go, but others will enforce the specifications of the blueprint to the nth degree. In any event, inspectors are in practice, if not in theory, held partly responsible if an operator runs scrap. Though formally accountable only for the first piece that is tagged as OK, an inspector will be bawled out if subsequent pieces fall outside the tolerance limits. Thus, inspectors are to some extent at the mercy of the operators, who, after successfully getting the first piece OK'd, may turn up the speed of their machine and turn out scrap. An operator who does this can always blame the inspector by shifting the tag from the first piece to one that is scrap. Of course, an inspector has ample opportunity to take revenge on an operator who tries to shaft him. Moreover, operators also bear the responsibility for quality. During my term of employment, charts were distributed and hung up on each machine, defining the frequency with which operators were expected to check their pieces for any given machine at any particular tolerance level. Moreover, in the period immediately prior to the investigation of the plant's quality-assurance organization by an outside certifying body, operators were expected to indicate on the back of the inspection card the number of times they checked their pieces.

The shift since the war is clear. Under Geer, as Roy describes it, the inspector was expected to check not only the first piece but also, from time to time, some of the subsequent pieces. When the operation was completed on all the pieces, operators had to get the inspector to sign them off the old job before they could punch in on a new one. The responsibility has now shifted toward the operators, who are expected to inspect their own pieces at regular intervals.[10] Furthermore, improved machining, tooling, fixtures, etc., permit greater worker control over quality. It is now also argued that problems with quality result, not from poor workmanship, but from poor design of the product. For all these reasons, we now find fewer inspectors, and the trend is toward decreasing their numbers even further.[11]

When an inspector holds up an operator who is working on an important job but is unable to satisfy the specifications on the blueprint, a foreman may intervene to persuade the inspector to OK the piece. When this conflict cannot be resolved at the lowest level, it is taken to the next rung in the management hierarchy, and the superintendent fights it out with the chief inspector. According to Roy's observations, production management generally defeated quality control in such bargaining.[12] I found the same pattern in 1975, which reflects an organizational structure in which quality control is directly subordinated to production. Not surprisingly, the function of quality control has become a sensitive issue and the focus of much conflict among the higher levels of Allied's engine division. Quality control is continually trying to fight itself clear of subordination to production management so as to monitor quality on the shop floor. This, of course, would have deleterious effects on levels of production, and so it is opposed by the production management. Particularly sensitive in this regard is control of the engine test department, which in 1975 resided with production management. The production manager naturally claimed that he was capable of assessing quality impartially. Furthermore, he justified this arrangement by shifting the locus of quality problems from the shop floor to the design of the engine, which brought the engineers into the fray. Engineering managment, not surprisingly, opposes the trend toward increasing their responsibility for quality. Therefore, the manager of engineering supported greater autonomy for quality control as a reflection of his interest in returning responsibility for quality to the shop floor. To what extent this situation has been preserved by the vesting of interests since Allied took over from Geer is not clear.[13]

After the first piece has been OK'd, the operator engages in a battle with the clock and the machine. Unless the task is a familiar one—in which case the answer is known, within limits—the question is: Can I make out? It may be necessary to figure some angles, some short cuts, to speed up the machine, make a special tool, etc. In these undertakings there is always an element of risk—for example, the possibility of turning out scrap or of breaking tools. If it becomes apparent that making out is impossible or quite unlikely, operators slacken off and take it easy. Since they are guaranteed their base earnings, there is little point in wearing themselves out unless they can make more than the base earnings—that is, more than 100 percent. That is what Roy refers to as goldbricking. The other form of "output restriction" to which he refers—quota restriction—entails putting a ceiling on how much an operator may turn in—that is, on how much he may record on the production card. In 1945 the ceiling was $10.00 a day or $1.25 an hour, though this did vary somewhat between machines. In 1975 the ceiling was defined as 140 percent for all operations on all machines. It was presumed that turning in more than 140 percent led to "price cuts" (rate increases), and, as we shall see in chapter 10, this was indeed the case.

In 1975 quota restriction was not necessarily a form of restriction of *output,* because operators *regularly* turned *out* more than 140 percent, but turned *in* only 140 percent, keeping the remainder as a "kitty" for those operations on which they could not make out. Indeed, operators would "bust their ass" for entire shifts, when they had a gravy job, so as to build up a kitty for the following day(s). Experienced operators on the more sophisticated machines could easily build up a kitty of a week's work. There was always some discrepancy, therefore, between what was registered in the books as completed and what was actually completed on the shop floor. Shop management was more concerned with the latter and let the books take care of themselves. Both the 140 percent ceiling and the practice of banking (keeping a kitty) were recognized and accepted by everyone on the shop floor, even if they didn't meet with the approval of higher management.

Management outside the shop also regarded the practice of "chiseling" as illicit, while management within the shop either assisted or connived in it. Chiseling (Roy's expression, which did not have currency on the shop floor in 1975) involves redistributing time from one operation to another so that operators can maximize the period turned in as over 100 percent. Either the time clerk cooperates by punching the cards in and out at the appropriate time or the operators are allowed to punch their own cards. In part, because of the diversity of jobs, some of them very short, I managed to avoid punching any of my cards. At the end of the shift I would sit down with an account of the pieces completed in each job and fiddle around with the eight hours available, so as to maximize my earnings. I would pencil in the calculated times of starting and finishing each operation. No one ever complained, but it is unlikely that such consistent juggling would have been allowed on first shift.[14]

How does the present situation compare with Geer? As Roy describes it, the transfer of time from one operation or job to another was possible only if they were consecutive or else were part of the same job though separated in time. Thus Roy could finish one job and begin another without punching out on the first. When he did punch out on the first and in on the second, he would already have made a start toward making out. Second, if Roy saved up some pieces from one shift, he could turn those pieces in during his next shift only if the job had not been finished by his day man. Accordingly, it was important, when Roy had accumulated some kitty on a particular job, that he inform Joe Mucha. If Mucha could, he would try to avoid finishing the job before Roy came to work. Shifting time between consecutive jobs on a single shift was frequently fixed up by the foreman, who would pencil in the appropriate changes. Nonetheless, stealing time from a gravy job was in fact formally illicit in 1945.

> Gus told me that Eddie, the young time study man, was just as bad, if not worse, than the old fellow who gave him the price of one cent the other day. He said that Eddie caught the day man holding back on punching off a time study job while he got ahead on a piecework job. He turned the day man in, and the day man and the time cage man were bawled out.
> "That's none of his damn business. He shouldn't have turned in the day man," exclaimed Gus angrily.
> Gus went on to say that a girl hand-mill operator had been fired a year ago when a time study man caught her running one job while being "punched in" on another. The time study man came over to the girl's machine to time a job, to find the job completed and the girl running another.
> Stella has no use for time study men. She told me of the time Eddie caught Maggie running one job while being punched in on another. Maggie was fired. [15]

I shall have much more to say about time-study men in chapter 10, but these examples do suggest that, while chiseling went on, it was regarded as illegitimate at some levels of management.

What can we say about overall changes in rates over the past thirty years? Old-timers were forever telling me how "easy we've got it now," though that in itself would hardly constitute evidence of change. To be sure, machines, tooling, etc., have improved, and this makes production less subject to arbitrary holdups, but the rates could nonetheless be tighter. However, an interesting change in the shop vernacular does suggest easier rates. Roy describes two types of jobs, "gravy" and "stinkers," the former having particularly loose and the latter particularly tight rates. While I worked in the small-parts department, I frequently heard the word "gravy" but never the word "stinker." Its dropping out of fashion probably reflects the declining number of jobs with very tight rates and the availability of kitties to compensate for low levels of output. How do Roy's own data on output compare with 1975 data? Recomputing Roy's output on piecework in terms of rates rather than dollars and cents, I find that during the initial period, from November to February, his average was 85 percent and that during the second period, from March to August, it was 120 percent.[16] During the first six months of 1975, the average for the entire plant was around 133.5 percent. For the different departments this average varied from 142 percent among the automatic screw machines and automatic lathes to 121 percent in the small-parts department, where I worked. The small-parts department functions as a labor reservoir for the rest of the plant because turnover there is high, rates are notoriously tight, and it is the place where newcomers normally begin. Nonetheless, of all the departments, this one probably most closely resembles Roy's Jack Shop in terms of machines and type of work. Thus, overall rates are indeed easier to make now, but my experiences in my own department, where most of my observations were made, bore a close resemblance to Roy's experiences.[17]

What is the foreman's role in all these operations? He is seen by everyone but senior plant management as expediting and refereeing the game of making out. As long as operators are making out and auxiliary workers are not obstructing their progress, neither group is likely to invite authoritarian interventions from the foreman. For their part, foremen defend themselves from their own bosses' complaints that certain tasks have not been completed by pointing out that the operators concerned have been working hard and have successfully made out. We therefore find foremen actively assisting operators to make out by showing them tricks they had learned when they were operators, pointing out more efficient setups, helping them make special tools, persuading the inspector to OK a piece that did not exactly meet the requirements of the blueprint, and so on. Foremen, like everyone else on the shop floor, recognize the two forms of output restriction as integral parts of making out. When operators have made out for the night and decide to take it easy for the last two or three hours, a foreman may urge more work by saying, "Don't you want to build up a kitty?" However, foremen do not act in collusion with the methods department and use the information they have about the various jobs and their rates against the operators, because rate increases would excite animosity, encourage goldbricking, increase turnover, and generally make the foreman's job more difficult.

However, the operator's defense, "What more do you want? I'm making out," does have its problems, particularly when there is a hot job on the agenda. Under such circumstances, operators are expected to drop what they are doing and punch in on the new job, "throwing everything they've got" into it and, above all, ignoring production ceilings—though of course they are not expected to turn *in* more than 140 percent. On occasions like this, unless the foreman can bring some sanctions to bear, he is at the mercy of the operator who may decide to take it easy. For this reason, foremen may try to establish an exchange relationship with each individual operator: "You look after me, I'll look after you." Operators may agree to cooperate with their foreman, but in return they may expect him to dispense favors, such as the granting of casual days, permission to attend union meetings during working hours, permission to go home early on a special occasion, etc. One of the most important resources at the disposal of the foreman is the "double red card," which covers time lost by operators through no fault of their own at a rate of 125 percent. Red cards may be awarded for excessive time lost while waiting for materials because a machine is down or some other adventitious event occurs that prevents an operator from making out. Bargaining usually precedes the signing of a red card; the operator has to persuade the foreman that he has made an earnest attempt to make out and therefore deserves compensation. Finally, one may note, as Roy did, that rules promulgated by high levels of plant management are circumvented, ignored, or subverted on the shop floor, with the tacit and sometimes active support of the foreman, in the interests of making out.

In 1945 foremen and superintendent played a similar role in facilitating making out, although they seemed to view many of these activities as illicit. The ambivalence of Steve, Roy's superintendent on second shift, is revealed in the following conversation.

> I told Steve privately that I was made out for the evening with $10.00.
> "That's all I'm allowed to make isn't it?" I asked.

Steve hesitated at answering that one. "You can make more,"
he said, lowering his eyes.

"But I'd better not," I insisted.

"Well, you don't want to spoil it for yourself," he answered.[18]

Shop management frequently sided with operators in their hostility
to the methods department when rates were tight and making out
was impossible. Yet operators were always on the lookout and
suspicious of foremen as potential collaborators with the methods
department. The primary criterion by which foremen were evaluated
was their relationship with time-study men.

As already indicated, the second shift operators felt, in general,
that the "better" supervisors were on their shift. They cited the
connivance of Brickers, Squeaky and Johnson [day-shift super-
visors] with the enemy, the methods department, pointing out
that they were "company men," would do nothing for the
workers, would not permit loafing when quotas were attained,
and "drove" the operators on piecework jobs that were regarded
as "stinkers." On the other hand, the night shift supervisors were
known to have "fought for their men" against the "big shots,"
sought to aid operators in getting better prices from time study,
winked at quota restriction and its hours of loafing, did not
collaborate with methods in the drive to lower "gravy" prices,
and exhibited a pleasing insouciance when operators puttered
away on day work.[19]

Another possible change revolves around the attitude of the foreman
to goldbricking. Certainly, in 1945, foremen were not well disposed
toward operators' taking it easy when rates were impossible, whereas
in 1975 they tended to accept this as a legitimate practice. In
general, Allied operators appeared to be less hostile and suspicious
of shop supervision and exhibited greater independence in the face
of authoritative foremen. As suggested earlier, foremen are now also
relieved of some of the responsibility for the completion of particular jobs on their shift, this function being assumed by the
assertive presence of the scheduling man. In all these respects my
account of changes are similar to those described by Reinhard
Bendix, Frederick Taylor, Richard Edwards, and others, namely,
the diminution of the authority of the foreman and the parceling-
out of his functions to more specialized personnel.[20]

The Organization of a
Shop-Floor Culture

So far we have considered the stages through which any operation must go for its completion and the roles of different employees in advancing the operation from stage to stage. In practice the stages themselves are subject to considerable manipulation, and there were occasions when I would complete an operation without ever having been given it by the scheduling man, without having a blueprint, or without having it checked by the inspector. It is not necessary to discuss these manipulations further, since by now it must be apparent that relations emanating directly from the organization of work are understood and attain meaning primarily in terms of making out. Even social interaction not occasioned by the structure of work is dominated by and couched in the idiom of making out. When someone comes over to talk, his first question is, "Are you making out?" followed by "What's the rate?" If you are not making out, your conversation is likely to consist of explanations of why you are not: "The rate's impossible," "I had to wait an hour for the inspector to check the first piece," "These mother-fucking drills keep on burning up." When you are sweating it out on the machine, "knocking the pieces out," a passerby may call out "Gravy!"—suggesting that the job is not as difficult as you are making it appear. Or, when you are "goofing off"—visiting other workers or gossiping at the coffee machine—as likely as not someone will yell out, "You've got it made, man!" When faced with an operation that is obviously impossible, some comedian may bawl out, "Best job in the house!" Calling out to a passerby, "You got nothing to do?" will frequently elicit a protest of the nature, "I'm making out. What more do you want?" At lunchtime, operators of similar machines tend to sit together, and each undertakes a postmortem of the first half of the shift. Why they failed to make out, who "screwed them up," what they expect to accomplish in the second half of the shift, can they make up lost time, advice for others who are having some difficulty, and so on—such topics tend to dominate lunchtime conversations. As regards the domination of shop-floor interaction by the culture of making out, I can detect no changes over the thirty years. Some of the details of making out may have changed, but the idiom, status, tempo, etc., of interaction at work continue to be governed by and to rise out of the relations in production that constitute the rules of making out.

In summary, we have seen how the shop-floor culture revolves around making out. Each worker sooner or later is sucked into this distinctive set of activities and language, which then proceed to take on a meaning of their own. Like Roy, when I first entered the shop I was somewhat contemptuous of this game of making out, which appeared to advance Allied's profit margins more than the operators' interests. But I experienced the same shift of opinion that Roy reported:

> ...attitudes changed from mere indifference to the piecework incentive to a determination not to be forced to respond, when failure to get a price increase on one of the lowest paying operations of his job repertoire convinced him that the company was unfair. Light scorn for the incentive scheme turned to bitterness. Several months later, however, after fellow operator McCann had instructed him in the "angles on making out," the writer was finding values in the piecework system other than economic ones. He struggled to attain quota "for the hell of it," because it was a "little game" and "keeps me from being bored."[21]

Such a pattern of insertion and seduction is common. In my own case, it took me some time to understand the shop language, let alone the intricacies of making out. It was a matter of three or four months before I began to make out by using a number of angles and by transferring time from one operation to another. Once I knew I had a chance to make out, the rewards of participating in a game in which the outcomes were uncertain absorbed my attention, and I found myself spontaneously cooperating with management in the production of greater surplus value. Moreover, it was only in this way that I could establish relationships with others on the shop floor. Until I was able to strut around the floor like an experienced operator, as if I had all the time in the world and could still make out, few but the greenest would condescend to engage me in conversation. Thus, it was in terms of the culture of making out that individuals evaluated one another and themselves. It provided the basis of status hierarchies on the shop floor, and it was reinforced by the fact that the more sophisticated machines requiring greater skill also had the easier rates. Auxiliary personnel developed characters in accordance with their willingness to cooperate in making out: Morris was a lousy guy because he'd always delay in bringing stock; Harry was basically a decent crib attendent (after he took my ham), tried to help the guys, but was overworked; Charley was an OK scheduling man because he'd try to give me the gravy jobs; Bill, my day man, was "all right" because he'd show me the angles on making out, give me some kitty if I needed it, and sometimes cover up for me when I made a mess of things. In the next chapter I will consider the implications of being bound into such a coercive cultural system and of constituting the labor process as a game.

The Dispersion of Conflict

I have shown how the organization of a piecework machine shop gives rise to making out and how this in turn becomes the basis of shop-floor culture. Making out also shapes distinctive patterns of conflict. Workers are inserted into the labor process as individuals who directly dictate the speed, feed, depth, etc., of their machines. The piece wage, as Marx observed, "tends to develop on the one hand that individuality, and with it the sense of liberty, independence, and self-control of the labourers, on the other, their competition one with another."[22] At the same time, the labor process of a machine shop embodies an opposed principle, the operator's dependence on auxiliary workers—themselves operating with a certain individual autonomy. This tension between control over machinery and subordination to others, between productive activities and production relations, leads to particular forms of conflict on the shop floor.

I have already suggested that pressures to make out frequently result in conflict between production and auxiliary workers when the latter are unable to provide some service promptly. The reason for this is only rarely found in the deliberate obstructionism of the crib attendant, inspector, trucker, and so on. More often it is the consequence of a managerial allocation of resources. Thus, during the period I worked on the shop floor, the number of operators on second shift expanded to almost the number on first shift, yet there was only one truck driver instead of two; there were, for most of the time, only two inspectors instead of four; there were only two foremen instead of four; and there was only one crib attendant instead of two or three. This merely accentuated a lateral conflict that was endemic to the organization of work. The only way such lateral conflict could be reduced was to allow second-shift operators to provide their own services by jumping into an idle truck, by entering the crib to get their own fixtures, by filling out their own cards, by looking through the books for rates or to see whether an order had been finished, and so on. However, these activities were all regarded as illegitimate by management outside the shop.[23] When middle management clamped down on operators by enforcing rules, there was chaos.

In the eyes of senior management, auxiliary workers are regarded as overhead, and so there are continual attempts to reduce their numbers. Thus, as already recounted, the objective of the quality-control manager was to reduce the number of inspectors. Changes in the philosophy of quality control, he argued, place increasing responsibility on the worker, and problems of quality are more effectively combatted by "systems control," design, and careful check on suppliers, particularly suppliers of castings. But, so long as every operation had to have its first piece checked, the decline in the number of inspectors merely led to greater frustration on the shop floor.

A single example will illustrate the type of conflict that is common. Tom, an inspector, was suspended for three days for absenteeism. This meant that there was only one inspector for the entire department, and work was piling up outside the window of Larry (another inspector). I had to wait two hours before my piece was inspected and I could get on with the task. It was sufficiently annoying to find only one inspector around, but my fury was compounded by the ostentatious manner in which Larry himself was slowing down. When I mentioned this to him, jokingly, he burst forth with "Why should I work my ass off? Tom's got his three days off, and the company thinks they are punishing him, but it's me who's got to break my back." In this instance, conflict between Tom and the company was transmuted into a resentment between Tom and Larry, which in turn provoked a hostile exchange between Larry and me. "Going slow," aimed at the company, redounds to the disadvantage of fellow workers. The redistribution of conflict in such ways was a constant feature of social relations on the shop floor. It was particularly pronounced on second shift because of the shortage of auxiliary workers and the fact that the more inexperienced operators, and therefore the ones most needing assistance, were also on that shift.

Common sense might lead one to believe that conflict between workers and managers would lead to cohesiveness among workers, but such an inference misses the fact that all conflict is mediated on an ideological terrain, in this case the terrain of making out. Thus, management-worker conflict is turned into competitiveness and intragroup struggles as a result of the organization of work. The translation of hierarchical domination into lateral antagonisms is in fact a common phenomenon throughout industry, as was shown in a study conducted on a sample of 3,604 blue-collar workers from 172 production departments in six plants scattered across the United States:

> ...work pressure in general is negatively correlated to social-supportive behavior, which we have called cohesive behavior, and positively related to competitive and intra-group conflict behavior. Cohesive behavior is generally untenable under high pressure conditions because the reward structure imposed by management directs employees to work as fast as they can individually.[24]

The dominant pattern of conflict dispersion in a piecework machine shop is undoubtedly the reconstitution of hierarchical conflict as lateral conflict and competition. However, it is by no means the only redistribution of conflict. A reverse tendency is often found when new machinery is introduced that is badly coordinated with existing technology. Here lateral conflict may be transformed into an antagonism between workers and management or between different levels of management.

To illustrate this point, I will draw upon my own experience with a machine that is designed to balance pulleys so that they don't break any shafts when they are running in an engine. The balancing machine, introduced within the past five years, is very sensitive to any faults in the pulley—faults that other machining operations may inadvertently introduce or that may have been embedded in the original casting when it came from the foundry.

The pulley is seated on a fixture attached to a rotating circular steel plate. The balancing plate and pulley can be automatically spun, and this indicates two things: first, the place where excess stock should be removed to compensate for imperfections in the pulley and, second, the degree of imbalance in the pulley. When an area of excess weight is located, holes are drilled in the pulley to remove stock; the pulley is then spun again and more holes are drilled as needed. This process is repeated until the pulley balances to within one or two ounces, according to the specifications on the blueprint. The most difficult part of the job is getting the balance set up. Before any pulley can be balanced, it is necessary first to balance the fixture and plate by placing clay on the plate. This complicated procedure for setting up is designed to ensure that the pulley is indeed balanced when the dial registers it as being balanced—that is, when the pulley is turned through 180 degrees on the fixture, the recording is still within one or two ounces, or whatever the specification happens to be.

The small pulleys were easy. Often they didn't even need balancing. Just a touch from the drill to indicate they had been attended to was all that was necessary. That was gravy. But the big seventy-five pounders presented a very different picture. They were the most difficult to balance and naturally the most critical. It was tough enough hauling them up onto the balance and then taking them off, let alone balancing them to within an ounce. Both Bill and I tried to pretend they weren't there, although there were always a good number sitting by the balance, four or five layers of sixteen, piled on top of one another. We balanced them only when we had to, and then with extreme reluctance. They often posed insuperable problems, due to defects in the castings or in the taper, which meant that they would not fit properly on their fixture. On one or two occasions I came on second shift to discover the unusual sight of Bill cursing and sweating over the mess the pulleys were in and hearing him say how, after ten years on the miscellaneous job, he was getting too old to face it any more. "It's all yours, Englishman. Perhaps they'll give you a little bonus to keep you on," he laughed. It wasn't so much that the pulleys were not offering him enough money, since Bill would have his time covered with a double red card. It was more that he had been defeated; his job had taken over; he had lost control.

No amount of energy or ingenuity seemed sufficient to get those pulleys to balance, yet they still had to be delivered to the line. "They expect me to make pulleys on this machine. Well, I only balance pulleys, and if they won't balance, they won't balance. They don't understand that if they've got blowholes in them they just won't come down."

I came in one day at 3 p.m., and Bill warned me that the big shots would be breathing down my neck for the seventy-five pounders. "Those pulleys are hot, man!" Sure enough, no sooner had he left than I found myself encircled by the foreman, the night-shift superintendent, the foreman of inspectors, the scheduling man, the setup man, and, from time to time, a manager from some other department. Such royal attention had me flustered from the start. I couldn't even set up the balance properly. The superintendent became impatient and started ordering me to do this, that, and the other, all of which I knew to be wrong. It was futile to point that out. After all, who was I to contradict the superintendent? The most powerful thought to lodge in my head was to lift the pulley off the balance and hurl it at their feet. As the clay piled up on the plate, way beyond what was necessary to balance it, the superintendent began to panic. He obviously thought his neck was on the line, but he had little idea as to how the machine worked. He was an old-timer, unaccustomed to this new-fangled equipment. And so he followed the directions on the chart hanging from the machine—directions that Bill had instructed me to ignore because they were wrong. When the superintendent thought the plate was balanced, we started drilling holes in the pulley—more and more holes, until the surface was covered with them. Clearly something was wrong. I'd never seen such a mess of holes. But the superintendent was more concerned with getting the pulleys out of the department and onto the engines. He didn't dare ask me to turn the pulleys through 180 degrees to see if they were really balanced—the acid test. I knew they wouldn't balance out, and probably so did he. By the end of the shift I had managed to ruin twenty-three pulleys.

The saga continued the following day. When I arrived at the balance, the superintendent was already there, remonstrating with Bill, who was trying to explain how to balance the plate. He was surrounded by yellow-painted pulleys—the pulleys I had "balanced" the night before—which had been pulled off the engines just before they were due to be shipped out. Amazingly, no one was after my neck. The superintendent was fussing around, trying to vindicate himself, saying that the chart was misleading. It wasn't his fault, he complained, and how much better it was in the old days before we had these fancy machines that didn't work properly. Bill was not upset at all, even though he'd been on the pulleys all day. It didn't take much imagination to see why, since he was now a hero, having retrieved the situation. Management had come round to him in the morning demanding to know what incompetent had balanced the pulleys. Since he alone knew how to work the balance, Bill sensed his newly won power and importance. The superintendent, however, was in hot water, and his prestige, already at a low ebb, had taken a further dive. No one was particularly surprised at my ineptitude, since I had never demonstrated any mechanical skill or understanding.

I have just described two types of conflict that can result from the introduction of a new piece of technology. In my first example, the new machine was out of tune with the surrounding technology and as a result turned what was potentially a lateral conflict into one between management and worker. In my second example, the new machine allowed an operator to monopolize some knowledge (and this is quite likely when the machine is unique to the shop); this enhanced his power and led to a severe conflict between shop management and middle management when the operator was not around.[25] There is no space here to explore other patterns of conflict crystallization, dispersion, and displacement. All I wish to stress is the way in which the specific organization of work structures conflict and how direct confrontation between management and worker is by no means its most common form.

Indeed, over the past thirty years conflict between management and worker has diminished, while that among workers has increased. This was how Donald Roy reacted to my obeservations at Allied:

Your point in regard to the big switch of hierarchical conflict to the side of inter-worker competition pleases me immensely. . . . But in retrospect I see that in my time the main line of cleavage

was the worker managment one. With the exception of the mutual
irritations between machine "partners" of different shifts operator relations were mainly cooperative, and most of the auxiliaries
(stock chasers, tool crib men, etc.) were helpful. There were employees in the Jack Shop then who recalled the "whistle and whip"
days before the local union was organized.[26]

There are a number of suggestions in his dissertation as to why there
should have been greater antagonism between management and
worker and less competition and conflict among workers. First,
because of wartime conditions, there were more auxiliary workers
for the same number of operators. Second, there was a generalized
hostility to the company as being cheap, unconcerned about its labor
force, penny-pinching, and so on,[27] whereas the attitudes of workers
at the engine division of Allied were much more favorable to the
company. This was exemplified by the large number of father-son
pairs working in the plant. If your son had to work in a factory,
many felt that Allied was not a bad place. Third, Allied treated its
employees more fairly than Geer. Part of this may be attributed to
the greater effectiveness of the union grievance machinery in 1975
than in 1945. Furthermore, as part of Allied, a large corporation,
the engine division was less vulnerable to the kinds of market
exigencies that had plagued Geer Company. It could therefore
afford to treat its employees more fairly. Also, Allied did not appear
to be out to cut rates with the militant enthusiasm that Roy had
encountered. Fourth, as Roy himself notes above, the period of CIO
organizing was still close at hand, and many Geer employees remembered the days of sweatshops and arbitrary discipline. Among
the workers I talked to, only the older ones could recall the days of
the "whistle and whip," and, when they did, it was mainly in reference to the tribulations of their fathers.

Conclusion

Between Geer Company of 1945 and Allied Corporation, thirty years
later, the labor process underwent two sets of changes. The first is
seen in the greater individualism promoted by the organization of
work. Operators in 1975 had more autonomy as a result of the
following: relaxed enforcement of certain managerial controls, such

as inspection of pieces and rate-fixing; increased shop-floor bargaining between workers and foremen; and changes in the system of piece rates—changes that laid greater stress on individual performance, effort, and mobility and allowed more manipulations. The second type of change, related to the first, concerns the diminution of hierarchical conflict and its redistribution in a number of different directions. As regards the relaxation of conflict between worker and management, one notes the decline in the authority of the foreman and the reduction of tensions between those concerned with enforcement of quality in production and those primarily interested in quantity. The greater permissiveness toward chiseling, the improvement of tooling and machines, as well as easier rates, have all facilitated making out and in this way have reduced antagonism between worker and shop management.[28] The employment of fewer auxiliary workers, on the other hand, has exacerbated lateral conflict among different groups of workers.[29]

These changes do not seem to support theories of intensification of the labor process or increase of managerial control through separation of conception and execution. What we have observed is the expansion of the area of the "self-organization" of workers as they pursue their daily activities. We have seen how operators, in order to make out at all, subvert rules promulgated from on high, create informal alliances with auxiliary workers, make their own tools, and so on. In order to produce surplus value, workers have had to organize their relations and activities in opposition to management, particularly middle and senior management. We shall see in chapter 10 how workers actively struggle *against* management to defend the conditions for producing profit. For Cornelius Castoriadis, this represents the fundamental contradiction of capitalism:

> In short, it [the deep contradiction] lies in the fact that capitalism . . . is obliged to try and achieve the simultaneous exclusion and participation of people in relation to their activities, in the fact that people are forced to ensure the functioning of the system half of the time *against* the system's own rules and therefore in struggle against it. This fundamental contradiction appears constantly wherever the process of management meets the process of execution, which is precisely (and par excellence) the social moment of production.[30]

But if the self-organization of workers is necessary for the survival
of capitalism, it also questions the foundations of capitalism.

> When the shop-floor collective establishes norms that informally
> sanction both "slackers" and "speeders," when it constantly con-
> stitutes and reconstitutes itself in "informal" groups that respond
> to both the requirements of the work process and to personal af-
> finities, it can only be viewed as actively opposing to capitalist
> principles new principles of productive and social organization
> and a new view of work.[31]

But is making out as radical as Castoriadis claims? Or is it, as
Herbert Marcuse would argue, a mode of adaptation that reproduces "the voluntary servitude" of workers to capital? Are these
freedoms and needs, generated and partially satisfied in the context
of work and harnessed to the production of surplus value, a challenge to "capitalist principles"? Does making out present an anticipation of something new, the potential for human self-organization,
or is it wholly contained within the reproduction of capitalist relations?[32] We can begin to answer such questions only by examining
more closely the relationship between making out and the essence of
the capitalist labor process—the simultaneous obscuring and securing of surplus value. To this I now turn.

3

The Production of
Consent

Five

The Labor Process as a Game

Following Marx, twentieth-century Marxism has too often and too easily reduced wage laborers to objects of manipulation; to commodities bought and sold in the market; to abstractions incapable of resistance; to victims of the inexorable forces of capitalist accumulation; to carriers, agents, or supports of social relations.[1] It has been left to industrial sociology to restore the subjective moment of labor, to challenge the idea of the subjectless subject, to stress the ubiquitous resistance of everyday life. But in upholding the subjective moment, industrial sociology looks down upon the objective moments as immutable. It presents wage labor and the deprivation of industrial work as the unavoidable and eternal concomitants of material existence in what it regards as a regime of scarcity.

Not surprisingly, industrial sociology finds its confirmation in attitude surveys conducted among workers, which show that they too are resigned to the inherent deprivation of working and adopt what Michael Mann refers to as "pragmatic role acceptance."[2] At the same time, workers go to great lengths to compensate for, or to minimize, the deprivations they experience as inexorable and inevitable:

> [A worker] clings to the possibility of a last remnant of joy in his work. . . . All activity, however much brutalized by mechanization, offers a certain scope for initiative which can satisfy after a fashion the instinct for play and the creative impulse. . . . Even when the details of performance have been prescribed with the utmost minuteness, and in accordance with the latest dictates of the Taylor system, there will be left for the worker certain loopholes, certain chances of escape from the routine, so that when actually at work he will find it possible now and again to enjoy the luxury of self determination.[3]

More than any other sociologist, William Baldamus has examined the nature of the compensations available to industrial workers:

> Hard work is not necessarily reflected in feelings of discomfort only. It can also produce certain satisfactions. As a matter of fact, all work deprivations may be connected with what I shall call "relative satisfactions." They are feelings of temporary relief from the discomfort of certain work realities, feelings which arise when these factors have become part of the worker's customary interpretation of his situation. They are, to this extent, only apparent satisfactions, which are actually derived from deprivation.[4]

Work realities (physical conditions, repetitiveness, and routines) give rise to deprivations (impairment, tedium, and weariness), and deprivations engender relative satisfactions (inurement, traction or tractableness, and contentment).[5]

As many writers have observed, these relative satisfactions are often constituted in the form of games, which reduce the strain of an "endless series of meaningless motions."[6] In their assessment of such supposedly autonomous responses of workers to the demands of capitalist work, sociologists express a deep ambivalence. On the one hand, they recognize that these relative satisfactions contribute to the psychological and social health of the laborer, but on the other hand they see these satisfactions as undermining management objectives. William Foot Whyte formulates the dilemma: "Can the satisfaction involved in playing the piecework game be preserved in our factories at the same time that the attendant conflicts are reduced?"[7] Games create opposition of interests where before there was only harmony. In their classic study, F. J. Roethlisberger and William Dickson argued that "employees had their own rules and their own 'logic' which, more frequently than not, were opposed to those which were imposed on them."[8] "This standard [of output] was not imposed upon them, but apparently had been formulated by the workmen themselves."[9] In his interpretation of the Bank Wiring Room Experiment, George Homans claims that group norms, such as restriction of output, were "spontaneously produced" so as to preserve the integrity of the group.[10] The view that the workers at the Hawthorne Plant evolved their own autonomous principles of work reaches its apotheosis in the writings of Elton Mayo, who speaks of the formation of a "social code at a lower level in opposition to the economic logic [of management]."[11] Michel Crozier argues, similarly, that in a wide variety of industrial settings uncertainties in the labor process are exploited by subordinates, leading to power struggles and noncooperative games aimed against management.[12]

All these treatments share the view that workers autonomously erect their own cultural and production systems in opposition to management. Ironically, the very sociologists for whom a class analysis would be anathema are also the ones who offer the greatest support for such an approach. Unfortunately, their empirical evidence is as weak as their theoretical framework is inadequate. There is ample evidence in *Management and the Worker* that the group chief, section chief, assistant foreman, and foreman either connived or actively assisted in playing a game that was supposed to undermine management interests.[13] Jason Ditton shows how the creation of uncertainty through the relaxation of rules enhances the power of management at the same time that it provides the basis for the construction of games.[14] Stanley Mathewson offers numerous examples of management organizing the forms of output restriction that Elton Mayo attributes to the workers' instinctual and nonlogical opposition to management.[15] On the other hand, when games (such as doubling-up on assembly lines) really do threaten managerial objectives, that is, jeopardize profit margins, management does indeed come in with a stick.[16] Crozier himself points out that, "were it to take place without any check, the power struggle would bring paralyzing conflicts and unbearable situations."[17] In short, where games do take place, they are usually neither independent of nor in opposition to management.

These conclusions are confirmed by my observations of shop management's role in the making-out game at Allied and by Roy's observations at Geer. I have already referred to the different ways in which foremen actively assisted operators in making out—showing them angles, getting annoyed with the methods department's tight rates, using the idiom of making out in defending performances to their own bosses, and so on. When operators handed in more than the acceptable limit (140 percent), not only fellow workers but shop management might protest. Thus, the superintendent frequently returned time cards to operators when they showed more than 140 percent, requesting them to reduce the number of pieces and bank the remainder. Time clerks would also check to see that the 140 percent ceiling had not been violated. All levels of shop management had an interest in steady output and quota restriction; they loved the industrial engineer no more than the operator did.[18] Assigning a new rate to a job could mean turnover of personnel, since workers tend to transfer to jobs where the rates are easier to make. As a result, there would be training costs, lower levels of output, more scrap, and so forth. Alternatively, operators would engage in "goldbricking" because the new rate was "impossible," and this too implied lowered levels of output. I will discuss these and other deleterious consequences of tightening rates in chapter 10. Suffice it to say, shop management not only encouraged operators to produce their quota but was also found actively acquiescing in output restriction by operators; that is, management actively engaged in the game of making out. Indeed, foremen and scheduling men are players in the game.

By way of summary, then, the games workers play are not, as a rule, autonomously created in opposition to management, as claimed by Elton Mayo, who views the matter from one perspective, and by Cornelius Castoriadis, who views it from another. Rather, they emerge historically out of struggle and bargaining, but they are played within limits defined by minimum wages and acceptable profit margins. Management, at least at the lower levels, actively participates not only in the organization of the game but in the enforcement of its rules. The stimulus to engage in such work games derives as much from the inexorable coercion of coming to work, and subordination to the dictates of the labor process once there, as from the emergence of "radical needs," "a new vision of work," or a "nonlogical code." The game is entered into for its *relative* satisfactions, or what Herbert Marcuse calls *repressive* satisfactions. The game represents a need that is strictly the product of a society "whose dominant interests demand repression." [19] The satisfaction of that need reproduces not only "voluntary servitude" (consent) but also greater material wealth. We must now turn to the concrete examination of how participation in a work game contributes to the reproduction of capitalist relations and the expansion of surplus value.

Obscuring and Securing
Surplus Labor

Making out, as described in chapter 4, inserts the worker into the labor process as an individual rather than as a member of a class distinguished by a particular relationship to the means of production. Workers control their own machines instead of being controlled by them, and this enhances their autonomy. They put their machines into motion singlehandedly, and this creates the appearance that they can, as individuals, transform nature into useful commodities. The system of reward is based on individual rather than collective effort. Second, the combination of autonomy with respect to machines and dependence with respect to auxiliary personnel has the consequence of redistributing conflict from a hierarchical direction into a lateral direction, in which individual laborers face one another in conflict or competition. The constitution of the worker as one among many competing and conflicting others masks their common membership in a class of agents of production who sell their labor power for a wage, as distinct from another class of agents who appropriate their unpaid labor.

The significance of creating a game out of the labor process, however, extends beyond the particularities of making out. The very activity of playing a game generates consent with respect to its rules. The point is more than the obvious, but important, assertion that one cannot both play the game and at the same time question the rules. The issue is: which is logically and empirically prior, playing the game or the legitimacy of the rules? Here I am not arguing that playing the game rests on a broad consensus; on the contrary, consent rests upon—is constructed through—playing the game. The game does not reflect an underlying harmony of interests; on the contrary, it is responsible for and generates that harmony. The source of the game itself lies not in a preordained value consensus but in historically specific struggles to adapt to the deprivation inherent in work and in struggles with management to define the rules.

The rules, which in the case of making out present themselves in the form of a set of social relations in production, are evaluated in terms of the defined outcomes of the game—making out or not making out—and not in terms of some broader set of outcomes that are also the consequence of the game, such as the generation of profit, the reproduction of capitalist relations of production, and so forth. Therefore, to the extent that it is institutionalized—as it is in making out—the game becomes an end in itself, overshadowing, masking, and even inverting the conditions out of which it emerges. As long as workers are engaged in a game involving their relations to a machine, their subordination to the process of production becomes an object of acquiescence. Equally, incorporation into a game involving other agents of production (workers, foremen, etc.) generates an acquiescence in the *social* relations of control inscribed in the labor process, that is, the relations in production. Two consequences of game-playing have so far been delineated: first, game-playing obscures the relations of production in response to which the game is originally constructed; second, game-playing generates consent to the social relations in production that define the rules of the game.

Individual (as opposed to collective) violation of rules leads to ritual punishment, which has the effect of reinforcing these obscuring and consent-producing consequences. That is, a violation of rules has the consequence of strengthening their hold over productive activities and relations. Thus, attempts by management to squeeze a little extra out of workers frequently enhanced consensual relations on the shop floor. Operators at Allied continually complained about "being screwed" by the company, and initially I associated this with some vague notion of exploitation. Soon I discovered that such anguish referred to the company's failure to provide the necessary conditions to play the game of making out; for example, drills might have burned up, the blueprint might have disappeared, the machinery might not have been functioning properly, etc. In other words, management was being accused of "cheating," of not playing according to the rules of the game; and these accusations served to reassert the legitimacy of the rules and the values of making out. In this way the consensual framework was continually being reestablished and reinforced.

It is not enough to obscure property relations and to generate consent to production relations; workers have to create a surplus over and above their wage. How are workers persuaded to cooperate in the pursuit of profit? Obviously, one way—but, generally, not a very efficient one—is by the continuous application of coercion, that is, by firing those who do not achieve a given quota. Coercion, of course, always lies at the back of *any* employment relationship, but the erection of a game provides the conditions in which the organization of active cooperation and consent prevails.

The purpose of the piece-rate system, as Taylor and his associates presented it, was to coordinate the interests of management and worker through their common interest in the financial gain that could be secured from labor's extra effort. It was the monetary incentive that brought forth the additional exertion. Studies in the human-relations tradition drew attention to output restriction as indicative of the failure of the economic incentive. As Roy pointed out, and as must be apparent from what I have said so far, restriction of output was in fact in conformity with maximization of economic gain. At the same time, both Roy and I observed events that suggested that monetary incentive was not an adequate explanation of the cooperation produced by making out.

It would be easy, *if the "verbal" behavior of operatives were accepted as indicative of action tendency* [italics added], to explain the partial success of the piecework system in terms of "economic incentive"; and it would be easy to account for its *partial failure* as due to maladministration of that incentive. . . . On the other hand, the writer's attention was drawn to a few "negative cases" that seemed to deny the all-powerful influence of the "economic incentive" and to point to a need for still closer examination of response to piecework. For instance, on some occasions operators either failed to put forth effort toward the attainment of "quota" earnings, when "quota" achievement was recognized as possible, or they stopped

production at levels short of the "quota" line. Also, operators on
occasion showed an indifference toward maximization of "take
home" earnings (a) by disinclination to work overtime, (b) by
"quitting early" after working partial shifts when jobs did
not suit them, or (c) by "laying off" to avoid "day work." In
addition, on occasion the "verbal" behavior of operators indicated that they did not "care about money." [20]

During my time at Allied I observed similar patterns of behavior
that contradicted the theory of economic motivation as the basis of
making out, but these patterns of behavior were couched in the
idiom of economic gain. Furthermore, if economic motivation were
at the basis of shop-floor activities, then the preference-ranking of
jobs would be in accordance with economic reward. This was not the
case. Many of the service jobs on day rates were widely regarded as
preferable to piece-rate jobs, even though the latter brought home
more money. Rather, the labor process is organized into a game,
and the goals that the game defines constitute the values current on
the shop floor. As always, Roy puts it graphically:

Could "making out" be considered an "end in itself"? It might
be suggested that the attainment of "quota" marked the successful completion of an "act" or "task" in which the outcome
was largely controllable by the operator; although "chance"
factors were also important determinants. "Making out" called
for the exercise of skill and stamina; it offered opportunities
for "self expression." The element of uncertainty of outcome
provided by ever-present possibilities of "bad breaks" made
"quota" attainment an "exciting game" played against the
clock on the wall, a "game" in which the elements of control
provided by the application of knowledge, skill, ingenuity,
speed and stamina heightened interest and lent to the exhilaration of "winning" feelings of "accomplishment." Although operators constantly shared their piecework experience as a chief
item of conversation, and always in terms of "making money,"
they were, in reality, communicating "game scores" or "race
results," not financial success or disappointments. It is doubt-
ful if any operator ever thought that he had been "making
money." It is likely that had anyone been able to communicate
accurately such a conviction, he would have been laughed out
of the shop. [21]

In other words, making out cannot be understood simply in terms of the externally derived goal of achieving greater earnings. Rather, its dominance in the shop-floor culture emerges out of and is embodied in a specific set of relations in production that in turn reflect management's interest in generating profit. The rewards of making out are defined in terms of factors immediately related to the labor process—reduction of fatigue, passing time, relieving boredom, and so on—and factors that emerge from the labor process—the social and psychological rewards of making out on a tough job as well as the social stigma and psychological frustration attached to failing on a gravy job.

It is not so much the monetary incentive that concretely coordinates the interests of management and worker but rather the play of the game itself, which generates a common interest in the outcome and in the game's continuity. Any game that provides distinctive rewards to the players establishes a common interest among the players—whether these are representatives of capital or labor—in providing for the conditions of its reproduction. Insofar as games encompass the entire labor process, the value system to which they give rise will prevail on the shop floor. Activities are evaluated and interests established as a consequence of the game. In other words, interests are not given primordially, nor are they necessarily brought to the shop floor from socialization experiences outside work. Rather, they are organized by the specific form of relations in production; in our example, interests are defined by relations to the game of making out. The day-to-day experience emerges out of the organization of work and defines the interests of the various agents of production once their basic survival—which, as far as workers are concerned, is an acceptable wage—is assured.[22] When the labor process is organized into some form of game involving the active participation of both management and worker, the interests of both are concretely coordinated. In other work situations the labor process organizes different constellations of interests, of a kind that may render the interests of workers and management irrevocably antagonistic.

To repeat, ordinarily the conception of work in terms of games has sprung from assumptions of irreducible harmony. Games are the spontaneous, autonomous, malevolent creation of workers; they generate power struggles and conflict with management. In denying the primordiality of interests and stressing their emergence out of the organization of work, I have come to different conclusions. Games do, indeed, arise from worker initiatives, from the search for means of enduring subordination to the labor process, but they are regulated, coercively where necessary, by management. Once a game is established, however, it can assume a dynamics of its own, and there is no guarantee that it will continue to reproduce the conditions of its existence. On the contrary, it is possible that playing the game will tend to undermine the rules that define it. Thus, in Marx's conception of piecework, workers are not sufficiently strong and well organized to enforce restriction of output.[23] Instead, they are compelled to compete with one another in producing at an ever faster rate, and this stimulates management to cut piecework prices. The piecework "game" becomes a self-defeating spiral of labor intensification unless it is stabilized by operators' transforming the rules and restricting competition, as in making out. Until then, workers find themselves in a "prisoner's dilemma": what is in the interests of the individual worker—the maximization of output—operates to undermine the workers' collective interest— higher piecework prices. Peter Blau describes the same conflict between individual and collective rationality in output games in a state employment agency. There competition among workers increases individual output but at the expense of collective efficiency. That is, the game itself produces conditions that make the game more difficult to play. Blau adds, "This poses the interesting question, which cannot be answered here: What conditions determine whether this process ultimately levels off or reaches a climax in a revolutionary transformation of the competitive structure into a cooperative one?"[24] Or, more generally, one can ask: What are the conditions for the reproduction of games? Under what conditions will the game's own dynamics undermine the harmony it also produces and so lead to a crisis? More specifically, what are the conditions under which making out can be continually played on the shop floor? Does this game have consequences other than the production of consent and profit—consequences that continually threaten its reproduction? Does making out sow the seeds of its own destruction?

Uncertainty and Crises

Numerous writers of both Marxist and non-Marxist persuasion insist that the promotion of organizational effectiveness and efficiency is contingent on the minimization of uncertainty.[25] Here I shall suggest that securing worker cooperation rests on a minimal uncertainty, the possibility that workers will assert some control over the labor process, if only of a limited kind:

> But operator interest in "quota" piecework jobs seemed to have
> its "diminishing returns." McCann, for instance, spoke of
> boredom on one "gravy" piecework job, [saying] that he had
> had so much that he could "run them in his sleep." His experi-
> ence suggests that "making out" on piecework was a stimulat-
> ing "game" only as long as the job represented a "challenge"
> to the operator, only as long as elements of "uncertainty" were
> present in the activity's outcome. . . . If "making out" lost its
> value as a "game" when operator control over the job became
> so complete that "winning" degenerated into mere routine, it
> also lost such value if the element of uncertainty became too
> predominant over the element of control; that is, if "bad
> breaks" became too frustrating to the application of skill, the
> job became "nerve-wracking."[26]

A game loses its ability to absorb players under any of the following three conditions: first, when uncertainty is too great and outcomes are entirely beyond the control of players; second, when uncertainty is too slight and outcomes may become completely controlled by players; third, when players are indifferent to the possible outcomes. Let us take an example of each. One of my jobs, which I particularly disliked, involved drilling 3/16-inch holes twelve inches deep into steel "slides." Bill's jumping jack, as it was called, was permanently set up for the job. It drilled two slides at a time, using thirteen-inch drills. After cutting a short depth, the drill would jump up to bring out chips, plunge back in again to drill another short depth, and so on until the hole was complete. Once started, the jumping jack continued automatically until the hole was finished. Because the drills were long and sometimes dull, they frequently broke, and, if they were not caught in time, the pressure could send pieces of steel flying in all directions. The job was not only dangerous but frustrating, because the rate did not allow for the breaking of drills. Furthermore, the conditions in which breaks might occur were largely unpredictable: the depth in the steel at which the drill might break, the speed at which it would break, and the number of times it could be used before breaking. The job gave me the jitters, and I never even tried to make out after I had broken one or two drills, preferring to stay alive and psychologically healthy. However, Bill, my day man, with ten years' experience on the miscellaneous job and not one to balk at a challenge to his ingenuity and skill, did, always, try to make out and, in fact, generally did so, at around the 125 percent mark. But he didn't like the job either. Thus, what was too much uncertainty for one was a challenge to another. But the moral remains: when there is too much uncertainty, players cease to play the game.

At the opposite extreme were the jobs on the automatic saw, which guaranteed 125 percent. Such a job was boring, since it required little attention, particularly when the stock was bar steel, eight inches in diameter, for then the saw cut only about four pieces an hour. Faced with this, I would go and find some other job to do while the saw was running and in that way build up my kitty.

Finally, what can we say about the evaluation of outcomes? I have already referred to the disdain with which both Roy and I regarded making out when we first entered the shop and how, eventually, we both succumbed to its dictates. Indeed, we both got hooked on the game and became avid players. I must confess that, at least in my own case, part of my initial contempt was a defense, to cover my inability to make out or to foresee any prospects of ever doing so. But then, what sort of game would it be, involving how much uncertainty, if any Tom, Dick, or Harry could walk in off the street and immediately begin making out without any previous experience? In other words, the fact that it took both Roy and me—and virtually anyone else who comes in green to machine shops—several months to achieve incentive pay serves to establish the worth and esteem associated with making out. Newcomers are given jobs with the tightest rates, a practice that in the short run generates withdrawal and bitterness but in the long run reinforces commitment to the values of making out. As both Roy and I soon came to appreciate, if we were to be anyone in the shop we had better begin making out. Until we did, we would continue, as objects of scorn and derision, to be ostracized.[27] The longer we delayed, the poorer our reputation would be and the more socially unacceptable we would become. Pressure to make out came not only from management (in my own case there was very little of this) but from fellow operators and auxiliary workers. Moreover, playing the game brought other than social rewards—namely, physiological ones. When one is trying to make out, time passes more quickly—in fact, too quickly—and one is less aware of being tired. The difference between making out and not making out was thus not measured in the few pennies of bonus we earned but in our prestige, sense of accomplishment, and pride. Playing the game eliminated much of the drudgery and boredom associated with industrial work.

> It cannot be claimed in this analysis of piecework response, that "economic" motivation played no part in "quota" attainment in the situation investigated. But it is suggested that piecework may provide a complex of incentives. The "piecework incentive" may include, but is not synonymous with, "economic incentive." Therefore, if piecework "works" under certain conditions, i.e., stimulates machine operators to put forth productive effort in a given situation, it does not necessarily follow that this stimulation may be attributable to economic incentive. Nor would the "failure" of piecework provide evidence of any inherent inadequacy of economic incentive. It could be that such worker expressions as "I don't care about the money" indicate not the inadequacy of economic incentive per se, but an absence in the situation of possibilities of economic reward of sufficient magnitude to stimulate "caring."[28]

Participation in the game is predicated on two limits of uncertainty in outcomes: on the one side, workers have to be guaranteed a minimum acceptable wage and, on the other side, management has to be assured of a minimum level of profit. While playing the game of making out never directly threatens the minimum wage, it can under certain circumstances endanger profits. I shall term this first kind of crisis a *system crisis*. A crisis of a second kind stems from workers' withdrawal from the game either because of too much or too little uncertainty in the attainment of making out (*legitimation crisis*) or because making out no longer has any value to the players (*motivational crisis*).[29]

The system crisis goes to the heart of the question: How is it that a capitalist can make a prior commitment to a wage and yet at the same time be assured of an acceptable level of profit? In the Geer days, the extraction of surplus value represented Geer's survival as a company, and in their anxiety for profit, that is, to avoid a crisis of the first kind, the Geer management frequently precipitated a crisis of the second kind. Raising rates, changing rules, cutting costs of retooling, and so forth, all contributed to a legitimation crisis, expressed finally in a walkout. By contrast, Allied could survive a system crisis without precipitating a legitimation crisis. Thus, when the engine division made a loss (as it did in 1974), for reasons unrelated to participation in making out (as I shall show in chapter 8), management made no significant attempt to undermine the basis of making out by changing rules or rates. The loss was absorbed by the corporation or was passed on to the customer, and a new general manager was installed at the engine division.

The paradox of the system crisis is that it cannot be known before the event. Individual output levels in the small-parts department for the first eleven months of 1975 suggest that consistent performance below 75 percent of the standard rate set by the industrial engineers is unacceptable. But there is no way of knowing what actually should be the minimum level to assure profit, since this depends on the outputs of all the operators in the machine shop, and these outputs are continually changing.

A crisis of the second type can be gauged by comparing levels of output for different jobs. Whenever uncertainty falls outside acceptable limits, either below or above, outputs will cluster around the 140 percent or the 80 percent mark, or both.[30] The existence of outputs in between indicates that some operators, at least, are playing the game, the level of uncertainty is acceptable, and operators are not indifferent to the outcomes of their activities. As operators gain in experience and seniority, they can move onto machines that offer a steady output of 140 percent—for example, the automatic chuck and bar lathes or the automatic screw machines. On these machines setups require considerable skill and practice, but, once they are mastered, uncertainty is eliminated and making out is no longer a significant game *for these operators;* however, as long as there is no motivational crisis in the shop, they will continue to turn in at 140 percent. That is, as long as others are struggling to achieve 125 percent, they remain at the top of the prestige ladder.

Many of these more senior employees basked in the glory of their power and status. Other things being equal, such employees should have been more class conscious than those who played the game of making out more actively. And, indeed, a number did express considerable hostility to the company, while others became active in the union. However, in comparisons between these workers and others in the plant, there is the complicating factor of seniority, which on the one hand generates greater commitment to the company (based on the rewards of seniority, such as pension and job security) and on the other hand enhances the opportunity for involvement in the union. As an expression of the former tendency, one or two operators risked their reputation by handing in suggestions to the company as to how rates could be increased on their own machines! Al McCann notwithstanding, a legitimation crisis is more likely to emerge out of tight rates rather than loose rates. Since Roy left Geer, rates have generally been easier to make, and transfers are facilitated by the bidding process. The result is that, after a few months, operators can hold jobs that offer all the challenges and rewards of making out. In such circumstances, legitimation crises are unlikely to occur.

We must finally pose the question of the relationship between system crises and legitimation or motivational crises. Certainly a crisis of the second type will precipitate a crisis of the first type. But a crisis of the first type can result from factors other than the breakdown of making out, for example, unusually high training costs or excessive overtime and so forth (see chapter 8). On the other hand, can a system crisis be the consequence of playing the game of making out according to its rules? If so, under what conditions will making out precipitate such a crisis? Clearly, the answer must lie in the possible types of distribution of percentage outputs of operators. One fact that might push the distribution to the low side is an increase in mobility between jobs. Under what conditions will a crisis of the second type be precipitated by a system crisis? That is, under what conditions will management attempt to undermine the conditions of making out when faced with declining profits? In other words, will management precipitate struggle when there is a profit crisis? I shall return to some of these questions in chapter 10.

The conditions for participating in making out and its effectiveness in obscuring and securing surplus labor provide a basis for distinguishing between at least two types of games. First, there are games that are confined to workers' relationship to technology, such as those described by William Baldamus, Donald Roy, and Harvey Swados.[31] If they can be sustained, such games may generate consent to the structures of deprivation inherent in work. But as Donald Roy points out, his "clicking" game did not absorb him for very long, since he could easily master every nuance and eliminate the essence of any game—uncertainty. Games limited to single workers and their relationship to the labor process offer only diminishing distraction from deprivation and, above all, do not generate consent to the relations in production. To achieve this consent, a second type of game must be established, one that involves other agents of production. Such group games are potentially more permanent, since they engage the attention of workers more deeply and enlarge the scope of uncertainty. They require skills, not merely in mechanical technique but in the more uncertain context of human relations.

In obscuring and securing unpaid labor, games are more effective the more broadly they encompass everyday life on the shop floor. Making out is perhaps a polar type in this regard. By contrast, subordination to an assembly line imposes limits on the scope of the possible games, although the scope is by no means as restricted as one might imagine. Presumably, the more tightly organized the labor process, the more likely it is that antagonistic class relations will emerge. To understand how such class struggles are contained, two other areas where surplus labor is obscured and secured—the internal labor market and the internal state—will have to be examined.

Conclusion

In this chapter I have tried to show how the constitution of the labor process as a game contributes to the obscuring and securing of surplus labor. However, the concept of "game" is more than a tool of explanation. It is also, and necessarily, a tool of critique.[32] First, it represents the link between individual rationality and the rationality of the capitalist system. Just as players in a game adopt strategies that affect outcomes, but not always in the ways intended, so in our daily life we make choices in order to affect outcomes. The possible variation of outcomes is limited but is not entirely beyond our control. That is, we do make history, but not as we please. We make history "behind our backs" through the unintended as well as the intended consequences of our acts. The game metaphor suggests a "history" with "laws" of its own, beyond our control and yet the product of our actions. This is as true of making out, playing chess, buying a new car, electing a president, or fighting a war as it is, unfortunately, of making a revolution.

Second, just as playing a game generates consent to its rules, so participating in the choices capitalism forces us to make also generates consent to its rules, its norms. It is by constituting our lives as a series of games, a set of limited choices, that capitalist relations not only become objects of consent but are taken as given and immutable. We do not collectively decide what the rules of making out will be; rather, we are compelled to play the game, and we then proceed to defend the rules. Third, just as the game defines a set of goals, so capitalism generates a set of interests. Although these interests are not unique and may change over time, they are nonetheless the product of capitalism, just as making out and the interests it defines are the product and, indeed, as I have suggested, a changing product of a particular way of organizing the labor process. The interests are taken as given, and, like the rules, they are not formed through democratic consensus.[33] Fourth, just as the possibility of winning or maximizing one's utility makes a game seductive, so the possibility of realizing one's interests, of satisfying one's needs, defined by capitalism in general or by making out in particular, is the very means for generating consent to rules and relations, presenting them as natural and inevitable. Alternatives are eliminated or cast as utopian. By the same token, dissatisfaction is the failure to satisfy the needs produced by capitalism in general, or by making out in particular, rather than the failure to satisfy some transcendent set of "radical needs" or even the need to decide collectively what those needs should be. In short, dissatisfaction, of which there is much, is directed not against capitalism but toward its reproduction.

As an instrument of critique, the game metaphor implies some notion of an emancipated society in which people make history themselves for themselves, self-consciously and deliberately. There are no unintended consequences, and the distinctions between norms and laws is obliterated. That is, there is a coincidence of individual and collective rationality. There is rational and undistorted discourse over means and ends, if indeed the distinction itself is still valid. Needs are not pregiven but are subject to collective determination. But even in such a society there would be conflict and contradiction, clashes between the realization of different needs; but these differences would be resolved through open and public political discourse.[34]

In focusing on the discrepancy between means and ends and between norms and laws, on the derivative nature of needs and the production of consent through the possibility of their satisfaction, we unavoidably construct an unrealistically static image of society—an image that the game metaphor forces us to go beyond. As we have seen, participation in a game can undermine the conditions of its reproduction. I have already suggested what these conditions are and have pointed to the corresponding crises that can develop. In this way we can draw from the game metaphor a dynamic that enables us to understand the significance of certain changes under capitalism. Thus, the differences between the organization of work at Geer and Allied suggest ever greater "quantitative" choice within ever narrower limits. In identifying the separation of conception and execution, the expropriation of skill, or the narrowing of the scope of discretion as the broad tendency in the development of the capitalist labor process, Harry Braverman missed the equally important parallel tendency toward the expansion of choices within those ever narrower limits. It is the latter tendency that constitutes a basis of consent and allows the degradation of work to pursue its course without continuing crisis. Thus, we have seen that more reliable machines, easier rates, the possibility of chiseling, and so forth, all increase the options open to the operator in making out. The tendency is also expressed more generally in schemes of job enrichment and job rotation. As we shall see in the next two chapters, this expansion of choice within narrower limits is particularly well illustrated by the rise of the internal labor market and the consolidation of an internal state.

Six

The Rise of an Internal Labor Market

Recent work by economists, prompted by dissatisfaction with the assumptions of neoclassical models and directed to the understanding of economic institutions, has stressed the importance of "internal labor markets."[1] An internal labor market is defined as

> an administrative unit, such as a manufacturing plant, within which the pricing and allocation of labor is governed by a set of administrative rules and procedures. The internal labor market, governed by administrative rules, is to be distinguished from the external labor market of conventional economic theory, where pricing, allocating, and training decisions are controlled directly by economic variables.[2]

Or, as Edwards writes, "The analysis of internal labor markets attempts to break open the 'black box' of the neo-classical firm by viewing social relations at the work place in part as a system of labor exchange within the firm, regulating promotion, job placement, the setting of wage rates, and so forth."[3] As economists, these writers have generally tried to examine whether it is more efficient to establish an internal labor market or to rely on an external labor market.[4] But the question of efficiency cannot be considered apart from the way the internal labor market helps to promote an ideological basis for masking and securing the extraction of surplus value. It is this latter aspect that concerns me here.

Karl Polanyi attributes the inevitability of the decline of the untempered reign of the labor market to the "clash of organizing principles of economic liberalism and social protection."[5] The appearance of the internal labor market is a necessary corollary of this decline. To sociologists, who have never taken too seriously the neoclassical assumptions about economic organizations, the internal labor market is just a new label for phenomena intensively studied in a long tradition, stretching back to Weber and Michels. Nonetheless, for present purposes the concept of the internal labor market is important in sensitizing one to the linkage between internal and external changes in the emergence of the modern firm. More specifically, functions hitherto performed by the external labor market have been progressively absorbed into the firm—a quite literal internalization. But what is of importance, here, is *not* the contrast between internal and external labor markets but their commonality. Competition is by no means eliminated by the internalization of the labor market, as Doeringer and Piore imply, but rather takes on a new form, regulated by different sets of constraints and rules.[6] In this chapter I shall explore the mechanism and consequences of reproducing "possessive individualism" at the point of production.

The function of any labor market—external or internal—is the allocation of individuals to places. Any particular labor market defines (*a*) a population of places (occupations), (*b*) a population of individuals (workers), and (*c*) a set of transformation rules that map the one onto the other. The transformation rules involve a matching of formally free preferences of workers for jobs and of jobs for workers. The final upshot of the allocation process is the result of the relative scarcity of jobs and workers. The difference between internal and external labor markets is based on the degree of delimitation of the population of workers, on the one hand, and of the corresponding population of jobs, on the other. In addition, the transformation rules may differ as between markets. In the pure type of external labor market, to which Britain in the first half of

the nineteenth century may be the closest approximation, the entire
labor force, considered as an undifferentiated population, would
constitute candidates for places in the entire economy—places that
also are considered as an undifferentiated population. When supply
and demand do not define the distribution of individuals into
places, one may postulate transformation rules based on some
random process. At some places in *Capital,* Marx saw capitalism
developing in this direction. The pure type of internal labor market
is probably most closely approximated in today's large Japanese
firm.[7] There the relevant populations of individuals and places are
the employees and occupations in a given firm. The distribution rules
within the firm are based on some combination of seniority and
ability, frequently leaning more in the direction of the former.
Replenishing the supply of individuals involves tapping a wider
labor market, but the entry points are only at the lowest levels of any
particular hierarchy. In a perfectly sealed internal labor market,
new employees would be drawn only from the families of incum-
bents. In the context of a wider external labor market, the problems
for the internal labor market are to ensure that individuals do not
seek places outside the firm, on the one hand, and that, in filling
places within the firm, priority is given to employees. This pattern of
mobility may be accomplished either by coercion or through a
combination of institutional arrangements and incentive schemes.
In the following account I will suggest that the thirty years since Roy
worked at Geer have seen increasingly diminished mobility of individuals out of the firm, increased mobility within the firm, and
reduced recruitment of workers from outside the firm and entering
at only the lower levels.[8]

Changes in the Internal
Labor Market

The emergence of an internal labor market requires, on the one
hand, that workers, once recruited, generally choose to remain with
the company rather than seek employment elsewhere, and, on the
other hand, that the company tries to fill job openings by selecting
from among its own workers before it recruits workers from an
external labor market. In other words, incentives must be provided

for workers to stay with the company and for the company to recruit workers from its own labor pool. With these points in mind, I will discuss six conditions or aspects of the internal labor market, namely, a differentiated job structure, an institutionalized means of disseminating information about and submitting applications for vacancies, nonarbitrary criteria for selecting employees for vacancies, a system of training on the job, ways of generating a commitment to the firm that makes jobs in other firms unattractive, and, finally, maintaining the allegiance of employees after they have been laid off.

In 1945, transferring between jobs was not regarded with much enthusiasm by workers at Geer. On the contrary, job transfer was most often used as a disciplinary measure when operators failed to meet expected performance standards. The lack of interest in transfers lay in the undifferentiated nature of the job structure. Thus, in 1945, there were, according to the contract, only three grades differentiated from one another by their minimum guaranteed wage, or the day rate, as it was called. However, the price of pieces was assessed in the same way for all jobs, that is, it was based on what an operator might reasonably be expected to accomplish and took no account of requisite skill or experience. In other words, the reward for effort on a lathe or automatic screw machine was assessed on the same basis as the reward for effort on a simple speed drill. Apart from a slightly higher minimum wage, the only other attraction of alternative jobs would be the maximum wage that would be permissible before management would increase rates. Thus, on the turret lathes the accepted ceiling on what could be turned in was around $1.35 an hour, whereas Roy on his radial drill was limited to $1.25.[9] But actually making that $1.35 on the turret lathe was apparently a quite different matter.

> I met Desplains, one of the lathe men, in the I.C. [Illinois Central commuter train] station. I asked him if he was making out consistently. He answered in the negative.
> "Too much tool trouble. I'm allowed to make $1.30 an hour but I can't make it."
> I talked for a while with the turret lathe man who was operating Dooley's drill. He is allowed to turn in $1.40, but never turns in more than $1.37 or $1.38.
> "We're allowed to turn in $1.40, but we don't make that much

all the time. Maybe we get a good streak for a couple of days, or maybe all week. Then we don't make out the next week." [10]

There was little advantage in moving to another job. On the contrary, it was probably a better idea to gain more experience on one machine, so as to improve one's chances of making out.

In 1947, following such large corporations as United States Steel, Geer introduced a job-classification scheme upon which the present structure is based. In 1975 there were twelve labor grades with different base earnings, ranging from $4.62 an hour to $6.30 an hour for day workers (auxiliary workers) and from $4.40 an hour to $5.52 an hour for incentive workers. Jobs were allocated to a labor grade on the basis of a job-description and job-evaluation scheme. Piece rates were no longer computed in prices but in pieces per hour. Incentive earnings were calculated as a percentage of base earnings corresponding to the percentage of output that exceeded a standard measured rate (so many pieces per hour, determined by the industrial-engineering department), pegged at 100 percent. Thus, a 140 percent output meant that a worker had produced 40 percent more than the standard rate and would receive a bonus of 40 percent of the base earnings. Although jobs might be timed at the same rate per hour, the earnings on each extra piece would vary with the labor grade. Equally significant was the tendency for the rates of jobs in the higher labor grades to be easier to make than those in the lower grades. As a result, jobs that in 1945 were subject to considerable turnover were more attractive in 1975. Roy provides the following insight into the situation that prevailed in 1945.

> Hanks said that the boys on the turret lathes are not making out. "They're just getting the day rate over there. You notice they're quitting all the time, don't you?"

> Hanks scoffed, . . . saying that Ed was getting no $1.40 an hour on the automatic screw machines, that there had been a great turnover on the screw machines because there was no money in them. He said that he knows Ray, the day man on the machines, and Ray told him that he got very poor jobs, that he made only 85 cents an hour. [11]

This situation must have been expensive in terms of training costs. By giving easier rates to the more skilled jobs in the higher labor grades, despite the increased opportunities for mobility, Allied management has been able to reduce turnover on such machines as the lathes and automatic screw machines. At the same time, newcomers are subjected to the "impossible" rates on the speed drills and are thereby socialized to shop discipline and the ordeals of not making out.

Apart from establishing a differentiated job structure, which places jobs in hierarchies of attractiveness, an internal labor market requires a system by which employees may choose and compete for job openings. In 1945 employees might request transfers by approaching the superintendent. Roy mentions two instances, the case of Jonesy in the tool crib, who could no longer tolerate the frustrations and pressure there, and the turret-lathe operators who couldn't make out.[12] For the most part, the superintendent would direct or offer employees alternative jobs on his own initiative.[13] The 1945 contract, which only briefly alludes to transfers, does suggest that they were made at the discretion of management:

> Employees *accepting promotions* within the unit and failing to qualify in ninety (90) days may return to their former or equivalent positions.
> Employees who *decline promotions* may do so without discrimination or loss of seniority. [Art. IV, sec. 21; italics added]
> When there is a job opening, employees shall be considered on the basis of their seniority in the department and their qualifications. [Art. IV, sec. 6]

There was no system for informing employees when job openings appeared, for applying for such openings, or for ensuring that employees were given preference over outside applicants. Furthermore, the emphasis on departmental seniority tended to lock employees within a single department.

By 1975 the contract contained a full-fledged bidding system, which involved the posting of job openings, a system for applying for the jobs, and a system for selecting among applicants. It worked as follows:

> Job openings shall be filled in accordance with seniority when ability of the employees involved to do the work available is relatively equal. Job openings shall be made known to the employees of the department before they are filled by posting the same on a standard form furnished by the Company on the bulletin board

from 10 A.M. on the day of posting to 10 A.M. on the following
working day, and if the opening is not filled, the job shall be posted
plant-wide from 1:00 P.M. on the day of posting to 1:00 P.M. on
the following working day for all employees. The Company recognizes its responsibility to train accepted personnel on job openings.
[Art. IV, sec. 5]

Employees submit their bids to their foremen on special forms. If
there are no acceptable bids from within the department, the job
goes plantwide. Only when there are still no bids is the job filled
from outside. Accordingly, only the lowest-paying and most unattractive jobs, such as the speed drills, go to newcomers. The
bidding system is open to a certain amount of managerial abuse and
manipulation. Thus, job openings were suspiciously canceled when
certain operators handed in their bids. There were complaints that
criteria for assessing the final candidate were not based on the
stated combination of seniority and ability. For example, a number
of blacks complained that racial prejudice affected management
decisions, but such accusations are notoriously difficult to sub-
stantiate. Other employees were frustrated when they were repeatedly told they were not qualified for the jobs they had bid on. In
general, however, the system did function effectively, because employees could always find another job if their present one was not to
their liking, provided they had passed through the probationary
period of fifty days.

An internal labor market can function only if there is provision
for training on the job. In 1945 there was no reference in the
contract to training being a management responsibility, but there
were occasions when operators were requested to break in other
employees:

> The four-spindle man (his name is Hanks) told me of an at-
> tempt made by Squeaky, the day foreman, to get the day man on
> the four-spindle to train another man to operate his machine. The
> day man consulted the shop steward, who advised him that he
> should get set-up man's pay for breaking in a new man. So he
> demanded set-up man's pay from Squeaky. Squeaky refused,
> saying, "You know we can't do that! Why, the man you break in
> will be a help to you, and you can turn out more pieces!"
> "He'll be more of a hindrance!" replied the day man, and re-
> fused to break the man in. [14]

Unfortunately, Roy began his field notes only after his first month in the Jack Shop, and he makes no reference to being broken in himself. Nor does he mention the training system anywhere in his dissertation.

In 1975 some of the ambiguity remained. The contract did stipulate that the company "recognizes its responsibility to train accepted personnel on job openings," but it failed to mention how this responsibility was to be carried out. The most frequent arrangement was for operators to break in new employees and to receive setup-man pay (the highest pay scale) for the period if they did not make out after adding the new employee's pieces to their own. In other arrangements, those breaking in were to receive a fixed number of hours, say four, at setup-man pay. But training is still the subject of bargaining and negotiation between operator and foreman. Part of the reason for this lies in the ambiguity of the trainer's obligations to the trainee. As the shop euphemism puts it, one doesn't have to "show everything" to the new employee. Hostility between trainer and trainee may be particularly severe when the newcomer poses some threat to the incumbent. For example, it is possible for the newcomer to have greater seniority than the incumbent; if this is the case, he can displace the incumbent in times of layoff. One story was told to me of an old operator who, after taking up the job of crib attendant, decided to bid back on the machines. Every time he tried, the incumbent operator refused to show him anything, and eventually the old man left the company in frustration. Antagonism of trainer for trainee may also appear when the trainee threatens to eliminate the incumbent's overtime. George, a lathe operator, had been working a twelve-hour day for some time and wanted to keep it that way. He was an old hand, and his fellow operators considered him to be the best lathe operator in the shop. Every time he was asked to break someone in on his machine, he made sure that they would sooner or later be disqualified. There was nothing management could do except continue the overtime—they needed George too badly. Similarly, the older operators on the automatics had a reputation for marked reluctance to show youngsters the intricate setups. In my own case, Bill initially remained aloof and showed me a bare minimum. When he realized that I was going to stick with the miscellaneous job on second shift and I got to know him better, he showed me lots of angles on the operations we had to do. In general, despite occasional friction and hostility, the system of breaking-in tended to operate adequately, and few operators were disqualified.

So far, we have discussed the introduction of a differentiated job structure and the institutional arrangements for filling vacancies. However, creating hierarchies of jobs in terms of attractiveness and facilitating movement between these jobs do not in themselves guarantee that employees will not look outside the firm for jobs. How has the company attempted to reduce the separation rate? We have already seen that seniority places employees in a stronger position in bidding for jobs; the longer an employee remains with the company, the better are his or her chances of obtaining an attractive job within the plant and the less are the chances of finding an equivalent job in another firm. Since 1945 there have been other changes that reward seniority and so make employment in other firms unattractive. In 1959 a pension scheme was introduced, directly linked to length of service. In 1975 the various options, including early-retirement schemes, applied only to employees with ten or more years of credited service. Under the normal scheme the retirement age is sixty-five, and an employee receives $11.00 per month for each year of credited service. With thirty years of service, for example, an employee receives $330 from the company each month. In 1956 a supplementary unemployment-benefit scheme was introduced; in 1975 this applied to all workers having one or more years of continuous service. The amount paid each week during a layoff, combined with unemployment compensation, comes to about three-fourths of normal earnings; the duration of payments varies with length of service, but it is limited to twelve months. After twelve months the company distributes a separation payment, which varies according to years of service. Vacations also are determined by length of service. In 1945 the paid vacation was one week for those with more than one year of seniority and two weeks for those with five years or more. In 1975 paid vacations varied in length from one week for those with one to three years of continuous service to six weeks for those with twenty-five years or more. In summary, the longer that employees remain with Allied, the greater is their commitment to the company. The rewards for seniority discourage employees from seeking employment in other firms.

What happens when the strength of the company grows and

diminishes in response to the fluctuating demand for its products—
in Allied's case, for engines? In 1945, layoffs were made according
to seniority where ability was equal, but those with five or more years
of service and who were in jeopardy of a layoff could exercise their
plant-wide seniority and "bump" any employee in any other department who had less than five years' service, provided they had the
ability to do the work involved. In 1975, employees could exercise
their plant-wide seniority in bumping other employees after only one
year of service with the company. This, of course, involves considerably more mobility when a layoff occurs, but at the same time it
offers employees much more job security based on seniority.[15] In
addition, the supplementary unemployment benefit is a means of
retaining the attachment of the same labor pool even after a layoff
has taken place. By contrast, employees laid off in 1945, when there
were no compensation payments, found it difficult to wait for a
recall. They were more likely to seek employment elsewhere. In
other words, recent developments in the internal labor market have
organized the continued availability of a labor pool even during
depressed periods by allowing layoffs to proceed on the basis of
plantwide, rather than departmental, seniority for all employees
with more than one year's seniority.[16]

Consequences of the
Internal Labor Market

The internal labor market promotes mobility within the firm and
reduces mobility between firms. The choice open to employees
within the firm, albeit a choice within definite limits, fosters the
same competitive individualism that has been normally associated
with the external labor market. But it also has a significant impact
on the patterns of conflict on the shop floor. The opportunity to
move between jobs has the effect of diminishing conflict between
workers and the lower levels of management—the foreman and the
industrial engineer. As long as operators are locked into a single job,
they have to fight with the time-study man for better rates. This is
one reason why the time-study man loomed so large over shop-
floor life in 1945. When employees can transfer with relative ease,
and at will, to other jobs with easier rates, they no longer have the

same vested interest in fighting the methods department on any particular operation. Moreover, they even have a diminished interest in *protecting* existing rates. Rate-busting by senior employees who then transfer off their jobs is not the uncommon occurrence it was in Roy's day. Equally, when operators resent the treatment they receive from their foremen, they can quite easily move to another section or department, though foremen have been known to try to obstruct such transfers. Concerned to limit mobility in and out of their sections and, above all, to avoid the costs and frustrations of training new operators, foremen are less eager to throw their weight around than they were in 1945. As suggested in chapter 4, the foreman's role has gradually shifted from one of control to one of service. As one older foreman complained, "We have all the responsibility but no authority."

Just as mobility mitigates conflict in a hierarchical direction, it tends to generate conflict in a lateral direction, both among operators and between operators and auxiliary workers. In chapter 4 I discussed the conflict between auxiliary workers and operators and how this was exacerbated by mobility. Over time, networks of social ties are established that bind workers into a system of mutual obligations and trust. Thus, had I gotten to know Morris, the trucker, he would probably have been less enthusiastic in frustrating my attempts to make out. The same applies to the competition between operators that developed, untempered by social ties, when incumbency was short. Rivalry for better jobs led to obstructionist tactics directed at other operators. For example, Larry, one of the grinders on day shift, had been with the company for more than twenty-five years. He generally managed to obtain for himself the tasks with the looser rates. From long experience he knew which jobs were coming up next on his machine, and by virtue of his seniority he exercised considerable influence over the scheduling man. Steve and Ken, the young second- and third-shift operators, usually found themselves saddled with the difficult operations. They decided to collaborate and between them arranged tasks so that, when Larry came in on day shift, Ken would have just set up on a task with a very poor rate. Larry had no alternative but to continue with it. Operators on lathes often changed their setups before the end of the shift so that the following operator could not exploit their ingenuity.

In extreme situations, when operators were out to destroy each other, they might hide tools or fixtures. This is, however, but one side of the picture, for there were notable instances of collaboration between operators on different shifts, and operators did sometimes cover up for another's mistakes, share a kitty, or reveal angles on making out. Cooperation was of course more frequently established between operators on the same shift than with those on consecutive shifts. Immediate competition was less, and the time to establish social bonds was greater. Though the evidence is meager, Roy's comments suggest that collaboration may have been greater in 1945. Among workers on the second shift, there was definitely more cooperation then, but Roy says little about relations between operators on different shifts. In his own case, the relationship was generally cool, but he cites the example of Jack Starkey and Al McCann as sharing a kitty. Between radial-drill operators today, such sharing would be extremely unlikely to occur, but Jack and Al had been "going together" for many years. It may be surmised that, the greater the mobility between jobs, the less opportunity there is to develop the necessary relationship of trust that would counteract tension and competition between workers.

Training on the job is another feature of the internal labor market that breaks down collectivities based on skill groups and promotes individual autonomy. Skills are acquired as if they are specific to jobs in the particular machine shop. There are no training barriers to movement between skill levels or labor grades. At the same time, as already suggested, the training relationship is one based on bargaining and individual autonomy. The internal labor market not only redistributes conflict in a lateral direction and fosters individualism and autonomy through limited mobility; it also provides a material basis for presentation of the company's interests as the interests of all. The rewards of seniority—better jobs, improved fringe benefits, job security, social status, and so forth—engender a commitment to the enterprise and its survival.

Conclusion

The internal labor market contributes to both the obscuring and securing of surplus value in a number of ways. First, it internalizes the features most characteristic of the external labor market—namely, the competitive individualism of "free and equal" laborers. Second, the mobility it engenders at the point of production dissolves some of the tensions between worker and management and generates new tensions among workers. In both these ways the interests of the worker are constituted as those of one individual agent against other individuals rather than those of one class opposed to another class. On the other hand, in fostering a commitment to the enterprise by rewarding seniority, the internal labor market concretely coordinates the interests of capitalist and laborer in the generation of surplus value.

This interpretation diverges from that of Doeringer and Piore, who see the internal labor market as an adaptation to enterprise-specific skills. Although this is a by no means unimportant feature, it is difficult to square their theory with Braverman's compelling degradation thesis: the decline of enterprise-specific skills and the ease with which they are acquired. How can one reconcile the rise of internal labor markets with the increasing separation between conception and execution? Certainly Braverman makes no such attempt. Richard Edwards, borrowing from Max Weber, Michel Crozier, and Alvin Gouldner, argues that the internal labor market is part of a system of bureaucratic control that

> rationalized the enterprise's power by making its application more predictable and stable, and hence bureaucratic control evoked more stable and predictable behavior from workers; that is, bureaucratic control tended to legitimize the firm's exercise of power, and translate it into authority.[17]

Although his analysis goes beyond Doeringer and Piore, in that it focuses on control, how the exercise of power is legitimized through rules is as unclear in Edwards' writing as it is in Weber's.

By contrast, I am arguing that what is significant about rules is not that they increase stability and predictability but that they confine increased uncertainty within narrower limits. Thus, the internal labor market bases itself in a complex of rules, on the one hand, while expanding the *number* of choices on the other. Nor should these choices be belittled by saying that one boring, meaningless job is much the same as any other. The choice gains its significance from the material power it gives to workers in their attempts to resist or protect themselves from managerial domination. Workers have a very definite interest in the preservation and expansion of the internal labor market, as the most casual observation of the shop floor would demonstrate. Moreover, it is precisely that interest that draws workers into the bidding system and generates consent to its rules and the conditions they represent, namely, a labor process that is being emptied of skill.

Seven

Consolidating an Internal State

In the preceding chapter I examined the consequences of the partial absorption of the external labor market by the industrial enterprise. I now propose to examine the implications of another process of internalization—the growth of the "internal state." Writing about the Progressive Era, James Weinstein describes the endeavors of corporation leaders in the National Civic Federation to solve social problems by "extrapolitical" means, that is, by keeping them out of the arena of public debate.[1] At that time, institutional arrangements for this kind of "depoliticization of the public realm" were still primitive. Since then, corporations have managed to provide solutions to many of their social and economic problems by establishing political processes within their own jurisdiction in the form of collective bargaining and grievance machinery. According to Jürgen Habermas, a distinguishing feature of advanced capitalism is the emergence of political class compromise between worker and capitalist, or what he refers to as the "repoliticization of the relations of production."[2] In a somewhat different vein, Selznick has called attention to the rise of private government within industry and the constitution of the industrial citizen. "It follows that if collective bargaining 'creates' a system of government, it does so by helping to reconstruct the managerial process. Management becomes more conscious of rights, and more capable of building that consciousness into the routines of institutional life. The administration of 'things' becomes the governance of men as this reconstruction proceeds."[3]

The term "internal state" refers to the set of institutions that organize, transform, or repress struggles over relations in production and relations of production at the level of the enterprise. It is in no way a new phenomenon, although it takes on a radically different form under monopoly capitalism. Under competitive capitalism, except where craft organization existed, the regulation of relations in production was largely carried out by the despotic overseer. The relationship between management and labor was modeled on master-servant laws. With the rise of the large corporation and trade unionism, the institutions of the internal state have become disentangled from the managerial direction of the labor process and embodied in grievance procedures and collective bargaining. The emerging internal state protects the managerial prerogative to fashion and direct the labor process by imposing constraints on managerial discretion and by endowing workers with rights as well as obligations.

The Union and
Its Members

The transformation of the internal state from its despotic to its hegemonic form rests on a limited participation by representatives of labor in the government of industry. The trade union must be sufficiently strong and responsive to labor in order to command the allegiance of its members and yet not sufficiently strong to present a challenge to management prerogatives in the organization and control of the labor process. Changes since 1945, slight though they have been, suggest, if anything, that worker support of the union is stronger, while the union's challenge to management is weaker.

As mentioned in chapter 3, union activities were curtailed during the war. A no-strike pledge took away the union's strongest sanction, and a maintenance-of-membership clause in the contract dampened the recruitment drive:

In recognition of the Government's wartime labor policy as expressed by the National War Labor Board, the Company agrees to the following maintenance-of-membership and checkoff clause. All employees covered by this agreement who on the effective date of this agreement are members of the union in good standing in accordance with the Constitution of the United Steelworkers of America–C.I.O, dated May 13, 1944, a copy of which is attached hereto as Appendix 1, and all such employees who thereafter join the Union, shall as a condition of employment remain members in good standing in accordance with the said Constitution for the duration of this agreement. [Art. I, sec. 3]

No strikes, security of membership, and a checkoff system made for a passive union. Roy knew of no operators on night shift who would speak favorably of the union:

The union was rarely a topic of Jack Shop conversation, and when it was mentioned, remarks indicated that it was not an organization high in worker esteem. Characteristic of machine operator attitude toward the union was the scornful comment: "All the union is good for is to get that $1.00 a month out of you."[4]

There was no union shop steward on night shift, and Roy had little contact with the one on day shift. In his eleven months at Geer, Roy interacted with him directly only twice. On the first occasion, the steward wanted him to sign the checkoff form. On the second, Roy went to complain about the price on one of his operations; the operation had been retimed, but the rate was still impossible to make. The steward showed interest but did nothing.

Since Roy had so little contact with the union, changes in union-management relations are difficult to gauge. Though he presents us with no accurate data on the matter, his observations suggest that there were fewer shop stewards. There have been some changes in the contract, and these have affected union-management relations. A union shop has been introduced, so that union membership is a condition of employment once the initial probationary period has been served. The disciplinary procedure has been rationalized to include a series of steps that must be taken before a worker can be discharged. At each step but the first (verbal warning), the union is notified and involved in the disciplinary procedure. Finally, a qualifying paragraph has now been added to the management clause; this stipulates that the company "will advise the Union in advance of initiating any major action that would cause a direct and adverse effect over the job and wage security of employees."

Nonetheless, attitudes among rank and file remain much as they were in 1945. There is a pervasive cynicism as to the willingness and ability of union officials to protect the interests of the membership. In part this is because union leaders in their day-to-day activities exercise so little *visible* power and so rarely initiate interventions on behalf of the members. But the role of the union is to preserve the status quo, and its power is generally *invisible*—designed to prevent arbitrary action by management. Nonetheless, this power is significant. The union's very presence acts as a deterrent to management's violation of the contract. Therefore, to the extent that management "plays it fair," the union is seen to do nothing. Indeed, it is to management's advantage to violate the contract from time to time if only to assist the union in preserving its legitimacy and its appearance of autonomy vis-à-vis management. Though much attention is drawn to union incompetence, feathering of nests, corruption, being in collusion with the company, and so forth, union leadership must, to retain minimal legitimacy, present itself as independent. Management recognizes the need for a legitimate union with which to bargain, and it therefore accepts the appropriate constraints on its discretion.

Comparison with nonunion shops, where punitive sanctions are applied more arbitrarily, unchecked by grievance machinery, highlights the importance of the union's presence. One of Roy's informants corroborates the point:

> The man that I deal with had formerly worked at Geer as an inspector. I noticed that he made no comment, but remained silent when I told him I worked for Geer. "I guess Geer is not regarded very highly," I said. "It's been better since the CIO got it," he said. "Before the union came in they did not treat the workers fairly. They'd come to work at seven, wait around for materials, and get sent home at nine without pay for the wait, if there were no materials. They had no regard for the workers."[5]

In 1975, at Allied, a certain discrepancy between action and attitude pointed to a continuing ambivalence on the part of workers. On the one hand, there were continual complaints that the union "ain't worth shit," that its officials were corrupt, and that it was good only for collecting and spending the dues, which in 1975 amounted to around ten dollars a month for each worker, depending on his earnings. On the other hand, whenever the workers had a grievance, felt that management was cheating them, that a fellow operator was endangering their job, and so on, their first move was to the union. Moreover, the union was wielded as a threat to any offender. "I'll get the union onto you," I was told when I ran someone else's job— which indicates that it was not regarded as so ineffectual as some of the comments might suggest. The complaints appeared to be directed at the *individuals* who held office rather than at the union as an institution, which generally defended workers against management encroachments, irrespective of the incumbent leadership.

Creating the Industrial Citizen

Everyday life under the internal state inserts the laborer into the political process as an industrial citizen with a set of contractually defined rights and obligations, together with a commitment to a more tenuous "social contract." This commitment to the enterprise finds its material expression, first, in the rewards for seniority, such as the pension scheme, supplementary unemployment benefits, bumping rights, and so on, and, second, in the grievance machinery, which is designed to guarantee equality of treatment and "industrial justice." The union acts as an umpire, both in protecting the rights of industrial citizens and in overseeing the punishment of offenders against contractual obligations.

> We think, you see, that the union is an attempt to extend the democratic processes in the industrial community; that organized society is based upon the principle that within the framework of a given society the people who make up that society have to work out rules and regulations to govern the relationship of one to the other. [6]

As a corollary, meetings of the union local, held every month, are interspersed with comments from Jim—the president—to the effect: "Our [sic] biggest problem is absenteeism," or "I'm proud of you guys, absenteeism is half what it was in December." [7] (In fact, a major reason for this was a doubling of the unemployment rate.) In its day-to-day dealings with the rank and file, the union leadership plays an individualizing role. The most intense interaction between union membership and union executives—in particular, Jim—occurs when grievances are discussed at the monthly meetings of the local—grievances that have been, have not been, or are in the process of being dealt with. Tempers may flare over the union's efforts, or rather lack of efforts, to protect a particular member. The meeting becomes a safety valve for the release of accumulating frustration on the shop floor, at least for the 6 to 9 percent of members who attend. Each time a *collective* grievance or an issue of principle outside the contract, affecting the entire membership or even a section of the membership, is raised, Jim insists, "Have you got a grievance? If you have, let's hear it. If you haven't, give the floor to someone else." Each case is dealt with on an individual basis, its merits being considered in light of the rules of industrial government, laid down in the sacrosanct contract.

Complaints by workers about particular shop stewards or other union officials revolve around whether they are discriminatory in their handling of grievances. Thus, one of the most explosive issues concerned the racial bias of the union executive. (Over one-third of the membership is black, but the entire union executive group is white.) In other words, ritual and sometimes quite deliberate and even violent condemnation of shop stewards, grievancemen, etc., only reinforces the normative assumptions of industrial government, namely, that everyone is equal before the law. The interests served by the "law" were never explored, let alone questioned.

Concrete Coordination
of Interests

In their day-to-day activities, union officials referee and enforce the rules embodied in the contract and in such customary practices as making out. Their enthusiasm to protect the rules stems in part from their role in bargaining for, and agreeing to, changes in these rules every three years. In Roy's time new contracts or extensions were negotiated almost every year. Now, as in many industries, the three-year contract has been firmly institutionalized.

Collective bargaining on the one hand *displaces conflict* between different agents of production from the shop floor, where it can lead to work disruptions, and on the other hand *reconstitutes conflict* in a framework of negotiation. In reorganizing conflict in this way, collective bargaining *generates a common interest* between union and company, based on the survival and growth of the enterprise.[8] Collective bargaining is a form of class struggle, that is, a struggle in which workers are represented as a class in opposition to capital. In this particular form, class struggle revolves around marginal changes, which have no effect on the essential nature of the capital-labor relationship. On the contrary, as a result of negotiating about marginal changes, capitalist relations of ownership and control become the object of consent. In other words, collective bargaining can be viewed as another game—this time a *game about rules and outcomes of other games,* such as making out. As before, the context that defines the rules of collective bargaining is, as a result of playing the game, taken as given. Violations of the established rules of collective bargaining, or failure to come to a mutual agreement, may lead to a strike or to compulsory arbitration at some higher level. In the particular industry or firm where collective bargaining fails, capitalist relations may be questioned, but outside the affected industry or firm the consequences of the breakdown are as likely to *reinforce* the commitment to collective bargaining and a common interest in the survival and growth of the company. When I confronted one of the leading officials of the union local with its timidity and cooperative spirit, he pointed to the example of Cog Company, across the road. "A few years ago negotiations with the union broke down and there was a strike. Then the company closed up and moved to the South. Lots of the men tried to come and join Allied." This is not to say that enforcement of a collective-bargaining agreement cannot itself push a company out of business. This is possible, since the wage commitment is prior to the securing of profit. But such an eventuality stems not from a rejection of the organizing principles of capitalism but from the inability of a particular enterprise to generate sufficient product to satisfy the distributive demands of both capital and labor. Collective bargaining, then, represents an institutionalized creation of a common interest between the representatives of capital and labor, that is, between management and union, but it rests on a material precondition—the growth of profits.[9]

The Relative Autonomy of
the Internal State

The rise of the internal state is characterized by the subordination of both workers and management to the impersonal rule of law. Moreover, the law assumes an autonomy of its own, in that it can be changed only in a prescribed, nonarbitrary fashion—most frequently through collective bargaining and joint regulation. Selznick describes the evolution of the employment relation as moving from "prerogative contract"—according to which the sale of labor power carries with it few, if any, proscriptions or prescriptions on its consumption by management—to the "constitutive contract" and to "creative arbitration," which does establish procedures and regulations for the utilization of labor.[10] Restrictions on managerial discretion and arbitrary rule, on the one hand, and enhanced protection for workers, on the other, reflect not only the ascendancy of unions and *internal* government but also indirect regulation by agencies of *external* government. This is revealed "in (1) the use of government procurement to impose standards on industries that enter contracts with public agencies and (2) regulation developed as a by-product of legislation or administrative policy directed primarily toward other problems, such as civil rights or the control of industries affected with public interest."[11] Rarely threatened with outside intervention or regulation, industrial government has been the bearer of a privatization of public policy. "It followed that public policy would develop less through an accumulation of regulations than through a process by which parties invoke the authority of public purpose in support of new demands and claims of right."[12]

Selznick is documenting the relative freedom of the internal state, first from the intervention of external public bodies, and second from the imposition of the immediate economic interests of capitalists or managers. We will have more to say about the relationship of the individual firm to external bodies in subsequent chapters. Suffice it to say that Selznick's analysis finds its expression in affirmative-action programs at Allied. Management submits annual plans, laying out targets for the racial and sex composition of its labor force, which are then passed on to government for approval. In other words, outside agencies do not intervene and dictate to Allied the precise proportion of blacks, women, and so on; instead they fulfill the more passive functions of ratification and constraint.

The second area of relative autonomy is more important to the argument of this chapter. Here the internal state is relatively autonomous in three related senses. First, it subjects management and workers alike to the rules and regulations inscribed in the contract. The autonomy is therefore relative, because it ensures the reproduction of relations in production by protecting management from itself, from its tendencies toward arbitrary interventions that would undermine the consent produced at the point of production. Relative autonomy in this sense is the autonomy necessary for securing and obscuring surplus value. Second, the autonomy of the internal state is relative in the sense that it is preserved only as long as surplus value is obscured and secured. The advent of a crisis can threaten this autonomy, and workers can then become subject to the arbitrary discretion of management. Third, the relative autonomy of the internal state expresses the institutionalized power of management in the context of an organized working class, organized through a trade union having a certain degree of independence and power. Moreover, the negotiation of a contract implies that the union is also relatively autonomous, that is, autonomous within limits defined by the requirements of accumulation. It is in the interests of the company to uphold the relative autonomy of the union leadership if only to legitimate the union as a bargaining instrument. That is to say, agreements between the company and union leadership preserve the relative autonomy of the internal state as long as there is no visible "collusion," of the kind normally associated with "sweetheart" contracts, though it may sometimes assume more subtle forms, such as this super-seniority clause:

In the event of layoffs, the officers of the Union. . .shall be deemed to have more seniority than any other employee for layoff purposes only. . . . [Art. IV, sec. 10]

At the beginning of my employment at Allied, the results of the contract negotiations were announced and the union's legitimacy was temporarily impaired. The new collective agreement included, as the most significant gain for labor, a more liberal pensions scheme. It was cynically noted by the rank and file that most of the union executives were close to retirement. Sentiments expressed in my presence were almost entirely opposed to the new proposals. Indeed, everyone I spoke to told me that they were going to vote no. I asked Bill which way he voted. He replied, "They are offering a bigger pension, but that's no use to me; I've got another fifteen years to go. We're all voting no." What about the wage increase, I asked. "Five percent, that's all we've got. That's nothing. The union officials will accept it, but we won't.... They could do with a bigger pension—it suits them." Curiously, however, the official result declared the membership's support for the new contract by a margin of 408 votes to 307.

Management was no doubt aware that improved pensions would appeal to the union executives and felt that it was worth risking the consequences of rank-and-file disaffection to get a cheap contract. From the discussions I had with the personnel manager, it appeared that management recognized the importance of preserving the relative autonomy of the union and responsiveness to its membership; he was, for example, concerned about the lack of black representation among the union executives. He understood that the day-to-day policing function of the union can be effectively carried out over the three years between contracts only if the terms of the negotiations are minimally acceptable to the rank and file.

Failure to negotiate an acceptable contract may impair the union's ability to preserve the status quo, and it may also lead to the overturning of the incumbent officers, particularly the president, in the elections held every three years. Since officials usually wish to retain their positions, the mechanism of elections is one way of maintaining the union leadership's autonomy from management, though it is not as effective a mechanism as one might think. But elections have the more significant consequence that they generate among the membership the view that a poor contract, with few gains to labor, is the fault of the incumbent leadership rather than a result of the structure of the union and its relationship to the company. In other words, at the local level, it does not matter whether there is a one-party system or a two-party system in trade-union politics as long as there is an effective electoral mechanism for replacing officers;[13] for the electoral mechanism effectively masks and thereby protects the structural context of management-union relations. The relative autonomy of the union as an institution is consistently preserved even in the face of—and, indeed, sometimes because of—the frailties of its leadership. At Allied's engine division, the position of the president of the local has for some time now rotated between two senior operators. Contempt for the union is frequently leveled at one or another of these individuals. Some of the more senior employees occasionally talked of presidents in the old days, who used "to really fight for the guys" (one of these former presidents has since moved into a higher office in the international union). Others would say, "What we need now is some young blood in the union."

The relative independence of industrial government from the narrow economic interests of capital and from outside intervention serves to mask the property relations that collective bargaining and the dispensation of "industrial justice" protect.[14] Furthermore, when that autonomy is impaired, it is human frailty and not property relations that are revealed. In its turn, frailty is not regarded as a consequence of a set of structural conditions but as a given—as a part of human nature.

Conclusion

The internal state and the internal labor market serve similar functions. Thus, in this chapter we have seen how the internal state in its relatively autonomous form concretely coordinates the interests of union and management through their joint use of grievance machinery and collective bargaining. It concretely coordinates the interests of worker and corporation in the expansion of profit, which provides material concessions in the form of employee benefits and wage increases. It obscures capitalist relations of production in the labor process by constituting workers as individuals—industrial citizens with attendant rights and obligations—rather than as members of a class. Finally, struggles over relations in production are regulated in the grievance procedure and displaced into collective bargaining.[15]

On the other hand, the internal state and the internal labor market serve complementary functions in the production of consent. In this chapter and the two preceding it, I have suggested that changes in the labor process and the rise of the internal labor market expand the choices of workers and thus constitute the basis of consent to degradation. However, this consent emerges only if management does not arbitrarily dictate choices to workers—if, for example, transfers are always taken at the initiative of workers and through the bidding process and, further, if punitive sanctions are confined to the transgression of the limits of choice, as when workers decide to stay at home rather than come to the factory. Moreover, when restricted to violations of the rules that define the limits of choice, the application of force becomes the object of consent. The relative autonomy of the internal state guarantees that coercion will play a more restricted role in the regulation of production.[16]

Yet there is a certain ambiguity in the organization of the internal state. Just because it coordinates the interests of workers and managers, labor and capital, it also acknowledges those interests as potentially antagonistic, as when workers make demands for increased control over the labor process. Unlike the global state, which does not recognize the existence of classes in its structure, the internal state explicitly recognizes classes and thereby becomes, at least potentially, more vulnerable to class struggle. After World War II there was much uncertainty as to what would be negotiable in a collective contract, but this uncertainty has since been resolved in ways that establish management's prerogative to direct the labor process. Whatever the reasons for this outcome, the consequences are relatively clear.

Thus, in part 3, I have shown that, in the period between 1945 and 1975, the application of force was increasingly limited to violation of rules that defined an expanding arena of consent. In doing so, I have regarded the enterprise as obscuring and securing surplus value through the organization, displacement, and repression of struggles, through the constitution and presentation of the interests of the corporation as the interests of all, and through the promotion of individualism, and I have also assumed that the obscuring and securing of surplus value can be examined independently of such external factors as the global state, markets, and the reproduction of labor power. These factors can no longer be ignored, and the remainder of this study will pose the question of their relationship to the form, reproduction, and change of the capitalist labor process.

4

The Relative Autonomy of
the Labor Process

Eight

The Labor Process
in a Recession

Thus far I have shown how the generic features of capitalist relations of production lead to the formulation of the essence of the capitalist labor process as the simultaneous obscuring and securing of surplus value. I have discussed how this was concretely accomplished at Geer and Allied through varying combinations of force and consent. In this chapter I will examine the way the labor process is affected by variations in relations of production, conceived broadly as the relations embodied in the supply, product, and labor markets. I will therefore be addressing the criticism leveled at industrial sociology that it ignores the "environment."

Recent statistical analysis of the original data collected for the first relay-assembly experiment of the Western Electric studies shows that 78.7 percent of the increase in output can be attributed to the enforcement of tighter discipline, and a further 14.5 percent can be attributed to the onset of the depression.[1] Moreover, it might be argued that the impending depression was in fact a condition for the intensification of supervision. Nevertheless, the very success of industrial sociology to illuminate industrial behavior suggests that the

shop floor may normally be regarded as a "system" unto itself and
therefore as a legitimate object of analysis. Thus, Roy's analysis of
output restriction is relatively complete, despite his failure to consider
the context of Geer. But here, again, industrial sociology takes as
given what has to be explained. What is essential is not so much the
making of general statements or assumptions about the impact of the
environment on the labor process but formulating the "relative
autonomy" of the labor process as a problem.

It has fallen to organization theory to take up the problem of the
relationship of the enterprise to its environment. Although not
couched in our terms, the seminal work of James Thompson directly
addresses the problem of relative autonomy. Most relevant for our
purposes is his thesis that an organization attempts to insulate its
"technical core" from changes in the environment through "buffering," which absorbs environmental influences; through "leveling,"
which smooths fluctuations; through "forecasting," which facilitates
adaptation to penetration; and, finally, as a last resort, through
"rationing."[2] As I argued in chapter 1, Thompson, in presenting his
framework as one having universal applicability, fails to recognize its
relevance to a particular period of capitalism in which certain large-
scale enterprises are so powerful that they can to some degree contain
market uncertainties.

A major difficulty in using Thompson's framework revolves
around the definition and location of the technical core. Although he
does distinguish three types of technology—long-linked, mediating,
and intensive—his discussion is so general that the notion of "technical core" eludes conceptual elaboration. It is by no means clear what
it is that is being insulated, why it has to be insulated, or what criteria
can be used to assess the degree of insulation. As a corrective to
industrial sociology, organization theory has tended to place almost
exclusive emphasis on the behavior of organizations in differing
environments.[3] Organization theory is therefore most weak where
industrial sociology is strong, namely, in understanding processes
within organizations. Here I shall attempt to synthesize elements
taken from both traditions by placing them within a Marxist
framework.

If the technical core is considered to be the labor process, it
becomes important to distinguish its aspect as a set of relations from
its aspect as a set of activities. While the two necessarily exist

simultaneously, it may be the case that the expenditure of effort—the translation of labor power into labor—varies independently of the relations in production. If this is in fact the case, it contradicts the assumptions implicit in my analysis up to this point, in which I have regarded the shaping of activities by relations as independent of the attributes of the individuals "carrying" the relations and participating in the activities. Black or white, male or female, I have assumed that all played the game of making out in much the same way. We must now weaken that assumption and entertain the possibility that the translation of the same relations into activities may vary over time and among different people. To the extent that activities change independently of relations, it becomes necessary to incorporate a theory of how different people respond to the relations in which they are enmeshed—that is, to incorporate a psychology.[4] It becomes important, therefore, to examine how conditions outside the firm affect relations in production, the expenditure of effort, and their covariation both over time (the task of this chapter) and among different groups (the task of the next chapter).

Changes in Markets

My life on the shop floor from July 1974 to May 1975 can be divided into two periods, conveniently separated from each other by the firing and replacement of the general manager of the engine division in December 1974. When I arrived, the company had already begun to expand the number of employees. Spurred by record farm income and the expectation of further high crop production, retail demand for farm equipment was exceptionally high in 1974.

The Agricultural Equipment Group of Allied Corporation was selling everything it could produce; consequently, output of the engine division was expanded to full capacity as quickly as possible. Because of relatively full employment, machine operators were not easily recruited, and management was hesitant about increasing the strength of the plant with inexperienced employees. The choice was between, on the one hand, spending time and energy in training new employees, with the possibility of having to lay them off if demand declined, as seemed likely, and, on the other hand, a generous allocation of overtime. Management in fact adopted both strategies. We were working six days a week and sometimes even seven—up to eighty hours a week. At the same time, the labor strength of the plant began to increase, but slowly.

The effort to expand production was also being thwarted by the difficulty of obtaining supplies from outside. A declining foundry industry made castings difficult to obtain in a period of high demand. Their delivery was unreliable, and their quality was frequently very poor. At one time the company even considered buying castings from overseas. The result was that half-completed engines stood in the aisles, waiting for parts that had still to be delivered.

This unprecedented situation was in part the consequence of the engine division's subservience to other product divisions of Allied Corporation. Each year a plan is drawn up to establish the number of engines to be manufactured each month for sale to each division. If these orders are subsequently changed, the two parties negotiate as to who shall bear the costs. In 1974 there was an increase in the demand for engines, and from June onward the engine division overextended itself. Working at full capacity is notoriously inefficient, and this was apparent to all on the shop floor. Excessive overtime, frequent changes in jobs and setups to meet short-term demands, problems of scheduling, etc., sent production costs soaring. When a new delivery of castings came into the plant, "hot jobs" would appear, and operators would have to drop everything and rush the job through, breaking setups where necessary. The monomania for output was further stimulated by the drive and dominance of the manufacturing manager, whose departmental interests were directly linked to producing as many engines as possible, irrespective of costs. Late delivery of engines to customers incurred economic penalties. Since the quality-control manager reported directly to the manufacturing manager, quality standards could be relaxed. When it came to a conflict of production versus quality, production took priority. Most significant was the fact that the "engine test," in which each engine is subjected to a final test before being shipped out, was transferred to the jurisdiction of the manufacturing manager. While it is impossible to assess the actual amount of scrap produced in any period (since it is unrelated to *reported* scrap), it seemed from my own observations that quality was declining. Below-standard parts would sometimes get through, sometimes be scrapped. Excessive overtime, the use of new, inexperienced operators, and the persistent pressure to produce inevitably led to a decline in quality.

As I noted in chapter 4, pressure from above frequently led to antagonisms between operators and auxiliary workers, particularly when the number of operators increased at a faster rate than the number of auxiliaries.[5] Increasingly, operators were frustrated by poor tooling, shortage of fixtures, and poorer service from truck drivers. In December, what was apparent to all on the shop floor appeared in the end-of-year financial accounts. The engine division had fallen into the red; the cost of production had exceeded the price of the engines delivered. The general manager of the division was fired. In fact, he rarely knew what was happening on the shop floor. Only occasionally did he venture out of his office into the plant. His relationships with the shop were mediated by the manufacturing manager, who was pursuing his own departmental interests— meeting production targets—rather than the profits of the division.

A new general manager arrived in January with a new set of skills. Once with Allied Corporation, he was now returning from an executive position with General Electric. Less versed in sophisticated modern managerial techniques, he was skeptical of "scientific" business methods and relied more on experience and an intuitive feel for what was needed. He demanded much more from his staff, imposed greater control, and ruthlessly removed managers from their positions when he felt this was necessary. He had a much better feel and grasp of the problems on the shop floor. Finally, he came with the support and confidence of executives in the head office.

In his efforts to tighten up the organization of the shop, he was aided and abetted by rising rates of unemployment as the recession of 1975 moved in. On his arrival in January he began to phase out overtime and Saturday work altogether. Experienced lathe, mill, and drill operators were now lining up outside Allied's employment office, having been laid off by other shops in the region. At one point the engine division absorbed a group of workers laid off by another division of Allied Corporation, which had suffered a serious setback in production. Accessions of new workers, therefore, continued to increase, and it was only a matter of time before all three shifts had a full complement of workers. Though there was speculation that the market for construction equipment might weaken, agriculture was still booming, and the demand for engines remained strong. Because of the recession, foundries now had surplus capacity, and castings were delivered promptly. The same applied to other parts. Accordingly, toward the end of my employment, management was trying to introduce tighter control over inventories.

Finally, in a third period, beginning after I left in May 1975, layoffs began as the demand for engines slackened. After May, accessions fell below separations. Those laid off who had been employed for more than a year received supplementary unemployment benefits, which, added to state unemployment compensation, brought home around three-fourths of the normal income. As is characteristic of internal-labor markets, layoffs involved a complicated reshuffling process of "bumping." We shall discuss the consequences of such internal mobility in the next section.

Changes in Production Relations

In the preceding section I suggested, at a number of points, that certain labor controls (relations of domination) became less effective during the first period of my employment, when the increased level of production in some instances forced the circumvention of regulations and in other instances caused frustrating delays. Quality control appeared to become less stringent. Uncertainty about the arrival of supplies from outside made scheduling difficult, and bottlenecks were unavoidable. After December, organization improved; this was due to the initiatives taken by the new general manager and to the market changes already described.

The first change in production relations occurred when quality control was taken away from the jurisdiction of the manufacturing manager and given its own manager, who reported directly to the general manager. It appears, however, that in important decisions the position of the manufacturing manager was still dominant, and the organizational change altered little. The life of quality-control managers had generally been short. In December 1975 I interviewed the incumbent, who had been recruited by the new general manager. He told me that there had been four people in his position in the previous eighteen months and that he had survived the longest. Two months later I discovered that he, too, had been removed and that the general manager had himself assumed direction of quality control. In 1975 the engine division also failed to obtain certification for Quality Assurance, and this, of course, reflected adversely on the quality of the engines and pointed up the ineffectiveness of quality control.

I gathered figures on the costs of scrap and rework as a percentage of direct labor costs. They show no consistent trend, although in the third period, when workers were being laid off, recorded "scrap and rework" did increase. For example, in the manufacturing department the costs of "scrap and rework" varied between 10 and 20 percent of direct labor costs in the period June 1974–May 1975. In June 1975 it rose to over 25 percent and in August to over 30 percent. This increase might reflect the considerable internal mobility that took place after May 1975.

Unfortunately, these official figures do not measure the actual level of quality each month, since there is a world of difference between scrap produced and scrap reported. From my conversations with the incumbent, I learned that each new quality-control manager begins by putting out a memo instructing each department to gather the accumulated scrap from the shop floor, record it, and, where possible, begin some "rework." This initial burst of enthusiasm is designed to get rid of all the scrap the previous manager had left unrecorded, so that it will not blot the new manager's copybook. In short, what the fluctuations in quality costs reflect is not so much actual scrap but the methods for recording scrap. The same applies to the quality of castings, etc., from the foundry. From time to time there would be a clampdown on the supplier and careful inspection of incoming castings; then this would be relaxed. To sum up: there is no evidence that shifts at the managerial level or in quality controls had any effect on the relations between operators and inspectors.

A second change occurred when stricter controls over productivity-accounting procedures were introduced, also in January 1975. Industrial engineers began to produce a weekly report that recorded, on a departmental basis, "measured performance" (average percentage achieved by operators on piecework during the week), "measured coverage" (percentage of operations covered by the piece-rate system), and "expense ratio" (proportion of labor hours spent on nonproductive labor).[6] When higher management insisted on improved performance levels, the industrial engineers frequently manufactured "improvement" by manipulating recording methods in preference to instituting organizational or time-study changes on the shop floor. From my conversations with industrial engineers and my

examination of their records, I could discover no consistent trend or
regular pattern in the savings they achieved by reorganizing the labor
process or by retiming jobs.

Here again, the recording methods were poor. It was difficult to
discover the actual date of particular "methods" changes or revisions
as distinct from the date for which they were recorded. Ironically,
industrial engineers themselves operated a procedure of chiseling and
"banking," shifting dollars saved from good months to bad months.
The industrial-engineering department had certainly not grown in
size; if anything, its strength had declined. From the shop floor things
looked a little different. The only two cases of rate increases in the
small-parts department during my employment both took place in the
second period (see chapter 10). It seemed to us that the methods
department was coming out of hiding, now that they were in a strong
position and the division had to cut costs. At the monthly meetings of
the union local, officers began warning operators to expect a managerial offensive, now that unemployment was so high. Members
should protect themselves by not going absent and by not turning in
more than "135 percent." Foremen sometimes appeared to be exercising greater pressure. On one occasion, when I was resisting new
inspection controls, a foreman came up to me, shook his fist angrily,
and reminded me that a few days ago hundreds of auto workers had
been laid off. But this was exceptional, and I noticed no overall
intensification of relations of domination. There were some feeble
attempts to control the crib, the distribution of double red cards, and
the retention of production cards by operators, but these were soon
relaxed and appeared to be random occurrences throughout my
sojourn on the shop floor.

Variations in Labor Output

If there were no clearly discernible changes in the relations on the
shop floor, what can we say about the actual performance of the
laborers? Could they have responded autonomously to fluctuations in
the labor market—for example, out of fear of losing their jobs? Had
this been the case, one might have expected higher levels of output.
However, the data I collected, both for the small-parts department
and for the plant as a whole, show only small variations in output, and
these were in no way consistent with changes then occurring in the

labor market. The data therefore do not invalidate, and possibly they support, the view that consent organized at the point of production is the immediate source of cooperation on the shop floor, not fear of unemployment.

There are, however, two qualifications. First, there was a slight dip in output when layoffs began in May 1975, but the original level was restored and even exceeded in the following months. The dip could have been due to a temporary disorganization, caused by the confusion created by bumping, or it could have been the result of a conscious attempt to restrict output in the face of a work shortage. Since I had already left, I have no way of knowing.

The second qualification is perhaps more significant: during 1975, that is, during the second and third periods, the rate of absenteeism fell by 80 percent. I attribute this decline, and a corresponding one in tardiness, to rising levels of unemployment.[7] But why should absenteeism and tardiness be affected by changes in the labor market while other indices of industrial behavior remain unaffected? One reason is that absenteeism is one form of effort withdrawal that invariably incurs a disciplinary charge. (Given the increase in fixed fringe benefits, absenteeism now represents a considerable cost to the company.) The union recognizes management's "right" to bring disciplinary charges for repeated absenteeism and tardiness. Absenteeism is widely recognized as illegitimate.[8] Furthermore, as with other aspects of the distribution of work (overtime and layoffs), it is relatively easy for management to impose both stringent and "fair" controls over absenteeism and tardiness.

By contrast, management's control over the quality and quantity of effort expended on the shop floor is very much more difficult. The responsibility for low levels of output and for the production of scrap cannot, like absenteeism, be easily attributed to particular workers. Changes in the labor and product markets are unlikely to directly affect job performance when employees are only rarely disciplined for low levels of output (one or two cases a year) and when layoffs are conducted on the basis of seniority. Indeed, many workers welcome layoffs, since the supplementary unemployment benefits can provide an adequate standard of living for no work.

Finally, what effect do changes in the supply market have on worker behavior? From my description of the two periods of my employment at Allied, one might have suspected that the relative order that prevailed in the second period, contrasted with the organizational chaos of the first period, would have facilitated making out. In fact, the data show no such trend, and this suggests that operators were able to manipulate conditions through the use of double red cards, the sacrifice of quality, etc., during the first period. The costs of an unreliable supply market are borne by management, not by the worker—at least in the short run.

The contrast between lower levels of absenteeism and tardiness, on the one hand, and the absence of an increase in output on the shop floor, on the other, serves to highlight the distinction between "coming to work" and "working." The data I collected suggest that fluctuations in conditions outside the factory, in particular in the labor market, do not directly affect the labor process. They also suggest that, while coming to work may result in part from coercion— the fear of losing one's job—activities on the shop floor are more likely to be the object of consent.

Indeed, it might be argued that fluctuations in the markets enhance rather than diminish the consent organized at the point of production; for the major changes that occurred within the plant as a result of changes in the supply, product, and labor markets were of a distributive nature, related, in particular, to jobs and hours of work. When the labor force expands or contracts, there is always a considerable amount of bidding, bumping, and reshuffling of laborers between jobs. A single vacancy can create a long vacancy chain. As I stated in chapter 6, job mobility recharges individualism, competition, and lateral conflict and reduces hierarchical conflict. At first sight, fear of losing one's job may appear to undermine consent, but three factors work against this hypothesis. First, loss of job affects only those recently hired. Second, losing one's job is generally unrelated to job performance. Third, employees with more than a year's service frequently look forward to a layoff. The seniority system and the internal labor market therefore serve to buffer the effects of fluctuations in levels of employment and, paradoxically, at times of recession and cutback even promote consent. The absence of an internal labor market and a developed internal state at the Hawthorne plant in 1933 might explain, in part, why job performance there was more sensitive to the approaching depression than it was at Allied.

Conclusion

We have observed that the engine division was, to a considerable degree, able to protect its "technical core" from the uncertainties and contingencies of a recession. However, it did so not merely by buffering, leveling, forecasting, and rationing but by *externalizing certain costs* as well. In 1974, for example, the engine division made a loss, and this was absorbed by the corporation as a whole and ultimately passed on to the consumer. This is a factor that Thompson ignores. The insulation of the technical core is more easily accomplished by large corporations, which have the power to externalize costs by raising the prices of their products. Thompson's formulation of the problem is therefore valid only for the era of advanced capitalism. Since the end of the nineteenth century, corporations have merged through vertical and horizontal integration and, as a result, increasingly control both supply and product markets. Thus, Allied Corporation no longer relies on an external supplier of engines but directly controls its own supply, made to its own specifications. By amalgamating their competitors, corporations have come to control larger shares of the product market and thereby, to some extent, the prices of products as well. Two processes of control are involved here. On the one hand, the corporation internalizes or incorporates part of the environment; on the other hand, it seeks to dominate those parts of the environment it cannot incorporate. This is as true of the political and ideological arenas as it is of the economic arena. The corporation attempts to protect itself from the vagaries and limelight of the external political and ideological processes in two ways: by exercising indirect and informal control over the apparatuses of the state and, as I have shown, by erecting its own internal state.

But it would be wrong to conclude that corporations are always successful in insulating their technical cores. Although my field notes are not adequate for presenting a precise picture, there is little doubt that there were changes on the shop floor during the development of the recession, though these changes were minor and were strongly mediated by the internal state and the internal labor market. Despite these changes, largely occasioned by the redistribution of personnel and working hours, the level of output for each department remained fairly constant. Two alternative explanations present themselves.

Either the expenditure of effort and level of output are in fact largely independent of changes in relations *or* workers went to greater lengths and expended greater effort in maintaining the same levels of output—in which case changes in relations do give rise to changes in activities. Although I tend to favor the second alternative, it is difficult to come to any firm conclusion. A clearer picture will, it is hoped, emerge in the next chapter, when I explore the effect of consciousness, imported from outside the workplace by different groups of workers, on the translation of relations into activities.

Nine

The Labor Process and Worker Consciousness

Marx defines labor power as the set of mental and physical capabilities exercised in the labor process. These capabilities are objective qualities. Mental capabilities refer to learned skills and not to subjective orientations, such as willingness to work. For Marx such subjective orientations were largely irrelevant in both coming to work and in the expenditure of effort. Coercion was the paramount factor in shaping what people did. In part 3 I argued that the organization of consent becomes increasingly critical as wages become more independent of the individual expenditure of effort. I also argued that whatever consent is necessary for the obscuring and securing of surplus value is generated at the point of production rather than imported into the workplace from outside. This position flies in the face of conventional wisdom, which claims that the attitudes, beliefs, theories—in short, consciousness—acquired in the family, school, church, etc., shape the relations and activities of the labor process. Curiously, the pioneering studies in industrial sociology largely ignored the "values" or "orientations" that workers brought with them to the shop floor. Industrial behavior was for the most part assumed

to be independent of externally derived consciousness, or at least it
could be taken as an unexamined given. In this chapter I shall argue
that industrial sociologists, instead of being wrong in their assumptions, as their contemporary critics maintain, simply failed to
examine why they were right. They did not examine *why* externally
produced consciousness does not significantly affect the labor
process; they simply ignored it.

External Orientations to Work

These "closed system" studies have received their most far-reaching
criticism in the influential work of John Goldthorpe and his associates.[1] In stressing the importance of "orientations to work,"
Goldthorpe et al. attempt to establish a corrective to two dominant
schools of industrial sociology—the school of human relations (and
"neohuman relations") and the school of "technological determinism" and sociotechnical systems. To the first they counterpose the
view that workers do not attempt to fulfill social needs through work
but that work is purely a means to an end—a source of income to
support external commitments. To the second they counterpose the
argument that external orientations to work determine the relationship between technology and behavior. They conclude:

> It may then be argued that in *any* attempt at explaining and under-
> standing attitudes and behavior within modern industry, the prob-
> ability at least must be recognised that orientations to work which
> employees hold in common will need to be treated as an important
> *independent* variable relative to the in-plant situation. . . . In this
> way, therefore, the possibility—indeed, the necessity—arises, as it
> does not with the other approaches we have considered, of explain-
> ing and understanding the social life which goes on within the
> enterprise by reference ultimately to the structure and processes of
> the wider society in which the enterprise exists.[2]

The transformation of relations in production into patterns of behavior is mediated, they argue, by orientations that workers carry
from the home into the plant and activate there.

   Their study raises and offers answers to four sets of questions.
First, does the so-called instrumental orientation arise from life

outside work or within the workplace? Second, and related, is this instrumental orientation on the increase, and, if so, why? Third, can one examine industrial behavior through the analysis of attitudes? Fourth, what significance should one attach to discrepant attitudes? I shall deal with each in turn. The authors claim that the instrumental orientation, which regards work as a means to an end, is not a product of the factory but of the geographical and social mobility peculiar to the Luton workers they studied.[3] Yet the variation in instrumentality among the workers seemed less related to social and geographical mobility than to the type of job.[4] Moreover, another study, conducted by Dorothy Wedderburn and Rosemary Crompton, concludes that an "instrumental" orientation also characterizes a labor force with very different life-experiences than the Luton workers.[5] Their study suggests that the orientation measured by Goldthorpe et al. did not emerge from a particular type of community life. As Goldthorpe et al. themselves recognize, one of the problems of validating their hypothesis is that all their comparisons are confined to a single sample of workers. The conclusions of Wedderburn and Crompton contradict those of the earlier study in that they stress the importance of technological constraint on worker behavior.

Second, Goldthorpe et al. claim that the instrumental orientation of workers is a product of recent changes in urban society and is therefore likely to become even more typical in the future. Their argument rests on the existence of "traditional" workers, who look upon work as an end unto itself. But until they can demonstrate that the so-called traditional worker exists or existed and does not exhibit instrumental orientations to work, their conclusions are less than compelling.[6] Moreover, they do not offer evidence to show that instrumentality is either becoming more significant or was any less significant in the past. What were the orientations of the employees in the satanic mills if they weren't instrumental? Indeed, the formulations of such historians as Karl Polanyi and Edward Carr are precisely the opposite: the problem of the welfare state is to discover a replacement for the economic whip of the nineteenth century.[7] Goldthorpe et al. indulge in a false comparison of the attitudes of workers in the middle of the twentieth century with a stereotype of the workers of early capitalism. But even if one grants Goldthorpe et al. their increased instrumentality, individualism, and market orientation, these are just as likely to result from changes in the labor process as from urban life. Not only do Goldthorpe et al. not provide any evidence for the trends they postulate, but they appear to arbitrarily rule out the possibility that such trends may originate in the industrial context itself.

Perhaps the most telling weakness of their study, and this is the third point, is its failure to provide any data on what workers actually do—that is, data on industrial behavior. Instead they rely entirely on a survey of worker attitudes. When they are divorced from their context, how can one interpret the enumeration of a set of attitudes? To what reality do these attitudes refer? They appear to reflect a general attitude toward work in capitalist society, to a reluctance to engage in meaningless, boring, and coercive routines. Inevitably they miss the adaptations workers make to compensate for the deprivations they endure. Any familiarity with what goes on in a factory makes it obvious that Goldthorpe et al. are measuring something far removed from everyday life on the shop floor. Even the attitudes expressed while on the job do not necessarily correspond to behavior there. Thus, as I shall show in the next section, the very expression of racial hostilities serves to undermine race as a relevant category of interaction. More to the point are Roy's observations, confirmed by my own, that, while workers speak of making out in the *idiom* of making money—the cash nexus—their actual behavior reflects a particular "culture," organized at the point of production and independent of outside orientations. I have no doubt that, had Goldthorpe et al. interviewed workers at Allied and Geer, they would have discovered the same instrumental orientation, despite the very different background; and yet industrial behavior at both Geer and Allied was in fact consistently responsive to a *different* ideology. In short, the idiom in which workers couch and rationalize their behavior is no necessary guide to the patterns of their actual behavior.

Finally, on close examination, the tables presented by Goldthorpe et al. display a disturbingly high percentage of deviants from the norm of instrumentality. What do these discrepancies signify? Do they reflect different types of workers, different levels of consciousness, an ambivalence toward their circumstances, or did different workers assess different elements of their experience in answering the questions? Michael Mann has postulated the concept of dual consciousness to explain patently contradictory views held by workers.[8]

This concept might be profitably deployed to explain variations in the responses of the Luton workers. In a critique of the Luton studies, John Westergaard suggests that the discrepancies signify a latent class radicalism that Goldthorpe et al. obscure.[9] In addition, he shows that attitudes can change significantly within a short space of time. He recounts how, after Goldthorpe's interviewers had left the scene, the very workers studied at Vauxhall Motors went on strike. Westergaard remarks, "The 'cash nexus' may snap just because it is *only* a cash nexus—because it is single-stranded; and if it does snap, there is nothing else to bind the worker to acceptance of his situation."[10] He concludes, "But the single-stranded character of 'cash orientation' implies a latent instability of workers' commitments and orientations whch is virtually ignored in the interpretation put forward in the Luton study."[11]

Westergaard's criticism highlights yet another problem with the Luton studies—their failure to distinguish between coming to work, on the one hand, and working, on the other—that is, between the delivery of labor power and its transformation into labor. The cash nexus is an essential ingredient in bringing the worker to the factory gates, although, even here, ideology plays a critical role in presenting this as natural and inevitable. But the instrumental or cash orientation does not play the same role in the labor process, even under a piece-rate system, where monetary reward is directly linked to individual output.

To conclude: in presenting a corrective to the human-relations and sociotechnical-systems approaches to industrial behavior, Goldthorpe et al. tend to dismiss both when the task is rather to combine them. For the labor process is nothing but the "human" relations into which workers and managers enter as they transform raw materials with particular technical instruments of production. Roethlisberger and Dickson understood this only too well. In their interpretation of the Hawthorne experiments, they argue that it is not improved working conditions—achieved, for example, by fiddling around with heating, lighting, ventilation, and so forth—that increased output but the way the improvements were experienced or, as Gramsci might say, the way they were mediated by ideology. The question is, then, what is this ideology, and where does it come from? Does it emerge at the point of production, or is it imported from outside? This is a reformulation of the Goldthorpe group's original question, which they cannot answer because they do not distinguish between the delivery and transformation of labor power; because they are unable to distinguish "orientations" that originate in the workplace from those that originate outside the workplace; and because they do not have any measures of industrial behavior. In this chapter I will try to examine more carefully whether imported consciousness mediates the translation of relations in production into activities. But first it will be necessary to examine how relations in production are themselves affected by the consciousness that workers carry with them into the plant.

Race Relations at the
Point of Production

In deciding whether relations in production are independent of the consciousness that people bring with them to the shop floor, it is necessary to have some measure of that external consciousness. I shall work on the assumption that different roles outside work foster different experiences and thus different consciousness. In my own observations, however, not all external roles were recognizable. I could, of course, distinguish different age groups, sexes, and races without much difficulty. Although sex may have been a significant influence on the formation of relations in production, the fact that there were only two women on second shift in the small-parts department makes it impossible to draw any conclusions. The second variable—age—was too highly associated with other variables, such as family size and seniority, which determined which jobs were held. Race was the only variable that provided the basis for a distinctive consciousness and also cut across positions within the plant.

There have been one or two studies of the effect of racial differences on the organization of work. Everett Hughes gives striking examples of the control a dominant white group can exercise over a new black group, forcing the latter into subordinate, marginal positions that in some cases led them to quit their jobs. At the same time, he argues that managerial policy may have a significant effect on the work behavior of Blacks.

The individualistic or "rabble" hypothesis of industrial management—that each worker is an individual who may be induced, and

who ought to be able to be induced to work for his own ends without
regard to his fellows—is almost unconsciously applied with re-
doubled force to the Negro worker. The behavior it encourages is,
in its essence, the behavior of the ambitious person. The ambitious white worker may dissociate himself from his fellows to some
extent, and in spite of being somewhat disliked he may get promo-
tions for it. The Negro worker apparently feels and is made to feel
in some situations that he has to dissociate himself from others and
be a "solitary" in order merely to keep his job. [12]

In other words, it is not being black per se but the particular racial
bias of the organization of work that contributes to the different
patterns of behavior. What happens when there are no formal
managerial mechanisms for the reproduction of race relations on the
shop floor? William Kornblum, in his study of a South Chicago steel
mill and its community, writes, "Seniority and skill are the main
criteria in making work assignments, and attachments forged over a
lifetime in the mills often cut across the racial, ethnic, and territorial
groupings which may divide men in the outside community." [13] His
observations show that coalitions across racial and ethnic boundaries
are as natural within the steel mill as they are unnatural in the
community outside.

The situation at Allied is similar. There, cliques based on race, age,
and common interests (such as religious fundamentalism) tend to be
more important on informal occasions. On both first and second
shifts, race was the most significant basis of association at lunch
breaks. On first shift, the secondmost important criterion of association was seniority, followed by department and then job. On second
shift, employees were relatively new, and so seniority was less important than department and job in shaping informal ties. Interrupt-
ing work for gossip or drinking provided occasions for informal
interactions, which were frequently across racial lines. On the shop
floor a mate was often someone working on a similar machine, and
the association was established on the basis of mutual assistance in
setting up, etc. Again, this interaction frequently crossed racial
boundaries and extended to drinking at the vending machines.

Despite, or perhaps because of, everyday cooperation, racial and
ethnic prejudices were a persistent idiom of shop-floor life. At one
moment, operators, auxiliary workers, and foremen would be

privately uttering some racial or ethnic slur; the next minute they
would be assisting a member of the insulted race or ethnic group
(possibly along with bantering, friendly abuse) as readily as they
would assist a member of their own group. Thus *attitudes* or
prejudices were imported from urban settings, such as housing and
education, which continuously reproduce "race relations," while
activities on the shop floor were largely unaffected by racial divisions.

In this connection, joking relationships assume a central significance by allowing and even reproducing a dislocation between attitudes and behavior. Radcliffe-Brown describes the joking relationship as follows:

> Social disjunction implies divergence of interests and therefore the
> possibility of conflict and hostility, while conjunction requires the
> avoidance of strife. How can a relation which combines the two be
> given a stable, ordered form? There are two ways of doing this. One
> is to maintain between two persons so related an extreme mutual
> respect and a limitation of direct personal contact.... The alter-
> native to this relation of extreme mutual respect and restraint is the
> joking relationship, one, that is, of mutual disrespect and licence.
> Any serious hostility is prevented by the playful antagonism of
> teasing, and this in its regular repetition is a constant expression or
> reminder of that social disjunction which is one of the essential
> components of the relation, while the social conjunction is main-
> tained by friendliness that takes no offence at insult.[14]

Where continual rather than intermittent contact between different races is to be found, the exchange of racial insults in a friendly
manner reflects, on the one hand, the requirements of continuous
cooperation and, on the other, the recognition that in other contexts
racial hostility is a prevailing norm. The joking relationship is
therefore testimony to the irrelevance of racial divisions to productive
activities. Furthermore, the circumstances and direction of joking
relationships are based, not on external social relations, but on the
relative standing of the participants in the "status" system of the shop
floor. To indicate the way in which the work context determined
relations between races and how the joking relation served to seal off
the work context and its "culture" from external social relations, I
will now briefly discuss my own relationships with some of the black
workers.

Bill, a well-built Black, nearly fifty, broke me in on the miscellaneous job. My training was on first shift and lasted for three weeks. I then took up a permanent position on second shift. Because Bill was on two hours' overtime, our shifts overlapped, and I continued to interact with him, even after I had begun on second shift. Bill had been on the miscellaneous job for ten years. (I was convinced I had misheard him when he first told me; but as I got to know him and the job better, I began to see why he should have suffered its extremely unpleasant features rather than move on to a more pleasant job.) Bill was, in fact, the only one in the plant who knew all the tasks the job involved. He'd broken in many operators, but none stayed more than a few months because the job was so tough and dirty. At first he maintained a discreet distance, instructing me in only the bare essentials of what I had to know in order to get by. Frequently, he complained about how incompetent and slow I was and said that I would never make out at the rate I was going. "On this job there ain't no time to fuck around, you gotta work, man." In that early period I was more interested in staying alive and keeping my job than in making out. After our relations had mellowed a little and I had become more accustomed to the job, he began to show me a few angles on how to make out. Bill also began introducing me to others as "my Englishman." The hostility aroused by *my* racial identity was being drawn attention to and, in a joking manner, pushed aside as being of little relevance in the present setting. However, at this early stage I could not push aside *his* racial identity. Only later, when I had established a firmer association, assisting whenever I could, covering up for him, looking after his tools, and eventually sharing a kitty with him, would I dare to call him "superdude." That is, a *symmetrical* joking relationship emerged only when I no longer depended on his advice and assistance in order to carry out my work.

A few months later I was broken in on the broach by another black first-shift operator—Howard. Even though I frequently worked on the broach on second shift, I never established the cordial relations with Howard that I had with Bill. He consistently looked on me with contempt, either because of my incompetence (I was terrified of this machine, since I nearly killed myself twice when I did not remove a gear quickly enough and the steel broach, arching upward, burst into pieces that flew in all directions) or because I was taking away much of his overtime, or both. He *used* race to establish a distance between us, but the hostility was not based on racial antagonism—this was merely a convenient *idiom;* instead, it emerged out of our respective positions in the productive process. This conclusion is confirmed by the generally amiable relations Howard had with other white operators on first shift.

Intermittent interaction with Howard was negotiated on the basis of latent hostility. Intermittent interaction with Leroi—the black first-shift overhead-crane operator—was based on mutual respect. Leroi always worked overtime, and two or three times a week he would bring me stock to cut on the power saw before he went home. On those occasions we would talk about politics and economics. He would tell me how we were little men and how it was the big men who ruled the world and had all the money. I would talk about socialism, how capitalism was doomed, and how a depression was looming up. The different form of relationship I had with Leroi, as compared to Howard, stemmed from his different position in the productive process.

Joking relationships, whether symmetrical or asymmetrical, can be established only on the basis of at least a minimal trust. They are also defined by, and confined to, a particular situation. Without a minimal level of intimacy or in an inappropriate setting, an intended joke can quickly shade into hostility and can sometimes erupt into violence, as it nearly did when a time clerk once insulted a black operator whom he did not know very well. Until a new context has been established, relations of hostility are carried over from an external setting, and only a minimal cooperation binds the two races. Joking relationships were less frequent between myself and several younger Blacks on my own shift with whom I would discuss and debate but with whom I was not directly linked in the process of production. With such Blacks the *content* of my relationship was governed by our external roles—mine as a white student working his way through school and theirs as black workers in a racist society. While an irreducible racial hostility persisted, the *form* of our relationship was governed by our similar positions on the shop floor. Soon I was excused for being a White; I was, in their terms, "all right." But only once did I go drinking with them; in other words, I was "all right" only on the shop floor.[15]

In summary: the joking relationship permitted (1) the coexistence of racial prejudices and everyday cooperation between races and (2) the convergence of interests at work and their divergence outside work. The direction and the content of joking relationships both reflect the structure of production relations and not the antagonistic race relations of the urban community. External consciousness lives on in the joking relationship but only as an idiom that expresses unchanged production relations.[16] If the consciousness carried into the plant does not affect the relations in production, does it mediate the translation of these relations into activities?

Consciousness and the Transformation of Labor Power into Labor

Early studies of machine shops, conducted at the end of World War II, suggest the importance of social background in the determination of output.[17] Thus, Dalton characterizes the rate-buster as likely

> to come from a family of higher socioeconomic level than that of other members of the work group, or, if he does not, he is trying to reach such a level...to be a nominal Protestant,...to be an Anglo-American or an immigrant from Northwestern Europe,... to be a Republican and...read a conservative newspaper,...to be a family man, [all this] accompanied by a relative indifference to the community at large,.... [Further,] despite his restricted social life and extremely individualistic behavior, the rate-buster is not personally disorganized.[18]

Two comments are relevant. First, Dalton seems to miss the item that most significantly characterizes the nine rate-busters he considers—their age. Only one was younger than forty-five, and their average age was fifty-one.[19] Rather than age per se, it is probably seniority that is closely associated with rate-busting. The more senior the employee, the more secure he or she will feel in breaking group norms:

> Apparently a girl who is socially well established in the group can consistently break the rate a little with only mild teasing as punishment. But outsiders who break the rate are severely punished by

ridicule and scorn; if they persist, they remain outsiders and, if
associations are important to them, they may be forced off the
job.[20]

Second, with the rise of the hegemonic organization of industrial
work, the rate-buster is *increasingly* likely to be an employee whose
skill and seniority place him in a relatively strong position. Only
such a worker can escape the sanctions of fellow workers and plant
management. We have already referred to shop management's
opposition to rate-busting. Only an operator with considerable influence, such as an ex-president of the union local, can consistently
turn in well over the accepted ceiling and yet keep management at
bay—particularly, the methods department.

To further specify the significance of imported consciousness on
the transformation of labor power into labor, I have undertaken a
statistical analysis of the influence of external roles on the level of
individual output. I have included in my sample all operators (185)
in the small-parts department of the engine division of Allied
Corporation who recorded more than forty hours on piecework in
the first eleven months of 1975.

For interpreting the figures, four hypotheses present themselves.
The first argues that activities on the shop floor are unaffected by
externally produced consciousness, that relations in production
intervene between race, education, family size, and age, on the one
hand, and the level of output, on the other. To put it another way,
external factors may determine the job one holds in the plant and
thus the particular relations into which one enters, but these relations then determine activities of production. The second hypothesis
maintains that externally derived consciousness *does* have a direct
impact on shop-floor activities—that race, education, etc., shape
activities in the factory independently of relations in production. For
example, this would seem to be true for informal activities during
lunch breaks.

The next two hypotheses are not concerned with the direct impact
of external factors on production activities but with the way external
factors affect or *mediate* the transformations of relations into activities.[21] The third hypothesis therefore asserts that consciousness
imported from outside plays no mediating role, while the fourth

hypothesis asserts the opposite, that the way in which social relations affect output is determined by external factors.

The plausibility of these models or hypotheses can be evaluated through the development of two sets of variables. The first set corresponds to external systems of social relations, involving the family, schooling, and the community. I have been able to gather reliable data on only four such variables, namely, race, level of education, marital status, and age. I excluded sex because there were only six women in the sample. I excluded family size because the personnel records rarely updated this information. The second set of variables corresponds to relations *in* production. Because the number of different jobs was so great and the sample relatively small, it was impossible to use the particular machine being run as an index of social relations. Instead, I adopted seniority (measured in terms of the number of months between the date of recruitment and November 1975) as an index of relations in production. The decision was based on three assumptions. First, I assumed the existence of a commonly shared prestige-ranking of piece-rate jobs in the machine shop. Second, I assumed that operators would attempt, through the bidding system, to place themselves on the jobs with higher prestige. As a result, seniority of operators would reflect the prestige of the machines they ran. Third, I assumed that machines with similar prestige would be inscribed in similar sets of social relations. Therefore, seniority would be an index of social relations in production.[22] The second internal variable is experience, as measured by the number of hours spent on piecework in the first eleven months of 1975. Experience measures not only the acquisition of skill in the operation of machines but also the acquisition of skill in the manipulation of the social relations that characterize a particular job—relations with foremen, truckers, inspectors, setup men, and so forth. Thus, among operators holding the same job, relations in production will vary according to experience. Since the influence of seniority and experience on the social relations of the shop floor will diminish as time periods increase, in the actual analysis I decided to use the logarithms (to base ten) of these variables.

The relative influence of each of the six factors (log seniority, log experience, race, education, marital status, and age) on the percentage output (the average for the first eleven months of 1975) was ascertained by combining them into a simple multiple regression. The results are summarized in Table 2. Seniority explains 24.4 percent of the variation in output, and experience a further 12.7 percent, while race, age, marital status, and education together contribute only an additional 3.5 percent.[23] These results appear to support the first hypothesis and not the second. The direct impact of external roles on output is negligible.[24]

However, we are still left with 60 percent of the variation in output

Table 2   **Regression of Allied Workers' Output***
                                              on Various "Internal" and "External"
                                              Variables ($N = 185$)

Independent Variable	Unstandardized Coefficients	Standardized Coefficients	Contribution to R^2
Log seniority	18.62 (3.49)†	0.43	0.244
Log experience	12.87 (2.94)	0.26	0.127
Race (White =1; Black = 2)	- 1.70 (3.05)	- 0.03	0.003
Age	0.22 (0.15)	0.12	0.009
Marital Status (Married =1; Single = 0)	5.54 (2.84)	0.12	0.012
Education (< High school =1; ≥ high school =2)	5.35 (2.95)	0.11	0.011
Constant	51.20 (14.69)		
			$R^2 =0.406$

*"Output" in this and succeeding tables refers to the recorded rate of producing pieces expressed as a percentage of the rate established by the industrial engineering department and averaged over all piecework jobs the operator completed during the first eleven months of 1975.

†Standard errors in parentheses.

unexplained. What can we say about it? The first point to be emphasized is the indeterminacy of the outcomes of particular strategies. Operators may attempt to make out, but their success is uncertain. It is precisely *because* work is constituted as a game that the levels of output exhibit random fluctuations; for the feature responsible for drawing workers into the game is their lack of complete control over outcomes. Uncertainty is inscribed in the labor process—in the fastidious inspector, in the faulty casting, in the dull drill, and so forth. While social relations in production may be the most significant factor in determining the level of output, this determination usually displays some variability—it is neither so great as to make the game frustrating nor so small as to make it boring. Accordingly, the regression of average percentage output for any given week on the six independent variables, and on the internal ones in particular, is much weaker in its predictive power than the regression using an eleven-month average output. For example, the regression equation for the next-to-the-last week in November 1975 explained only 21.1 percent of the variation in output.[25]

The indeterminacy of the outcomes of activities inscribed in the game of making out is one source of unexplained variance. Another source lies in the crude measures we have used to measure social relations in production. It quite frequently happens that senior employees do not attempt to bid on the more prestigious jobs but are content to remain on one they know well. There could be a number of reasons for this. My day man, Bill, for example, said he was too old to start something new. More significant, however, was the satisfaction he derived from the challenge and power that the miscellaneous job offered. Al McCann, Roy's workmate, clearly found satisfaction in the prestige he commanded by virtue of his mastery of the angles in making out on the radial drill. At Allied the most prestigious jobs, such as the automatic lathes, were unattractive in terms of making out, since, once the setups had been mastered, they presented no challenge or uncertainty. A second problem with the seniority index lies in the possibility that vacancies on the more prestigious machines may be filled from outside. When management felt that there were no satisfactory bids on some of the more sophisticated machines, they sometimes brought personnel in from outside. In such cases, seniority would not be a measure of job

prestige. A third problem, involving a lack of correspondence between social relations and seniority, concerns the distribution of
difficult piece rates to prestigious jobs, as happened on some of the
lathes. Since piece rates are themselves expressions of social relations, any lack of correspondence between seniority and easy piece
rates will contribute to the unexplained variance in the first regression. Yet another source of error may be sought in the problem of
using experience as a measure of "within-job" variations of relations
in production. It often happens that an operator has had prior
experience on a particular machine, but this would not show up on
our measure of experience, which was confined to 1975. These are
just some of the factors that must be introduced if social relations at
the point of production are to explain more than 37 percent of the
variance.

It is also possible that the heterogeneity of the population of
workers may impose definite limits on the amount of variation in
output that can be explained by relations in production. So far, I
have assumed that workers respond to the social relations of the
machine shop in ways independent of their background. This
assumption is, in fact, our third hypothesis, which asserts that
workers may be regarded as supports or agents of particular sets of
social relations. These social relations are treated as prior to the
individuals who "carry" or "support" them and who act in accordance with the rationality that springs from them. Workers fill
"empty places" (lathe operator, crib attendant, scheduling man,
foreman, etc.) defined by the labor process. The relations in production give rise to a lived experience that is independent of the
particular individuals who fill the empty places but that shapes their
activities. Making out emerges out of the organization of empty
places and is prior to the individual worker who is inserted into the
game. Outcomes are dependent on an acquired skill at playing the
game of making out and on the social relations that define each
particular job. It might be argued that skill is somehow determined
by "external" factors, but our hypothesis claims, further, that skill
develops at the point of production, through experience and training
on the job.

The alternative and fourth hypothesis conceives of workers as
carrying around in their heads a consciousness formed by various

processes of "internalization" or "socialization." Consciousness acquired in one setting mediates the effects that relations have on activities in a different setting. Socialization patterns learned in the family, school, and community are activated at work and determine how operators will respond to a piece-rate system—whether they will play the making-out game or some other game or even no game at all.

In order to examine the mediating influence of imported consciousness, I divided the 185 operators into subpopulations: white and black; young and old; married and single; grade-school graduates and high-school graduates. In tables 3 and 4 I have compared the influence of log seniority and log experience on output for the different groups. Although it is difficult to draw any firm substantive conclusions from a comparison of regression equations where both coefficients and constant terms differ, there are, nevertheless, a number of interesting results. First, with the exception of the poorly educated, splitting the population up into subpopulations does not increase the explained variation in output, and for the younger operators the explained variance falls markedly. Second, with the exception of Blacks, the young, and possibly the unmarried operators, the standardized coefficients that measure the effects of log seniority and log experience on output for the subpopulations are close to the coefficients for the entire population. Both results suggest that the heterogeneity of the population, that is, the different backgrounds of the operators, has only a limited mediating effect.[26]

Without doubt the exceptions provide interesting material for speculation on the source of the mediating effects that do exist. Let me deal with each in turn. The most interesting deviant group is made up of people born after 1946. For this subpopulation the variation in output explained by relations in production is half that for the entire population, and the regression coefficients suggest that seniority is no more important than experience in determining output. It is plausible that the younger operators learn from experience, much like any other group, but tend to experiment among jobs rather than immediately seek those with easier rates. In other words, the younger workers play the game of making out as well as anyone, but they do not necessarily bid on jobs with the easier rates.

Rather, they attempt to accumulate skill on as wide a variety of machines as possible.

The opposite is true for the poorly educated. Almost 50 percent of the variation in output is explained by relations in production. For the grade-school graduates, experience contributes more to the explained variation than seniority, whereas for the population as a whole seniority is twice as important as experience. This suggests that grade-school graduates are more likely to pick up their skills at the point of production and to learn more through experience on the job than the high-school graduates do. Although Blacks and Whites have their output equally shaped by relations in production, the contribution of seniority relative to experience is nearly five times greater for Blacks than for Whites. One might infer the existence of two distinct groups of black operators: those who have been with the company a relatively long time and are "good" workers, and those who have arrived more recently and exhibit the greatest antagonism to the hegemonic organization of work. Thus, young Whites and young Blacks responded to the machine shop in different ways, reflected in the hostility that existed between the two groups and manifested in the weak link between relations and output for the entire group of young operators.

From these results it is clear that the labor process is not autonomous with respect to the translation of relations into activities. Consciousness molded in practices outside the factory do affect, although within narrow limits, the way operators respond to production relations. However, if the labor process is not autonomous, it may be *relatively autonomous.* That is, the labor process may itself determine the effect of imported consciousness. Or, to put it more specifically, does the effect of race, education, age, and marital status on the translation of relations into output vary with the position in the labor process? Unfortunately, my population was too small, the positions in the labor process too similar, and my measures too crude to supply a convincing answer to this question. The numbers in the subpopulations made subdivision according to position in the labor process (as measured by seniority) impractical. Instead, I split the population into those with seniority greater than three years and those with seniority less than or equal to three years and then examined the contribution of external factors to output,

Subpopulation	Independent Variable	Unstandardized Coefficients	Standardized Coefficients	Contribution to R^2	R^2
White ($N = 147$)	Log seniority	20.81 (2.92)*	0.48	0.22	
					0.373
	Log experience	13.36 (3.31)	0.27	0.15	
	Constant	48.28 (9.46)			
Black ($N = 38$)	Log seniority	26.45 (5.94)	0.59	0.34	
					0.391
	Log experience	8.55 (7.04)	0.16	0.05	
	Constant	53.55 (21.49)			
Born before 1947 ($N = 85$)	Log seniority	18.37 (3.18)	0.52	0.25	
					0.396
	Log experience	10.87 (4.17)	0.23	0.15	
	Constant	62.12 (11.81)			
Born after 1946 ($N = 100$)	Log seniority	24.19 (7.37)	0.30	0.09	
					0.191
	Log experience	14.18 (4.19)	0.31	0.10	
	Constant	39.85 (14.66)			
Total population ($N = 185$)	Log seniority	21.96 (2.59)	0.51	0.25	
					0.375
	Log experience	12.37 (2.97)	0.25	0.13	
	Constant	49.50 (8.60)			

Table 3   **Regression of Allied Workers' Output on Log Seniority and Log Experience, by Race and Age Group and for Total Population**

*Standard errors in parentheses.

Table 4

Regression of Allied Workers' Output on Log Seniority and Log Experience, by Marital Status and Educational Level and for Total Population

Subpopulation	Independent Variable	Unstandardized Coefficients	Standardized Coefficients	Contribution to R^2	R^2
Married ($N = 130$)	Log seniority	19.69 (2.80)*	0.50	0.24	0.375
	Log experience	11.10 (3.12)	0.26	0.13	
	Constant	58.23 (9.12)			
Single ($N = 55$)	Log seniority	23.92 (6.42)	0.43	0.18	0.329
	Log experience	18.31 (7.29)	0.29	0.15	
	Constant	26.19 (20.69)			
Less than high-school education ($N = 39$)	Log seniority	19.79 (5.12)	0.53	0.21	0.495
	Log experience	15.84 (8.29)	0.26	0.29	
	Constant	39.59 (21.34)			
High-school education or more ($N = 146$)	Log seniority	24.25 (3.37)	0.50	0.24	0.340
	Log experience	12.40 (3.23)	0.26	0.10	
	Constant	47.38 (9.91)			
Total population ($N = 185$)	Log seniority	21.96 (2.59)	0.51	0.25	0.375
	Log experience	12.37 (2.97)	0.25	0.13	
	Constant	49.50 (8.60)			

*Standard errors in parentheses.

controlling for log experience. The results are summarized in table
5. They indicate that, within the narrow limits that imported consciousness is effective, its impact does vary according to position in
the labor process.[27] Obviously, this is no proof of the relative
autonomy of the labor process at Allied. At best it is suggestive.

Table 5		Regression of Allied Workers' Output on Log Experience and on Race, Education, Age, and Marital Status, by Seniority		
Subpopulation	Independent Variable	Unstandardized Coefficient	Standardized Coefficient	Contribution to R^2
	Log experience	14.69 (3.74)*	0.31	0.101
	Race	- 3.96 (4.13)	- 0.08	0.003
Less than or equal to three years of seniority ($N = 137$)	Education	3.81 (3.96)	0.08	0.003
	Age	0.37 (0.22)	0.15	0.018
	Marital status	7.54 (3.59)	0.19	0.048
	Constant	78.78 (17.54)		
				$R^2 = 0.173$
	Log experience	13.90 (4.11)	0.48	0.178
	Race	2.35 (3.79)	0.08	0.007
More than three years of seniority ($N = 48$)	Education	5.72 (3.76)	0.23	0.042
	Age	0.22 (0.17)	0.19	0.012
	Marital status	- 0.80 (4.57)	0.00	0.000
	Constant	87.8 (16.95)		
				$R^2 = 0.239$

*Standard errors in parentheses.

Conclusion

In this chapter I have tried to show, first, that variations in imported consciousness do not give rise to different relations in production; second, that imported consciousness mediates the translation of relations in production into activities, but only within narrow limits; and third, that the mediating effect of such consciousness varies in accordance with position in the labor process, that is, its effect is shaped by the labor process itself. These very tentative conclusions, based on flimsy data, converge with those of chapter 8, where I tried to show how changes in markets, brought on by the 1974 recession, affected the labor process in ways determined by the organization of work, the internal labor market, and the internal state. From all these findings I concluded that the labor process at Allied is relatively autonomous—that is, it autonomously shapes the outcomes of external changes, and, as we shall see in the next chapter, it creates its own characteristic dynamics.

However, it would be wrong to conclude that what happens to workers outside the factory is of little importance to what they do inside it on the grounds that variations in imported consciousness do not significantly affect either the relations in production or the expenditure of effort. The variations in consciousness between Blacks and Whites, young and old, grade-school graduates and high-school graduates, and married and single persons may be merely small variations around a common consciousness that capitalism inculcates in all its subjects.[28] A more adequate assessment of the importance of externally produced consciousness would have to be based on a comparison of the responses of workers in a capitalist society with the responses of precapitalist workers. I address this problem in the appendix, where I suggest that the organization of work may vary with the social, political, and economic context but that the behavior of workers is in accordance with the organization of the labor process and largely independent of any precapitalist consciousness they carry with them.

The more we dissociate the experiences of workers outside work from the responses in work, the more we are forced toward postulating invariant human characteristics—that is, the more we are driven toward outlining a theory of human nature. Already I have made a number of assertions about how workers generally adapt to the exigencies of capitalist work by the construction of games, the "instinct" to control, and so on. Are these human universals? Ultimately, no Marxist can avoid advancing a theory of human nature—a theory of what Marx called species essence, of the potentiality inherent in the human species. Such a theory is indispensable to understanding the nature and possibility of an emancipated society.

Apart from what we all share, there is a second reason why what happens outside work can be critical for what happens on the shop floor. In normal times, variations in the form and content of schooling, family, and the mass media may not affect the subordination of workers to the labor process. However, at moments of crisis—when lived experience is momentarily questioned, when what exists no longer seems so natural and inevitable—a variety of theories can become an effective force, that is, can become ideologies. What is taught in schools, what is disseminated in the mass media, and what is experienced in the family can then become critical in organizing the collective will and in shaping workers' responses to capitalism.

5

The Motors of Change

Ten

Struggles on the
Shop Floor

In part 2 I described changes in the organization of work and in part 3 how these changes contributed to the obscuring and securing of surplus value. In part 4 I discussed the degree to which the labor process was insulated from external changes and the consciousness workers acquire outside the factory. I turn now to my last task: the explanation of changes in the labor process observed between 1945 and 1975 at Geer Company and Allied Corporation. In this chapter the discussion is focused on struggles on the shop floor, while the next chapter takes the discussion beyond the workplace.

Economic Struggles

The object of economic struggle on the shop floor is the effort bargain, that is, the monetary reward for labor expended or the reward for effort. Management determines the reward for effort through the piecework system. Thus, in 1945 each operation on each piece was assigned a "price." The hourly wage was computed by multiplying the number of pieces turned out by the price per piece.

In addition, workers were guaranteed a basic hourly wage when they failed to produce the expected number of pieces. In 1975 the system had changed from one based on prices to one based on "rates"; that is, each operation on a given piece had a standard rate, fixed at so many pieces per hour. If the operator exceeded the standard rate, he or she earned a bonus, worked out as a proportion of his or her hourly basic earnings. When they fell short of the standard rate, operators received the basic earnings. (For further discussion of "prices" and "rates," see chap. 4.) However, in both systems we can construct a "reward-for-effort curve" (see figure 1), which indicates the reward an operator receives for turning out so many pieces per hour, that is, for expending a certain level of effort. For any given operation we can also construct an "effort curve" that indicates the returns to capital and labor (measured in pieces or their equivalent value) for any given level of effort (see figure 2). Moving up on the effort curve constitutes making out.

We have already referred (chapter 4) to the hierarchical conflict that can attend the pressure and frustration of making out and how this can be redistributed into conflict among workers. This hierarchical conflict is *not* a form of struggle, since it is part and parcel of making out. Rather, it is a form of *competition,* and it takes as given the distribution of economic rewards, the rules of the game, and the hierarchy of preferred outcomes. Economic *struggle,* on the other hand, refers not to moving up on the effort curve but to the displacement or reshaping of the effort curve so that the relative returns to labor and capital change. Management seeks to cut prices (1945) or increase rates (1975), while workers strive to do the opposite. In the labor process, struggle of this nature is initiated, most usually, by the methods department, whose responsibility it is to establish the shape and position of the effort curve. However, since 1945, as we shall discover below, the methods department has increasingly withdrawn from the shop floor, and day-to-day struggle around the effort bargain has accordingly diminished.

Time Study in 1945

The methods department at Geer employed a crew of time-study officers as watchdogs of efficiency—emblems of scientific

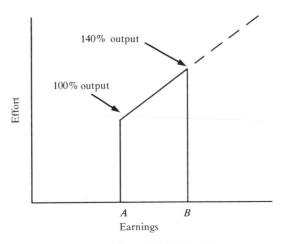

Figure 1   **Reward-for-Effort Curve**

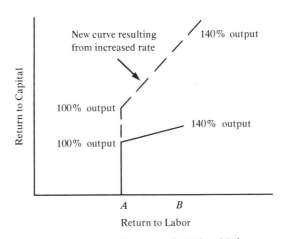

Figure 2   **Returns to Capital and Labor**

In both diagrams, *A* corresponds to "base earnings," achieved for output less than or equal to 100 percent. The segment *AB* is the bonus pay for 140 percent output. "Effort" is measured in terms of output. The standard output is 100 percent. Workers begin to earn an incentive bonus for levels of output in excess of 100 percent. (The "expected" rate of output is 125 percent. See chapter 4.)

management. They were to be found, stopwatch in hand, constantly prowling about the shop floor, timing jobs in their search for "good prices," which offered "gravy work" for the operator. Only perpetual vigilance on the part of operators kept them at bay.

> If the "Big Shots" were disagreeable to the operators as symbols of "more work," the time study men held the expanded significance of "more work for less pay." Worker hostility toward members of top management was tempered by manifestations of a sense of humour; relations with the time study men were "grim business" all the way.[1]

The time-study men were agents of "speedup," always trying to cut the piecework prices. It was even suspected that they received a commission or bonus for the amount of money they saved the company. This was not true, as Roy later discovered, but it is significant that many operators believed it. How else could they explain the persistent attempts to undercut the operators?[2] The tactics of the time-study men were met with unqualified opposition.

> The writer was further warned to "watch out for" the time study men whether he exceeded a quota or not, the implication being that the time study men did not rely solely on "clues" from the records, but performed "private eye" work in the field to detect "gravy" jobs.
> "The men you want to watch out for are the time study men. Whenever you see a man standing around with a watch attached to a board, watch out! Slow down! Take it easy!"
> Stella, a milling machine operator, and regarded as a skillful one, described some of the subtleties of the "detective work" of the time study sleuths.
> "I caught Eddie timing me with his back turned the other day. He was listening to the machine to see when I finished a piece. Later he came along and looked at the route sheet, just as I thought he would. He'll come along, get the number of a job, memorize it, and write it down later.
> "He'll come along to time old jobs that way. You won't think he's watching you, but he'll be listening to your machine."[3]

The consequences of the continual presence of the methods department is not difficult to imagine.[4] Obviously, operators were careful not to turn in more than their quotas and not to exceed them in front of time-study men. Anyone turning in more than his or her quota was subject to considerable social pressure and harassment. Operators, time clerks, foremen, and others were always on the lookout for operators who might be turning in more than the quota, either accidentally or intentionally.

> However, the "social climate" of the Jack Shop was evidently not congenial to the flowering of quota smashers. Either they were nipped in the bud, or they failed to sprout at all; for during the eleven month period the writer's attention was drawn to but several minor and isolated instances of quota exceeding. These dark deeds occurred under special conditions and their perpetrators were not "habituals." [5]

Indeed, Roy can offer only three trivial, isolated instances of rate-busting.

If there were no rate-busters, then what about price-cutting? The methods department could "legitimately" lower prices on any piece-work jobs by introducing some small change:

> It is understood and agreed that the Company may at any time change piecework rates because of mechanical improvements, changes in specifications, or engineering changes. [6]

If management wanted to change a price, it could therefore easily do so. During his eleven months at Geer, Roy himself never experienced a price cut, though he heard reports of a number. His own day man, Joe Mucha, experienced two cuts and one unsuccessful attempt. Roy also reports four other cases of price-cutting on other machines, but it is not clear whether Roy knew of any others. One technique frequently employed by the methods department was to remove the price on a job and then place that job in the category of "time study." This was a recognized precedent to retiming and repricing. "Whenever a price was removed, the operator had reason to assume that a price cut was in order." [7]

The timing operation itself was a game with no clearly defined rules:

> Job timing was to the operators a "game," a "matching of wits," with the rigorous codes of fair play characteristic of cricket not in evidence. The object was a "good price," and that end justified any old means that would work. [8]

Operators commonly tried to fight back by adding extra movements and running the job at low speeds; but the time-study officer was, of course, attuned to these and other tactics, and they therefore could not be relied upon to achieve a "good price," as Roy discovered to his own cost. Roy himself had three new jobs timed. He confesses that he was still green at the art of "screwing the time-study man," and he never scored a clear victory. The struggle brings workers together in solidarity against the methods department. Each gives the other his own tips on how best to deceive the time-study man. After the timing and the awarding of a price, there is a postmortem with fellow operators, inspectors, setup men, and so on, in which each offers advice for future encounters. Even foremen have a stake in operators' getting a good price, as already described, and on occasion they will intervene on behalf of the operator:

> Joe said tonight that I was given a poor price on the worm gear. He was looking for a price of ten cents or twelve cents instead of the six and a half cents I was given. He asked me if I put the feed up for the timing. I told him I ran it at 11 feed, and he threw up his hands.
>
> According to Joe, they were going to time him shortly before three o'clock, and tried to get him to run at 610 speed and 11 feed (he had been running 445 and 7). He tried a piece at 610 and 11, but Rosie (day foreman) told the time study man that the work was unsatisfactory at that speed and feed. Instead of timing the job at 445 and 7, the time study man walked away and came back later to time me at 445 and 11 (which I had been running at time study).[9]

On the other hand, operators were constantly on the lookout for foremen or other management officials who might be in collusion with the methods department. "Although the line foremen on the second shift were never accused of the greatest of offenses, collaboration with the methods department, were never branded with the epithet 'Company Man,' the feelings of the machine operators toward them were by no means of complete approval."[10] As has frequently been pointed out in the literature, foremen are middlemen and in an ambiguous position, inclining them to support different sides of industry in different situations.

Leaving the foremen aside, the pervasive influence of the time-study men and the constant fear of price-cutting served to generate a solidarity among workers. Struggle with management tended to counteract the patterns of conflict associated with making out, namely, the diffusion of hierarchical pressure into antagonisms and competition among workers. Animosity toward one's day man, toward the inspector, toward fellow operators and others was tempered by the continual creation of a common interest in opposition to management as represented by the methods department.

Industrial Engineering in 1975

Over the past thirty years the situation has changed dramatically, for reasons I will explore in the next chapter. Today, time-study men have been replaced by industrial engineers, who spend most of their time in some distant office with pencil, paper, and pocket computer. Time study has been professionalized and made more "scientific." There is a marked reluctance on the part of industrial engineers to appear on the shop floor with a stopwatch. Sometimes they have to, but they are careful to begin by trying to win the cooperation of operators and to dampen hostility. They certainly do not march up and down the aisles looking for loose rates or combing the output records in search of an occasional rate-buster. It is now difficult to find an industrial engineer on the shop floor, let alone find one retiming a job. Bill, my day man, tried to find an industrial engineer to give one of our jobs a permanent piece rate (to replace an estimated rate). That particular job must have come up about half a dozen times while I was there, but Bill never managed to get it timed. Indeed, neither Bill nor I had any job timed on any of our machines during the entire ten months I was at the engine division.

Yet the fear of rate increases remains a pronounced feature of shop-floor culture, and so it remains the basis for continued enforcement of "quota restriction." The fear is well founded, but, as I shall indicate below, rate increases do not result from the decision of an idiosyncratic, rapacious time-study man on the prowl; instead, they follow a predictable pattern. To my knowledge there were three instances of rate increases in the small-parts department during the ten months I was there. In each instance the rates on a number of jobs run on the same machine were affected. In one case the rates were first drastically increased but then, a few weeks later, were restored to their original level—for reasons that remain unclear.

A second case involved an automatic lathe. One of the operators, Ed, handed in "suggestions" for increasing a number of rates on his machine—a very unusual but not unprecedented event. Indeed, it was not the first time Ed had done this. If suggestions are workable and therefore save the company money, the operator receives a bonus. The bonus, of course, goes only to the worker who makes the suggestion, not to other operators on the machine in question. Once a step of this nature has been taken, there is little that any operator can do to convince management that the new rates are unfair. Not surprisingly, feelings of intense hostility are directed at the worker who makes the suggestion, and he is almost totally ostracized on the shop floor; for his action not only infuriates the operators who are directly affected but is a direct affront to the entire community. Ed himself, who was a senior employee, with over thirty years at Allied and Geer, appeared unconcerned about the animosities he had aroused. Helpless, his night-shift worker could demonstrate his hostility only by bidding off the job. However, given the existing high level of unemployment, management had little difficulty in finding a skilled substitute. Union officials stood by and watched. They claimed they could do nothing about the situation, but one steward intimated that, if he had been working on that machine, he would have given Ed something to think about.

The foremen were also disturbed by Ed's action, for it upset the policy of assigning "loose" rates to the more skilled jobs. As I pointed out in a previous section, this is necessary because tight rates lead to high mobility between jobs; and, when an automatic lathe is involved, mobility can be costly in terms of training, production of scrap, and efficient operation of the machine. For the simpler jobs in the shop, such as the speed drill, where most novices begin, little training is necessary; the rates are difficult to make and turnover is therefore considerable, but it is not costly. Operators who manage to get placed on the more sophisticated machines tend to stick with them. Thus, if rates on an automatic lathe are increased, the job is less attractive, and foremen are then faced with a problem of stability. However, the methods department, whose operations are evaluated on the basis of dollars saved by "methods revision" and "time study," was only too pleased to put Ed's suggestions into effect.

The third case of rate increases was contested more vigorously. It concerned one of the final operations in the production of gears: "shaving" the teeth. The job required a certain amount of expertise in setting up, and both of the operators who were involved were senior employees. Art had had over twenty years with the company and worked on day shift, while Bruce had had eleven years and worked on night shift. Art had been turning in 150 percent for the past year, and the company had eventually decided to intervene. To increase an established rate, the methods department had to introduce a technical change. It was decided to reduce the number of "passes" over the teeth. Since both Art and Bruce were experienced operators and gears are the most essential parts of the engine (assembly cannot begin without them), they were in a relatively strong position to fight the change. They adopted two strategies. First, they both submitted bids to one of the automatic screw machines; second, they staged a "go-slow." For two weeks management officials stood around the shavers, to monitor the quality of the gears that came through, following the technical change, and doubtless to discourage Art and Bruce from slowing down. The struggle continued by other forms of withdrawal from work, such as absenteeism and taking casual days. This had the planned effect: gears were not coming off the line quickly enough. Eventually a compromise was struck: if the operators would make every effort to catch up on the backlog, management would increase rates only on the small gears. A few weeks later, Bruce left the gear machine to take a job on one of the automatic screw machines. Art remained on first shift, and a new operator took over from Bruce. Throughout the struggle with management there was hostility between Art and Bruce, stemming from their different relations to the union (Bruce was a shop steward, while Art had been the previous president) and from Bruce's resentment of Art's rate-busting. This did not help in their fight against the changes. The greatest sympathy went to Bruce, who was a solid, hard-working operator. Art's rate-busting only reinforced the unpopularity he had acquired as president of the union.

Thus, with the exception of the mysterious first instance, operators lost their struggles with management. As Frederick Winslow
Taylor demonstrates so well in his narration of a similar case of
rate-increasing, the company, by virtue of its greater power, can
ultimately force operators into submission, if only because it can
easily replace operators by drawing on both the internal and the
external labor markets.[11] Rate increases do generate economic
struggles, but these struggles both reinforce the rules of making out
and intensify conflict among workers. By "playing the game according to the rules," that is, by increasing only those rates that operators have consistently and openly demonstrated to be "loose,"
management escapes confrontation with an antagonistic and cohesive group of workers. Instead of being directed at the methods
department, hostility is largely directed against workers who bust
rates or hand in suggestions. Everyone in the department comes to
hear about rate increases, and gossip surrounds the guilty operator
for years to come. Some operators threatened to beat up Ed; others
wanted to tinker with his setups or hide his tools. Foremen point out
to their subordinates that they have only themselves to blame for
rate increases. Breaking norms and its punishment—rate increases—
serve to restore or reinvigorate commitment to the rules that are
violated. Rate increases are the occasion for ritual affirmation of the
norms of making out and of the coincidence of management and
worker interests that they symbolize. As long as management re-
stricts itself to increasing only those rates where the 140 percent
ceiling has consistently been flouted, its action, far from generating
a cohesive opposition, strengthens consent to its domination.

In 1945 the time-study man was the focus of an emergent conflict
between the operators and the company. Instead of engendering
commitment to the rules of making out, the time-study man, by
precipitating an economic struggle, undermined the rules of the
game. In other words, economic struggle threatened to spill over,
and frequently did spill over, into political struggles—that is, struggles over the rules of making out, over the relations in production.
In 1975, by contrast, economic struggles engendered by the industrial engineer not only were fewer in number, but they reinforced the
rules of making out—that is, economic struggles did not promote
struggles of a political nature.

Political Struggles

It is in the nature of making out to attempt to avoid, negotiate, and even subvert certain rules in order to achieve one's quota. We have noted, for example, that one such strategy is to transfer time saved on one job to another job—the practice called "chiseling." In 1945 this led operators to subordinate and refashion some of the social relations in production that define the rules of making out. Specifically, chiseling requires the cooperation of time clerks, who tell the operator which job is next; of the crib attendant, who gives out fixtures and prints while the operator is still punched in on a previous job; of the stock-movers, who bring up the stock early, without a work order; of the inspectors, who sign the operator off the previous job after he has already begun a new job; and of the foreman, who connives in all of this. These "informal" practices, contrary to the "formal" rules, Roy called the "fix."[12] We have also noted in earlier chapters how other "angles," involving the subordination of social relations to the operators' interest in making out, were arranged with the cooperation of the foreman, who would, for example, "fix" time cards, or with the inspector, who might change the time of punching off setup, and so on.

Between March 1945 and May 1945, a new set of rules was promulgated from on high to restore and enforce the "formal" set of relations in production at Geer.[13] The first new ruling concerned the crib attendants, who were no longer to allow prints and fixtures out of the crib until operators brought them a yellow card, which showed that they had punched off the previous job. This only created more work for the crib attendants, since operators could no longer help themselves to fixtures and had to return them at the end of the shift. However, setup men could still steal into the crib to pick up the fixture needed for the next job. The next intervention was therefore more drastic: everyone but the superintendent and crib employees was barred from the crib. This created confusion and bottlenecks outside the crib, serving to frustrate operators, crib attendants, and foremen alike:

> At quitting time I noticed Gil [foreman] talking to Walt [crib attendant] at the crib window. Gil seemed very serious; Walt was waving his arms and otherwise gesturing in a manner indicating

rejection of responsibility. I didn't catch any words, but gathered that Gil was voicing disapproval or warning, and after Gil left I said to Walt, "Looks like you're behind the eight ball now!"

I noticed that Walt's hair was mussed, and he looked a little wild. He denied that he was in any trouble whatsoever; nor was he worried about anything whatsoever.

"I'm just working here!" he exclaimed. "I just go by the cards and beyond that I've got no responsibility!" [14]

Obviously accustomed to such "new rulings," Hanks predicted that this one would not last out the week. [15] In another move to reduce the autonomy of the operators, stock-movers were instructed to bring stock to the machines only when presented with a work order and not before. This meant that operators first had to punch off one job and onto another before they could receive any stock. Time clerks were no longer to pass out information about subsequent jobs. Johnny, the setup man, was rudely ejected from the time cage when he tried to find out what Roy's next job would be. Inspectors had to introduce "the red-tag system," which involved tagging any machine that was running scrap, checking pieces every hour, and recording that check on a work sheet. [16] But this was just too much work for the inspectors.

Sam was busy checking tonight, and he did not like it.

"To hell with this God damned system!" he remarked on one occasion as he made a routine check nearly three-fourths of an hour late. He "dated" his check back from eight-fifteen to seven-thirty.

I have never seen Sam so disgusted. I couldn't help ribbing him just a little.

"You'll have to get around a little earlier for your first check after this," I said solemnly, when he checked my first one at five-twenty. He responded with profanity.

I looked closely at Sam several times, and I actually think he was perspiring. [17]

Moreover, inspectors now had to count the pieces completed by the operator at the end of the shift, and their ability to connive in the chiseling process was also made more difficult. Even foremen were subject to restrictions. "During the 'crackdown' period Gil reported that his days of 'fixing' cards after the end of the shift were over." [18] These changes were introduced over a period of two months, but it was only a matter of weeks before things were back to normal.

I experienced a similar set of events. Inspectors were instructed to introduce a "green-tag system." The green tag, stamped with the date, operation, and inspector's number, was attached to the first piece OK'd by the inspector. If one assumed that operators did not switch the tag to another piece, the responsibility for scrap could be accurately attributed to a particular operator or inspector. New inspection cards were also introduced; these provided space for the operator to record periodic checks of the pieces he turned out. Foremen would come around to check whether operators were properly filling in the cards. There was also a crackdown on foremen who were handing out "double red cards" too liberally or were awarding too many hours, at setup-man pay, for breaking in new operators. Time clerks were instructed to keep production and setup cards in the time cage and not let them out on the floor. This may have been directed at operators, like myself, who were penciling in the times rather than having them punched in on the clock. But the bombshell of 1975 fell, as it had in 1945, when the crib was locked to all but the general foreman and crib attendants. This created havoc on second shift, where there was only one crib attendant. For example, one of the machines I frequently ran was the broach. A piston pulled a long steel shaft—the broach, tapered with sharp teeth—horizontally through the inside rim of a pulley or gear, cutting a keyhole of a prescribed size. The trickiest part of setting up was finding the correct broach with which to run the operation. The broaches were kept in the crib, but the crib attendant hardly knew one broach from another, and I always went into the crib to fetch them myself. With no one allowed in the crib, a crisis descended over the broach operations. I had to get special permission to enter and find what I needed. All these changes proved as unworkable in 1975 as in 1945, and it was not long before things were back to normal.

The Sources of Political Struggle

The crackdowns of 1945 and 1975 were not isolated or unusual events. They were, according to both Roy's and my own informants, integral to shop-floor dynamics and therefore recurrent events.

Hanks knew that the new rulings wouldn't last, just as Bill, my day man, did; as Bill put it, "They're always introducing some new shit like this." Hierarchical control produced intergroup tensions, but these in turn gave way to cooperation as informal alliances sought to circumvent managerial rulings. Sooner or later this process led to renewed attempts from on high to reimpose strict controls. But why has this been such a persistent feature of shop-floor life since before Roy's time?

Roy interprets these events as indicating that, under certain circumstances, efficiency can be maintained only through informal channels; that efficiency is not the prerogative of management; and that the informal work group does not necessarily obstruct but may in fact facilitate the pursuit of managerial goals. He is making a telling criticism of the Hawthorne experiments and providing an important corrective to those who see only mischief and obstructionism, from management's point of view, in the informal group. But if rules hamper production, as both Roy's and my own observations suggest, why does management persist in imposing them? Roy appears to have no answer. To argue that management does not understand the requirements of efficiency or is ignorant of what is going on at the shop-floor level is to commit the same mistake that Elton Mayo did when he charged workers with not understanding managerial efficiency. So what are we to make of the cyclical dynamics?

First, the dynamics are inscribed in the relations in production, namely, operators' autonomy vis-à-vis their machines, coexisting with their dependence on auxiliary workers. Departmental specialization means that auxiliary workers are responsible to their own managerial hierarchy, which is motivated by concerns different from those of production management. For example, during my last days at Allied I noted that "materials control" management was clamping down on the distribution of stock to the production departments. Up to that time, foremen had been able to inflate— doubling or tripling—the amount of stock specified on the shop order. In this way the high costs of frequent setups on the automatics were avoided, and operators would receive long runs on their jobs. Now the distribution of stock was limited to the amounts specified on the shop order. This move was part of a drive to cut back on inventories, but savings in this area were canceled by increased production costs elsewhere. Moreover, the change stimulated conflict between operators and foremen, on the one hand, and between operators and the stock distributor, on the other. Another focus of conflict is quality-control management, which is always at odds with production management. A new quality-control manager frequently begins by imposing stricter control over inspectors, and this in turn leads to antagonisms between operators and inspectors. Conflict can give way to continued production only if workers collaborate in breaking rules, where this is mutually advantageous, even though reimposition of the original rules by higher management appears to be the inevitable consequence. In other words, the dynamics stem from the juxtaposition of the *interdependence of production and auxiliary workers* and the *relative autonomy of the corresponding departments.*

But managers, who are often themselves products of the shop floor, must be aware of the consequences of enforcing restrictive rules—in particular, their inevitable demise. Why then do they persist in these apparently futile efforts? A possible explanation is that the cyclical intensification of "obsolete" rules constitutes a ritual affirmation of managerial domination. In the day-to-day play of the game of making out, workers exercise considerable control over their own activities; the occasional introduction of rules is designed to remind them, or has the consequence of reminding them, that they are indeed subordinates and that their autonomy is confined within definite limits. It serves, in other words, to discipline the labor force. The enterprise creates mechanisms to make itself independent of, or to supplement, a traditional source of discipline: the reservoir of unemployed labor. However, when the rise of internal labor markets and internal states produces greater security of employment for the workers, management has to find alternative means of discipline. But this explanation is not entirely satisfactory, since the organization of work, as I have described it, is designed to eliminate the need for discipline and to concretely coordinate the interests of worker and manager. Ritual punishment through the imposition of rules serves only to reintroduce hierarchical antagonisms and to undermine the organization of hegemony on the shop floor.

I am therefore led to look at the dynamics in another way—namely, as a struggle between shop management and higher management. Shop management is responsible for securing surplus value, which is at the same time obscured. Being unable to monitor its own success in securing surplus value, shop management allows the labor process to drift in accordance with the dictates of making out, which increases costs and reduces quality. The operators constantly interact with their foremen and pressure them to be lenient in distributing double red cards. They pressure inspectors to OK pieces that barely pass acceptable standards. They pressure the crib attendant, and this can lead to disorganization if operators enter the crib to help themselves or if they keep fixtures at their machines, where others can't find them. Pressure on the time clerks can lead to extensive chiseling. Since auxiliary workers frequently share the operators' interest in subverting rules and refashioning relations, these tendencies, if not reversed, can lead to a profit crisis. However, where it does not actually encourage them, *shop* management turns a blind eye to these practices.

It is *higher* management that introduces "new rules" with the object of protecting profit. Higher management is less involved with the direction of the labor process—the obscuring and securing of surplus value—than with the realization of surplus value in the form of profit. It falls to higher management, therefore, to impose limits on costs and quality. Since, however, it is distant from the shop floor, it can exercise control over these factors only by imposing rules—rules that turn out to be incompatible with the organization of the machine-shop labor process.[19] The continued obscuring and securing of surplus value rests on the relaxation of these rules, and the relaxation eventually produces another profit crisis.

In short, struggles over relations in production and the cyclical dynamics to which it gives rise are the concrete expression of the simultaneous obscuring and securing of surplus value. The obscuring of surplus value in the labor process leads higher management, concerned with the realization of surplus value, to impose rules to counteract tendencies that undermine the securing (production) of surplus value. It is in the nature of the machine-shop labor process that, as a remedy, these rules are worse than the disease. They have to be relaxed. Then the cycle begins again.

Conclusion

In this chapter I have distinguished two types of shop-floor struggles: economic struggles, whose object is the effort bargain, and political struggles, whose object is the relations in production. In 1945 the economic struggles could, at least potentially, lay the basis for political struggles; in 1975, the economic struggles had the effect of reinforcing consent to existing relations in production. Yet, in both periods, political struggles produced a cyclical imposition and relaxation of the rules created by higher management—rules that worked against the interests of shop management. The cyclical dynamics can be viewed as a specific expression of the defining character of the capitalist labor process—the simultaneous obscuring and securing of surplus value. Struggles between different levels of management, which are the result of the separation of the production of surplus value from its realization, do not always lead to a cyclical dynamics. Higher management is sometimes successful in imposing a lasting change in production relations,[20] and it is sometimes able, too, to respond to the pressures of realizing surplus value through economic struggles—for example, by speeding up the assembly line.

Although both Roy and I experienced economic struggle and a limited form of political struggle on the shop floor, only rarely did we observe struggles over production goals, over the ordering of preferred outcomes, or over whether to participate in making out or some other game. Isolated instances of such ideological struggle were regarded as "deviant," and, as such, they renewed commitment to, rather than undermined, the goals of making out. Yet, only when struggle has moved to an ideological plane—that is, when the terrain of political and economic struggles becomes the object of struggle—is the capitalist labor process directly threatened. Ideological struggles take us beyond capitalism, beyond the dictatorship of needs. They are struggles, not over the shape of the effort bargain, but over the very notion of reward for effort; not over relations in production, but over their basis in the relations of production. Ideological struggles distinguish that which exists from that which is natural and inevitable.

Eleven

Class Struggle and Capitalist Competition

In chapter 10 we saw that struggles on the shop floor are largely shaped by conflicts between different levels, and among different fractions, of management. These struggles give rise to a cyclical change, which acts as the vehicle for the introduction of long-term unidirectional change in the labor process.[1] That is, the rise of the hegemonic organization of work, the internal labor market, and the internal state are superimposed on the cyclical dynamics endemic in the machine shop. But what was the source of the changes between 1945 and 1975 that the cyclical dynamics mediated rather than produced? To answer this question, we must go beyond the shop floor and examine the interaction between "external" and "internal" factors in ways that we did not attempt in the discussion of short-term change in chapter 8. As we shall see, the longer the time span, the fewer are the variables that one can safely hold constant and the further afield must one search for the origin of change.

Forces beyond the shop floor usually make themselves felt through two channels—class struggle and capitalist competition—and these in turn affect the dynamics of the labor process in ways determined by the essential structure of the machine shop. Thus, class struggles and capitalist competition are organized in such a way as to prevent shop-floor struggles from themselves becoming the source of change in the labor process, except in the cyclical manner already described.

In the normal everyday life of the shop floor, workers are not organized as a class. For this reason I have avoided referring to struggles on the shop floor as class struggles. Instead, I have until now distinguished the different struggles by the *object* of struggle. Class struggles, on the other hand, are those that involve struggles between classes. They are struggles that both presuppose and shape the organization of workers and capitalists into self-conscious collectivities with common interests. In this chapter I will try to show how class struggle between the organized representatives of capital and labor—namely, management and union—contributed to changes in the labor process at Geer and Allied. Insofar as union and management struggle to reshape or maintain the distribution of economic rewards (economic class struggle) and the relations in production (political class struggle), they are organized representatives of their respective classes.[2] The fact that these struggles take the capitalist order as given, natural, and inevitable—that is, these struggles are not ideological and are rarely even political—does not mean that they are not class struggles.

The second motor of change is capitalist competition. In examining the impact of a recession on the labor process, I looked at relations among capitalists in terms of their interdependence. Each firm depends on other capitalists, both to supply it with its instruments of production and raw materials and to buy its products. Relations of interdependence are conditions for the realization of profit, while the rate of profit is shaped by competitive relations among capitalists. Competition may be waged over human and nonhuman inputs into the productive process, over the organization of production itself, or over consumer outlets. In other words, from the standpoint of the use value of commodities, relations among capitalists are those of interdependence, while, from the standpoint of the exchange value of commodities, relations among capitalists are competitive. Between 1945 and 1975 the competitive structure of the engine division radically changed, with consequences I explore below.

In this chapter, therefore, I will argue that changes in the labor process at Geer and Allied over the past thirty years are the product of a combination of class struggle and capitalist competition, themselves shaped by broader forces, which I shall briefly discuss in the concluding chapter. But first I will address a slightly different hypothesis—implicit in much of the literature, both Marxist and non-Marxist, on the organization of work—that changes in the labor process are part of an inherent dynamic toward rationalization, fostered through managerial foresight, the product of deliberate managerial strategies, promoted in anticipation of competition and struggle, or simply the result of the pursuit of efficiency.

Changes Instigated by Management

Since the consequences of the changes between 1945 and 1975 in Geer/Allied's engine division all contributed to the consolidation of a hegemonic organization of work, the obvious hypothesis is that management engineered the changes with this objective in mind. According to such a theory of "concessions," management initiates changes and dispenses benefits in order to forestall future conflict and to preserve industrial harmony. That is, management introduces change, not as the result of struggle, but in anticipation of struggle and in an attempt to secure the workers' active consent. There have indeed been periods in American history when an "enlightened" fraction of the dominant class has been influential and has managed to introduce limited concessions of this nature.[3] There is, however, ample evidence that management at Geer and Allied could not be characterized as "enlightened" in this sense. Many of the changes that have occurred have been the consequence of struggles between union and management, and those that were not, as I shall show, were the result of changes in the competitive position of the engine division or of competition within management.

Concession theory predicts that, in periods when struggle is temporarily muted, organizational changes will still occur. World War II was one such period. But an examination of the contracts signed between the union and management shows very few such changes at Geer. To be sure, a wage freeze was in effect during most of the war period, but there are no reasons why changes in working conditions could not have been implemented. Instead, it was just after the war, in the face of renewed labor strife throughout the United States, that changes were introduced. The 1947 contract for the first time included "superseniority" for union officials, provision for public announcement of job vacancies, a job-classification scheme, and a rationalized wage structure. Subsequently, management vigorously resisted reducing, from five years to two and then to one year, the length of continuous employment necessary before an operator could exercise plant-wide seniority.

Another observation casts doubt on the concession thesis. According to historians of "corporate liberalism," the distribution of concessions in the organization of work is a phenomenon most characteristic of the large corporation. However, an examination of the contracts and conversations with union officials suggest that many of the major organizational changes were made after the war but *before* Allied took over. According to one president of the local, whose term spread over both periods, Allied tended to be more liberal in dispensing benefits and correspondingly reluctant to negotiate changes in the organization of work. Geer, by contrast, having smaller funds and operating in a more competitive market, was less able to grant direct economic concessions and, as a result of bargaining, was more prepared to introduce organizational change. All of this is not to say that there is no "enlightened" group of corporate executives in American industry; however, they were not to be found in Geer or Allied's engine division, and, moreover, they were not the executors of the changes that contributed to the consolidation of the hegemonic organization of work.

In questioning the theory of concessions, I have stressed the changes that management resisted—changes that were the outcome of conflict between management and union. However, there have been other changes that *appear* to be "concessions" granted without struggle—in particular, those involving time-study men, inspectors, and foremen. Industrial engineers explain their own disappearance from the shop floor in a number of ways. First, they say that in 1945 Taylorism was still very popular and management retained its faith in the stopwatch; since then there has been a change in management philosophy. Second, methods have been professionalized; the industrial engineer now computes rates while sitting at his desk.

Third, it has become more important and lucrative to change technology than to change rates. An official of the American Institute of Industrial Engineers told me that industrial engineers are reluctant to go on to the shop floor to time jobs because of the hostility they arouse. He also complained that industrial engineers are now so unfamiliar with the jobs and operations that they cannot time them properly. Nor can they detect when operators are pulling the wool over their eyes.[4]

A similar set of reasons is given for the relaxation of quality control on the shop floor. Changes in the philosophy of quality control have led to the transfer of responsibility from the inspector to the operator. Moreover, the source of poor quality is now found less in workmanship and more in design. Rather than insisting on improved quality on the shop floor, more is to be gained by insisting that suppliers—of castings, for example—meet certain specifications for the quality of their products. One manager of quality control also assured me that he was trying to cut back even more on the number of inspectors because poor quality could just as easily be located with the use of sophisticated statistical techniques. It might be noted, parenthetically, that inspectors are regarded in the company's accounting system as overhead, to be cut where possible. Not surprisingly, a good quality-control manager is hard to come by, and the turnover in that position is considerable.

Changes from the authoritarian to the service-oriented style of supervision reflected, according to personnel management, the shift toward increased responsibility of the worker. One can no longer treat people the way one used to, the argument goes, because employees are now better educated and less prepared to tolerate arbitrary authority. Now one has to persuade rather than command, or, as Morris Janowitz puts it, manipulate rather than dominate.[5] This change in philosophy is reflected in the human-relations literature associated with such names as McGregor, Likert, Argyris, and Drucker. These writers hold that the democratic ethos that pervades the political arena has inevitably spread to the industrial setting. Changes on the shop floor are manifestations of a general trend in society away from coercion and in the direction of persuasion.

These changes in industrial engineering, in quality control, and in personnel management appear to be enlightened managerial ini-

tiatives. In reality they provide neither the necessary nor the sufficient conditions for the rise of the hegemonic organization of
work. Thus, the philosophical changes that management and its
intellectual representatives present as having causal efficacy are
largely rationalizations of changes brought about by other forces.
The tenacity of the human-relations view of industrial organizations, the retirement of the methods department from the shop
floor, and the reduction of the inspectorate are reflections of real
shifts in the relations in production and technology brought about
by struggle and competition. Yet it would be a mistake to dismiss
the changes in managerial philosophy as mere reflections of changes
in the labor process, having no causal efficacy of their own. They are
also reflections of the conflicting interests of different fractions of
management. The various interests within management are responsive to professonal associations, which exist to defend and advance
the interests of some fractions of management against those of other
fractions. The national institutes of personnel management, quality
control, and industrial engineering provide the ideological basis and
source of innovations that will promote and present their respective
particular interests as the interests of management as a whole.
However, the ability of these various fractions to further their
disparate interests is limited by their common interest in the survival
of the firm, that is, by the level of class struggle and capitalist
competition.[6]

Competition

Firms can respond to competition in different ways with different
consequences. I will consider four possible responses: first, introduction of new technology, which increases productivity; second,
cutting costs through low wages and low rates of capital replacement; third, speedup, that is, intensifying the expenditure of labor;
fourth, specialization and/or expansion, thereby introducing econ-
omies of scale. I will first examine Geer's and then Allied's response
to competition.

Smaller companies have fewer options in responding to competition. Thus, Geer did not have access to large funds for capital
investment in new machines, tooling, and so forth. Roy does note

that, as he was leaving, Geer was installing some new automatic lathes, but when Allied took over, in 1953, capital equipment was in a poor state of repair. Moreover, Geer had little choice but to manufacture a wide range of products. It was essentially a large jobbing shop, whose livelihood was based on relatively small orders tailor-made to the requirements of individual buyers. It was not large enough, nor did it have a sufficiently assured market, to specialize in any one product. Only when the war brought large government orders for engines for tanks and lifeboats did it experience an unprecedented expansion. After the war, when it had to cut back its production, it again became vulnerable to market fluctuations. Almost inevitably it merged with a larger corporation. Therefore, in responding to competition, Geer relied on maintaining relatively low wages and benefits and low rates of capital replacement. Roy and his coworkers were always complaining about the inadequate tooling and fixtures. Speedup, of course, was Geer's other response to competition, and this, as we have seen, took the form of price-cutting. Under Geer management, we may conclude, competition led to the intensification of struggle.

Allied has responded to competition in a different way, reflecting the larger resources at its command and the captive market of the engine division. Rather than speedup and low wages, Allied introduced new machinery, eliminated unprofitable lines, and ultimately limited production to diesel engines. In 1957 Allied brought in its own general manager. Tooling, machinery, and fixtures were all improved. The crib was reorganized. Product lines were eliminated, and in 1961 the division was split in two, with the engine plant moving into a new single-story building a mile from the old four-story Geer building. As a result of these various rationalizations, some of which may be attributable to developments in the machine-tool industry, certain auxiliary personnel became less important. Thus, there was a reduction in the number of layout men, who were responsible for a detailed setting-up when there were no standard fixtures. The function of the time-study man became less important because there were fewer jobs to time and, in other cases, standardization meant that a number of operations could be timed simultaneously. The methods department became increasingly involved in methods revision, that is, with improving technology and organization rather than rerating jobs. Once given a rate, an operation was rarely retimed. When improved and cheap inspection equipment became available, which employees could purchase for themselves, greater responsibility for quality control could be shifted to the operator. In contrast with Geer Company, at Allied *competition led to changes that brought about a diminution of struggle on the shop floor.*

Moreover, competition itself was cushioned by the plant's integration into a large corporation. In the first place, the engine division now had a captive market and was therefore not directly subject to the rigors of the open market. At the end of each year a plan is drawn up for the coming year, based on orders received for engines from other divisions of Allied and on estimated costs of production. Prices of engines are fixed annually, and profit margins are low. If the engine division meets the various targets embodied in the plan, senior management in theory receives a bonus. Failure to meet the targets and the incurring of financial loss occur frequently, but they do not have the devastating effects they would have if the plant were operating autonomously in the open market. The losses can be absorbed by the corporation, although the management of the division may incur penalties. (While I was employed, the general manager of the engine division was fired because of the plant's poor performance.)[7] As a consequence, failure to make a profit does not immediately redound on labor in the form of wage cuts, speedup, and so on, and therefore does not necessarily intensify struggle. At the level of the corporation, also, competition is subject to greater control than it would be for a smaller company. First, there are the various forms of informal price control (Allied was involved in a famous antitrust suit). Second, losses suffered in one product line may be balanced out by other more successful lines. Third, large corporations have all sorts of accounting devices for concealing or writing off losses—short-term losses, at any rate. In summary, Allied's takeover of Geer resulted in the diminution of struggle, for two reasons. First, the rationalization of production directly reduced the level of shop-floor struggle. Second, the role of the engine division within the larger corporation plus the oligopolistic position of the corporation itself facilitated the absorption of struggles through the externalization of costs.

Struggle

We have indicated how competition, in the Geer period, produced struggle on the shop floor, while, in the Allied period, it had the effect of diminishing struggle. But struggle takes place at the bargaining table as well as on the shop floor. What determines the struggle at the bargaining table, and what consequences does this struggle have for further struggle and competition? As I have already suggested, Geer appeared to be more willing to negotiate changes in the conditions and organization of work because it could not afford wage increases and fringe benefits. The rise of the internal labor market and the rationalization of the internal state therefore began—after the war, but before Allied took over. In 1954—under Geer management, but when Geer was already a part of Allied Corporation—after considerable conflict a breakthrough was achieved in consolidating the internal labor market: the period of continuous employment required before plant-wide seniority could be exercised was reduced from five years to two years. Later, under Allied, the bidding system was improved, and job openings had to be posted on departmental bulletin boards. It is important to note that the operation of the internal labor market was also facilitated by changes in technology. Since the improved machines did not require the same skill and experience as the older and less reliable ones, they provided conditions for increased mobility between jobs. Although it is true that Allied did give in to a few changes in the organization of work, such changes had in the main been initiated and established under Geer. However, Allied was responsible for introducing new fringe benefits, such as the supplementary unemployment benefit and pension scheme, and other benefits, such as vacation pay, were improved. Wages also increased relative to the average in manufacturing industry after Allied took over, as indicated in Table 6.

What were the consequences of these struggles at the bargaining table? As I showed in part 3, the rise of the internal labor market and the internal state, as well as the linking of wages and fringe benefits to seniority, served to diminish struggles on the shop floor. The rise of the internal labor market reduced the power of the foreman, reduced the struggle between the time-study man and the operator, increased competition and conflict among laborers, and so

Table 6			Changes in Workers' Earnings at Geer/Allied from 1937 to 1975	
	Minimum Earnings of Incentive Workers		Anticipated Rate of Grade-3 Operators*	
Year	Hourly Earnings	Percentage of Average in U.S. Manufacturing	Hourly Earnings	Percentage of Average in U.S. Manufacturing
1937	$0.62½	...	....	....
1942	0.75	95%	....	
1945	0.79	83	....	....
1947	1.09	92	$2.06	175%
1949	1.15	86	2.14	160
1951	1.26	83	2.28	151
1952	1.35	85	2.39	150
1954†	1.47½	85	2.54	147
1956	1.74½	92	2.79	148
1959	1.94	92	3.04	143
1962	2.26	98	3.38	146
1965	2.52	100	3.68	146
1968	2.83	98	4.22	147
1971	3.49	102	5.15½	150
1974	4.40	104	6.13	145

Source: Figures for Geer/Allied earnings come from union contracts. Data for average hourly earnings (excluding overtime) in manufacturing come from U.S. Department of Labor, *Handbook of Labor Statistics* (1974), Table 96, p. 21.

*Anticipated rate = 125 percent. Grade 3 is the highest labor grade for incentive workers.

†The 1954 contract was the first one signed with Allied Corporation.

forth. The consolidation of the internal state and the constitution of the industrial citizen with rights as laid down in the grievance machinery further regularized struggle. In short, struggle at the bargaining table had the effect of absorbing some forms and diminishing other forms of struggle on the shop floor. *Therefore, under Allied, the consequences of struggles reinforced, and combined with, the effects of competition in reducing struggle.*

A problem that must be raised, though its solution lies beyond the scope of this book, concerns the determinants of struggle at the bargaining table. In part, the struggle reflects the dynamics of the shop floor and the resources of the particular firm, as I have suggested; in part, it is responsive to general movements in bargaining patterns throughout United States industry. Contracts signed by the United Auto Workers with the major automobile corporations and by the United Steelworkers with United States Steel provided and continue to provide not only models for contracts but the agenda of items for negotiation, first with Geer and then with Allied. The introduction of job-classification schemes, bidding systems, fringe benefits, and so forth followed their introduction in the basic steel industry. Why the contracts followed the directions taken in these particular lead industries (autos and steel) is a matter for further inquiry.[8]

But the consequences are interesting. Once an internal labor market has been introduced, it becomes a terrain for future class struggle. Unions fight for the extension of bidding and bumping rights, so that these may be exercised, not just within individual departments, but on a plantwide basis. They then fight for a reduction in the seniority required to exercise plant-wide bumping, and so on. Thus, although management might originally support the introduction of an internal labor market as a means of rationalizing job structures, struggles subsequently waged over bidding and bumping are met with strong opposition from management, which is interested in the flexible deployment of its labor force. Similarly, the emergence of a system of benefits and regularized wage bargaining have meant that incentive earnings as a proportion of total earnings have diminished considerably since 1945. In other words, the monetary incentive for making out has fallen. Therefore, collective bargaining is not only a *form* of class struggle that guarantees management the support of the union in the enforcement of the contract. In addition, the *content* of the collective bargain, at least at Geer and Allied, contributes to a reduction in the level of militancy on the shop floor by promoting conditions for the organization of consent.

Ironically, the impetus that produced the trade-union locals of the thirties came from the militant rank and file. At Geer the union had to be organized clandestinely in the face of ruthless managerial resistance.[9] That early militancy was absorbed in the organization of class struggles at the bargaining table after the war. The very success of union struggles in the thirties had led to the introduction of changes that wrested control of the union from the membership. I would suggest, then, that the conservatism of the established trade unions in the United States is in part rooted in the shop-floor experience, which has permitted the emergence of a union bureaucracy unresponsive to the rank and file.[10] Whether union leaders are conscious of the self-serving consequences of their struggles with management for "industrial democracy" is a matter for further investigation.

Why should the experience of the United States be different from that of Great Britain, where there continues to be a strong shop-steward movement and a militant rank and file? In similar industries, workers in Britain have managed to retain greater control over the shop floor than in the United States,[11] and the internal labor market is there largely organized by the union rather than by management. In a machine shop like the one at Allied, for instance, the British union has a considerable say about who shall fill which job. But why should there be such a difference? One possible answer lies in the relative timing of unionization and mechanization. In Great Britain, unions had established themselves prior to the twentieth-century thrust toward mechanization, whereas the reverse is true for the United States. Thus, at the time of their formation, industrial unions in the United States had to take expropriation of control over the labor process as a *fait accompli,* whereas, in Britain, industrial unionism appeared earlier, was able to resist such expropriation, and in this way laid the basis for a more militant trade-union movement. More recently, large British corporations have been attempting to move toward more American patterns of organizing work, the internal labor market, and the internal state.[12]

Conclusion

Changes in the labor process between 1945 and 1975 have been the outcome of three interacting forces, namely, the rivalry between different levels and among different fractions of management, competition among enterprises, and class struggle. In attempts to advance their power within the corporation, different managerial groups draw upon national associations for support. These external bodies do exercise some indirect influence on the outcomes of struggles within management, but an examination of their practices would take us beyond the scope of this study. Suffice it to say that, as a result of interdepartmental rivalry, changes can occur in the labor process. This is perhaps particularly clear in the replacement of time-study men by industrial engineers.

Intramanagement conflict does not take place in a vacuum but in anticipation of responses from workers on the shop floor. The common interest in which the competing fractions of management all share—the interest in securing and obscuring surplus value—sets limits on the changes any one fraction can adopt. However, conflict within management is not limited simply by the anticipated reactions of workers—by the power of constraint; the more direct pressures of class struggle and competition with other enterprises also play a limiting role. When engaged in collective bargaining, management represents a common interest vis-à-vis the union. Similarly, when it is competing with other enterprises, management presents a united front. At Allied's engine division, senior management has a common interest in achieving the targets of its annual plan, since bonuses are attached to its fulfillment. Inevitably, however, individual departments will express their specific interests as matters of common interest.

Just as class struggle and capitalist competition set limits on conflict within management, so they also set limits on each other. On the one hand, the competitive standing of Geer constrained its ability to dispense economic concessions and compelled it to bargain over working conditions, whereas Allied's oligopolistic position and the engine division's service role with respect to other divisions of the corporation not only permitted increases in wages and benefits but were the necessary price of retaining control over the labor process. On the other hand, struggle, by extracting varying concessions from management, affects the competitive position of the company.

While struggle and competition set limits on their mutual variation, both are, within those limits, shaped by other forces. The competitive position of Geer changed after the war when the government stopped letting contracts, and it changed again when Allied took over. The changing position of Allied in its various product markets received cursory examination in chapter 3, and these fluctuations have affected the entrance of the engine division into markets outside the parent corporation. Significantly for our purposes, competition among firms leads to the introduction of new technology, which can reshape the labor process. If it were not protected by a captive market but instead were in direct competition with, say, General Motors, Allied's engine division would have to expand and/or specialize its production so as to be able to introduce more automated machine tools. If such technological changes can transform the labor process, what forces determine the form of new machinery? David Noble has implied that the development and production of automated (numerically controlled) machine tools was motivated by the twin concerns of large corporations to push small machine shops out of business and to enhance managerial control over the labor force.[13] If technology is in fact not neutral and its development is as much a political as an economic process, it becomes important to examine why one machine rather than another is developed and marketed.

Class struggle is also affected by forces that come from beyond the shop floor. First, it is the contracts negotiated at the largest corporations that establish the terrain of struggle at smaller companies. Second, the struggle itself is shaped by the ability of a company to offer concessions without jeopardizing its survival and by the pressure brought to bear on the union leadership by the rank and file. I have tried to show how changes in the lived experience on the shop floor, themselves brought about by struggle and competition, have, over the past thirty years, reduced the level of militancy among union members.

The importance of everyday life on the shop floor has implications for theories of the United States labor movement. It suggests that the role of trade unions, so important in the orthodox histories of the United States working class, cannot be adequately understood without reference to changes in the labor process. It suggests that the hegemonic ideology of corporate liberalism can be an effective force in coordinating the interests of capital and labor only if it is rooted in the daily life of the working class. In this study I have pointed to changes in the labor process that might be congruent with such a hegemonic ideology. By the same token, the claim that only a corrupt union leadership and a contaminating culture block the spontaneous and immanent tendency of the working class toward class struggle is also unsatisfactory. Leaders in part reflect the demands of the led, and the strength of a culture is linked to its roots in working-class life.[14]

To explain the sources of changes in the labor process, it has been necessary to move beyond the individual enterprise. At the same time, these more distant changes are conveyed to the labor process through their impact on class struggle and capitalist competition. Moreover, struggle and competition do not have any unique consequences for the labor process, such as the reduction of uncertainty, the separation of conception and execution, the intensification of shop-floor struggles, and so on. Rather, the effect of changes in pattern bargaining, in the competitive structure, in industrial engineering, and so on, is shaped by the already existing relations in production, that is, by the imperatives of obscuring and securing surplus value. The scope of this study does not allow me to explore the specific dynamics of these more distant changes. Instead, I will present, in the next and final chapter, a more general picture of the transformation of the political and economic context in which all these changes have occurred.

Twelve

From Competitive to
Monopoly Capitalism

I began this study by contrasting the capitalist mode of production with the feudal mode of production, in this way deriving what is distinctive about the capitalist labor process: the simultaneous obscuring and securing of surplus labor. We explored the generic features of capitalism that contribute to the obscuring and securing of surplus labor, namely, the system of wage labor, the subordination of the worker to the labor process, and the mystifying effects of the market. Beyond these, a variety of different mechanisms contribute to the same end.

Thus, in examining the labor process at Geer and then at Allied, I drew attention to the changing patterns of force and consent brought about through the development of a relatively autonomous internal state and the emergence of an internal labor market as well as changes in the organization of work and the system of piece rates. All these contributed to the growth of individualism, the dispersion of hierarchical conflict, and the concrete coordination of interests between capitalist and laborer, as well as between manager and worker, and thus to the obscuring and securing of surplus labor. We can extrapolate the differences between Geer and Allied into two different types of capitalist labor process. The first is the despotic organization of work, in which coercion clearly prevails over consent. Here the expenditure of labor on the shop floor critically determines the survival, not only of the laborer, but of the firm itself. Workers have no ways to defend themselves against the arbitrary whims of the manager or overseer who hires and fires at his own discretion, just as the entrepreneur or manager has few ways to defend himself against the caprice of the market. Anarchy in the market leads to despotism in the factory. The second type of labor process, the hegemonic organization of work, is based on consent predominating over coercion. Here the wage and therefore the survival of the laborer are only weakly linked to the expenditure of labor, and the firm is able to insulate itself from, or directly control, the market. Subordination of the market leads to hegemony in the factory.

How do our two types of labor process relate to changes in capitalism? In this study I moved outward from the shop floor to examine the impact of markets, professional associations, schooling, family, competition among capitalists, struggles between unions and corporations, and so forth. To appreciate the broader significance of changes in the labor process and, in particular, of the two types we have constructed, it is necessary to reverse the process by first briefly sketching the dynamics of capitalism in the advanced nations. Only then is it possible to return to the labor process and understand its transformation as part of an ensemble of changes in capitalist societies.

I will first trace out the rudiments of Marx's theory of the development of capitalism. As I stated in chapter 11, there are two motors of capitalistic development: struggle and competition. In order to survive as capitalists in a perfect market, capitalists must compete with one another in the search for profit. They do this, according to Marx, by increasing unpaid labor, either in absolute terms through the extension of the working day or, when this is no longer possible (as a result of, for example, the Factory Acts), through increasing relative surplus value, that is, through reducing the amount of the working day spent on producing the wage equivalent. This reduction in "necessary labor" can be accomplished by reducing real wages or by increasing productivity and the wage-goods sector so that the amount of labor necessary to produce the wage equivalent falls. While both of these methods produce lasting gains for individual capitalists, the more normal way to increase unpaid labor is through temporary competitive gains. By intensifying or mechanizing the work process, an individual capitalist can increase his profit—but only until his competitors catch up. There are three consequences for the capitalist class of this competitive innovation on the part of the individual capitalist. The first is intensification of class struggle between capital and labor. Second, when all the capitalists have adopted the new machine, pioneered by one capitalist, then, in terms of unpaid labor, all the capitalists are back where they began; but the rate of profit—that is, the surplus value regarded as a proportion of the wages, instruments of production, and raw materials used up—has fallen. Third, the continual expansion of production, with either falling or constant wages, leads to crises of overproduction, which force capitalists to cut back production and render their capital idle. In short, the market forces individual capitalists to innovate and gain competitive advantages over one another, but, when they do so, they threaten their own existence as a class by intensifying class struggle, bringing down the rate of profit, and creating crises of overproduction. That is, compelled to pursue their individual interests on pain of survival, they undermine their common interest in the survival of capitalism.

The logic of Marx's analysis led him to anticipate the overthrow of competitive capitalism. In this, of course, he was correct. However, in identifying the overthrow of competitive capitalism with the overthrow of capitalism and the inauguration of socialism, he was incorrect. As it turned out, competitive capitalism was pregnant not with socialism but with a new form of capitalism—monopoly capitalism—in which the patterns of struggle and competition have been transformed. What Marx missed was the possibility of tempering the worst effects of competition without undermining competition completely and the possibility that class struggle not only could be contained within the parameters of capitalism but could be harnessed to the reproduction of capitalism if workers extracted concessions that would make it more tolerable. Class struggle was not the gravedigger of capitalism but its savior.[1] Of course, both Marx and Engels were aware of the tendencies toward the preemption of the market through the emergence of joint-stock companies, trusts, cartels, and even nationalization. They also recognized the possibility of repressing struggles and ameliorating the conditions of the proletariat. But there were definite limits on such last-ditch attempts to save capitalism from itself. These reactive mechanisms to restructure capitalism were the death throes of capitalism, which was doomed to splutter into its revolutionary overthrow.[2]

If competitive capitalism gave birth to monopoly capitalism rather than socialism, the event was by no means foreordained, and the labor was neither short nor easy. During the first three decades of this century, particularly in Europe, there were indeed moments when the capitalist edifice seemed to be toppling.[3] The rise of fascism was as much a sign of capitalism's weakness as of its strength. Even from the vantage point of fifty years later, it is not obvious why Marx was wrong in anticipating the overthrow of capitalism or precisely how capitalism managed to save itself. Indeed, this has been a major problem for twentieth-century Marxism in its various forms, and many solutions have been postulated. The very acuteness with which Marx analyzed competitive capitalism and its inevitable demise made it necessary to revise his theories when one was trying to understand, first the appearance, and then the development, of monopoly capitalism. Some of the assumptions on which Marx based his analysis no longer held under monopoly capitalism. In short, with the consolidation of monopoly capitalism, history forced Marxism beyond Marx.[4]

Given that Marx and Engels saw the state as protecting "the common interests of the entire bourgeoisie," it is not surprising that twentieth-century Marxism has spawned numerous theories of the capitalist state. They all share the view that the state is the key agency, first in handling the conflict of competitive capitalism and then in guiding capitalism into a new era. On the one hand, the state takes over some functions of the market and complements others. It regulates both competitive and interdependent relations among capitalists through planning, nationalization, and the provision of infrastructures, such as roads and the postal service; through antitrust legislation and fiscal policies; and through absorbing "surplus" in order to prevent crises of overproduction.[5] On the other hand, the state becomes involved in organizing struggles—in con-

fining them within limits or repressing them—so that they do not
threaten capitalist relations of production. It does this by disor-
ganizing the dominated classes, which it accomplishes by transforming relations among agents of production (capitalists, managers,
workers, etc.) into relations among individuals constituted as citizens with equal rights before the law, in education, and in the
electoral system, or into relations among parties, races, religious
groups, or language groups. In this way the apparatuses of the state
appear to be above classes or autonomous with respect to classes, in
that they operate according to their own logic, which cannot be
arbitrarily changed at the will of any one class. Moreover, this
autonomy constitutes both a real and a necessary basis for preserving the political interests of capitalists—that is, their class interest in
the maintenance of the capitalist order. For, to preserve these
political interests, the state must frequently act against the capitalists' economic interests by granting concessions to other classes.
In normal times the state applies coercion in a more or less legally
prescribed manner and not at the immediate behest of the dominant
class; but in times of crisis the state may lose its relative autonomy
and become an instrument of the dominant class in the arbitrary
repression of struggle.[6]

In going beyond Marx to develop more sophisticated theories of
the state, Marxists have paid less attention to the equally fundamental changes taking place in the enterprise.[7] The consolidation
of monopoly capitalism involves not simply state intervention in the
working of the market; capitalists themselves have tried to conquer
and subordinate the market to their interests. This has involved both
concentration—the merger of enterprises producing similar commodities into large corporations—and centralization or vertical
integration—the extension of the single enterprise into both product
and supply markets. Allied's takeover of Geer clearly involved both
processes. Geer was producing lift trucks and engines in a competitive market, while Allied was one of a handful of corporations
that virtually controlled the production of agricultural machinery.
Geer was limited in the commodities it produced and was therefore
dependent on suppliers and buyers; Allied, by absorbing Geer,
sought to preempt one more market, namely, the market for engines, and thus reduce its dependence on outside suppliers.

Concentration and centralization have obvious implications for the organization of work. If competitive, supply and product markets are subject to control; it then becomes essential to control the labor market as well. To control some markets and not others would be a self-defeating process. Just as Allied brought the production of engines under its management, so it also sought to bring the supply and distribution of labor under its control, through the development of an internal labor market. In addition, it sought to regularize relations between workers and managers through the grievance and collective-bargaining machinery of the internal state.

Just as the internal labor market, the internal state, and the global state were involved in the taming of the market, so all three were also involved in containing the struggles that threatened to overthrow competitive capitalism. Just as the global state became involved in the organization of struggles in the wider political arena, so an internal state emerged to regulate struggles within the factory. This internal state was not so much a coercive instrument of the company as it was a set of institutions that organized struggles over relations in production—and, to some extent, relations of production at the level of the firm—in ways that fostered the smooth running of the enterprise.[8] Thus, the internal state and the internal labor market imposed constraints on managerial discretion, institutionalized the granting of concessions, and thus concretely coordinated the interests of management and worker, capitalist and laborer; constituted workers as industrial citizens with rights and obligations; and fostered competition, individualism, and mobility. But the internal state has the effect not only of organizing struggles but also of dispersing them among enterprises. It prevents struggles from reaching beyond the enterprise and coalescing in struggles aimed at the global state.

We have so far considered changes in the mechanisms for distributing people into places in the production process and for organizing struggles over relations among those places. But what can we say about the relations themselves and the activities to which they give rise? Have they changed with the transition from competitive to monopoly capitalism? Harry Braverman claims that the distinctive feature of monopoly capitalism is the destruction of skill, or what he calls the separation of conception and execution. In practice this process of craft destruction has been an uneven one, which took place as much under competitive capitalism as it has under monopoly capitalism. Furthermore, if we are to understand changes in the labor process, it is equally important that we note the way in which the labor process is reconstituted once skill has been expropriated, that is, we must note the particular mechanisms through which conception dictates to execution, once they have been separated. Inasmuch as these relations in production are shaped by technology, we can make few generalizations, since the impact of machinery on the labor process has been so varied.[9] However, we can draw some general conclusions about the way the internal labor market and the internal state have affected the relations in production and the corresponding activities. Both have offered workers a very limited but nonetheless critical freedom in their adaptation to the labor process. The rise of rules and, with them, constraints on managerial intervention, have opened up an area of choice within which workers can constitute work as a game. Workers are sucked into the game as a way of reducing the level of deprivation. But participation has the consequence of generating consent to the rules, which define both the conditions of choice and the limits of managerial discretion. Thus, it is not the rules themselves but the activities they circumscribe that generate consent.[10] Of course, the extent of this area of choice is affected by technological imperatives, but its existence, no matter how small, is crucial.

The hegemonic organization of work does not pervade monopoly capitalism. Different sectors of advanced capitalism employ different forms of labor process, and by no means all of them have elaborated an internal state and an internal labor market like the ones developed at Allied. Not even all of the largest corporations have erected hegemonic systems, as the organization of work in agribusiness clearly demonstrates. Since the labor process in the competitive sector is by definition less well insulated from markets, one may argue that in general there is less to be gained there by introducing the internal labor market and internal state. Nor can the costs of these institutions be absorbed simply by raising prices, as they can be in the monopoly sector. On the other hand, it would be a mistake to equate the labor process in the competitive sector of monopoly capitalism with the labor process under competitive capitalism. Even where they are not unionized, competitive

industries have developed rudimentary internal labor markets, grievance procedures, and collective bargaining. In short, the labor
process found in the competitive sector exhibits features of both
despotic and hegemonic systems. Just as the form of the labor
process is not uniform throughout monopoly capitalism or even
tending in that direction, so it is not the same across all advanced
countries. Thus, even in their monopoly sectors, the forms assumed
by the internal state and the internal labor market in Britain are very
different from the forms they assume in Japan; the forms they
assume in the United States lie somewhere in between.[11]

Marxist theories of the state have drawn their inspiration from the
formulations to be found in Marx's own writings, but the emergence
of a Marxist psychology has represented a more fundamental departure. For Marx, in all precommunist societies the social relations
in which men and women are involved are "indispensable and
independent of their will," that is, they compel people to act in
particular ways. Thus capitalists, if they were to survive as capitalists, had no alternative but to compete and to accumulate, just as
workers had no alternative but to sell their labor power for a wage.
Moreover, workers were compelled to work as fast and as hard as
the labor process dictated. There was no room for choice. Rationality
was embedded in social relations and independent of the people who
carried those relations, just as the experience of commodity fetishism was independent of psychic makeup. It was not that individuals
were motivated by the pursuit of material self-interest but rather
that the specific rationality of capitalism, the specific needs it
produced, led people to act in particular ways. The rationality and
needs generated by feudal relations led to very different types of
activities.

The turn to psychology was another way of explaining why Marx's
anticipations were not fulfilled. The link between relations and
practices was not as Marx supposed it to be. It was therefore
necessary to examine the operation of psychic mechanisms to explain, first, why the proletariat did not engage in the revolutionary
overthrow of capitalism and, second, why it embraced the restoration of capitalism. In its most simple form, Marxist psychology
argues that it is the consciousness men and women carry with them,
inculcated in different areas of life but particularly in the family

and school, that shapes their response to capitalist relations. A more
profound formulation is to be found in the Frankfurt School's
appropriation of Freud, specifically aimed at understanding fascism
and its appeal. The rise of monopoly capitalism realizes Marx's view
of individuals as merely carrying out the logic of capitalist relations.
But where Marx saw this as a matter of survival, the Frankfurt
School presents it in explicitly psychological terms, namely, as the
destruction of the autonomous ego. This does not contradict Marx's
analysis but reflects the transition to monopoly capitalism. Where
competitive capitalism retains an arena of resistance and class struggle, under monopoly capitalism the individual psyche is stripped of
its capacity to resist the structures of capitalist domination. The
family no longer nurtures the rebellious and independent individual
of early capitalism. Instead, people are directly shaped by and
subjugated to broader institutions: the mass media, the culture
industry, and so on. The arena of subjectivity, of conscious resistance to domination, disappears, giving way to the individual as a
mere object of manipulation. Monopoly capitalism has managed to
shape our very character in accordance with its rationality.[12]

Just as in the turn to the state, so in the turn to psychology the
transformation of the labor process gets left behind. In parts 3 and 4
of this study I have tried to return to Marx's original concerns by
arguing that the translation of labor power into labor is conducted
independently of the different psychic makeup—character or consciousness—that workers bring with them to the shop floor. Activities at work can be largely accounted for in terms of the organization
of the labor process, the internal state, and the internal labor
market. Consent is produced and reproduced on the shop floor and
is not dependent on legitimacy drummed into people's heads in
schools or on character formation in the family. Even in the marginal situations where imported consciousness does shape behavior,
its specific impact is determined by the workers's position in the
production process.

Of course, productive activities and the reproduction of consent
do depend on certain minimal human characteristics produced outside work and common to all workers, such as the capacity to
communicate through language and the inclination to participate in
socially constructed mechanisms, such as games, which compensate

for loss of control over the labor process. I do not maintain that what happens outside work has no bearing on what happens at work or that individuals are shapeless pieces of clay out of which the shop floor molds laboring men and women. Rather, variations in the character and consciousness that workers bring with them to the workplace explain little about the variations in the activities that take place on the shop floor. These activities are most adequately explained by reference to a person's position in the organization of work. At least two qualifying remarks are in order. First, I am talking here about hegemonic and despotic organizations of work. In those less-well-insulated labor processes where neither despotism nor hegemony reigns, there is more room for external factors to exert influence on work behavior. Second, in times of crisis, whether local or global, when the hegemonic system breaks down, the consciousness people carry in their heads and the characters they have formed become critical in the shaping of activities.

To summarize: to explain the restoration of capitalism in its monopoly form, twentieth-century Marxism has focused on areas that remained largely underdeveloped in Marx's own writings. At the same time, it has accepted Marx's view of the labor process and has therefore missed the significance of its transformation, in particular the ability of the factory to contain struggles and to produce consent. The state, the school, the family, culture, and the personality are not unimportant, but their importance can be assessed only by taking the transformed labor process as one's point of departure.

This is particularly important in the study of crises. It is very fashionable to pinpoint some contradiction and conjure up some crisis. Crisis theory is a blossoming area of Marxist discourse. Indeed, it seems that, the more stable capitalism appears, the more we lament the gap between what is and what could be and the more desperately we search for new crises. In this study, however, I have resisted the temptation. Instead, I have suggested that the prospects of a local crisis—that is, one emerging at the point of production—are bleak indeed. Others have persuasively argued that capitalists can buy peace in the economy only at the price of externalizing or displacing struggles into the wider political arena, where they become fiscal or legitimation crises. Unfortunately, these are abstract crises, as much a product of the Marxist imagination as of the real world.[13] Moreover, as Marx points out, crises present opportunities to the dominant classes as well as to the dominated classes. They are the means by which capitalism is able to restore stability and save itself from itself. Nowhere is this more clear than in the crisis of transition from competitive to monopoly capitalism.

This pessimism brings us to a third overtaking of Marx by Marxism, again brought on by the events of the twentieth century, specifically in the underdeveloped nations of the world. Marx's sometimes qualified anticipation that socialism would appear first in the most advanced capitalist societies was premised on the collapse of competitive capitalism. The transition to monopoly capitalism has not merely postponed the emergence of socialism in capitalist countries, but, it is convincingly argued, has made it more likely that socialism will first emerge in the underdeveloped nations.[14] The stability of monopoly capitalism has been won, not only by a restructuring of the economy and the state, but also by an incorporation of the "peripheral" regions of the world into a system of international capitalism. For the advanced nations this has meant a certain uneven development, while for the poor nations it has led to a greater underdevelopment. At the same time, the expansion of repressive apparatuses in the postcolonial states reflects a growing resistance to continued incorporation within world capitalism and the search for some alternative. It is therefore in the Third World, and possibly in some European countries, that the most significant experiments have been made and that socialism is very much on the agenda.

Appendix

Comparative Perspective: Change and Continuity in the Zambian Mining Industry

Changes in industrial behavior are primarily rooted in changes in the organization of work. That was a major theme in parts 4 and 5. I illustrated this relative autonomy of the labor process by examining the impact of short-term fluctuations in markets (chapter 8), the impact of variations in externally derived worker consciousness (chapter 9), the dynamics of shop-floor struggles (chapter 10), and the effects of changes in class struggle and capitalist competition over the past thirty years (chapter 11). The argument developed in these chapters should be as relevant to international variations in industrial behavior as it is to changes over time within a single country. According to that argument, differences in the behavior of machine operators of different countries should be largely explained by variations in the organization of machine shops. The more conventional view regards national work traits as a function of the attitudes, ideas, orientations, and so forth, that laborers carry around in their heads and that originate outside the workplace. Individuals are the vessels and executors of a national culture. This is the basis of development theory: workers in underdeveloped countries are "tradition"-oriented or bound to a set of primordial loyalties and are therefore ill-equipped to cope with the demands of the industrial order. A more sophisticated view argues that the national culture not only affects individual consciousness through agencies of socialization but, in addition, molds the form of the industrial enterprise.[1] This latter, eclectic, position does not attempt to comprehend the relative importance of two different theories of human behavior. Nor does it develop an understanding of the relationship of the industrial enterprise to its political and economic context.

Elsewhere I have shown how different political and economic contexts shape the organization of the machine shop and how these in turn mold the activities of workers on the shop floor.[2] That earlier study upholds the theory elaborated here, but a comparison of industries that produce very different forms of industrial behavior in different countries would be more useful. I therefore draw here on the history of the development of copper mining in Zambia, since this provides a vivid contrast with mining in other parts of the world. I will try to show how the organization of work emerged historically through forms of struggle shaped by a colonial political order. Only when the labor process had developed a compatibility with the colonial political economy did it become relatively autonomous. Accordingly, when the colonial order was transformed after independence, the relative autonomy of the labor process was placed in jeopardy. But even under these relatively turbulent conditions, in their activities in the mine the workers have continued to respond to the organization of work rather than to the changing political order.

Creation and Reproduction of Relative Autonomy

The distinctive features of mining organization originate in the inescapable environmental uncertainty of the underground ore bodies from which minerals are extracted. Unable to control the geological environment, work organization can adapt to uncertainty in two opposed ways. On the one hand, the work group can be constituted as its own decision-maker, independent of managerial supervision. A self-regulating group can make the necessary rapid

adjustments to the exigencies, dangers, and unpredictability of
underground mining.[3] On the other hand, rapid adjustments at the
underground work face can also be accomplished with a strict,
coercive, and well-disciplined hierarchical organization of work, in
which subordinates unquestioningly respond to the instructions of
superiors, who unilaterally decide how the organization shall adapt
to uncertainty. Such an organization is normally associated with
management's complete lack of trust in the willingness or ability of
subordinates to perform the work effectively.[4] In their study of
British coal mining, Trist et al. concluded:

> Long wall systems, because of their greater degree of differentia-
> tion, require much more integration than single place systems;
> but the conventional pattern of organization has broken up the
> traditional, self-regulating cycle group into a number of segre-
> gated single task groups each bound within its own concerns.
> These groups depend entirely on external control in order to carry
> out the indivisible primary task of completing the cycle. The exist-
> ing pattern of management through the wages system can only
> partially supply this control. Full control would require either a
> degree of coercion which would be both impracticable and unac-
> ceptable or a degree of self-regulation which implies a different
> organizational pattern.[5]

Despite mechanization, the autonomous self-regulating group controlled by the wages system is still the most effective form of work
organization.

By contrast, the organization of mining in southern Africa (gold
and diamond mining in South Africa, coal mining in Zimbabwe, and
copper mining in Zambia) would be characterized by a "degree of
coercion which would be both impracticable and unacceptable" in
Britain. Why does mining assume a very different form of organization in southern Africa? There is no space to go into the the details
of the historical development of mining in southern Africa; a brief
summary will suffice.[6]

The organization of both gold and diamond mining began in
South Africa in the last quarter of the nineteenth century as a
system of subcontracting. Africans were brought together in gangs
to work for small white "entrepreneurs," using rudimentary techniques of excavation. When such primitive operations no longer

paid dividends, mining companies were created, using foreign capital to establish large-scale industrial organizations based on wage labor from two sources. Skilled and supervisory workers were imported from Britain, while unskilled workers were recruited from the surrounding African territories. A rigid "color bar" separated the jobs reserved for Whites from those reserved for Blacks. Gangs of African labor were subordinated to the dictatorial command of a white "section boss."

The unrestrained coercion (often involving arbitrary physical brutality and verbal abuse) within the industrial organization was a continuation of the coercive mechanisms used to drive labor off the land. In South Africa a combination of expropriation of African land and taxation forced Africans into the cash economy. The compound—a total institution, erected to control a worker's activities outside work while employed in the mines—secured the final subordination to the untrammeled power of a colonial political economy. When not employed in the mining industry, African workers would be forced back to the diminishing areas known as "reserves" through the enforcement of a series of pass laws, which regulated (and still regulate) their movement. Whereas in Britain the enclosure movement permanently ejected laborers from the land, in South Africa expropriation of land stopped short of the creation of a completely landless proletariat. Instead, the areas known as "reserves" were established as a means of externalizing and absorbing problems of urban social control and reducing the costs to the mining companies of reproducing labor power. The political and economic subordination of Blacks stands in marked contrast to the strength of the white workers, who consistently made gains at the expense of the Africans. Against this setting, the origins of a coercive bureaucratic organization of work are clear. Colonialism in southern Africa implied particular types of external labor markets and a particular form of political and economic domination. In combination, these stamped their character onto the organization of work.

The South African gold mines have provided a model for the colonial organization of work in other territories of southern Africa. The widespread adoption of this coercive form of mining casts grave doubts on any theory of technological determinism. It suggests that the form of the labor process reflects the requirements of and the possibilities open to the colonial order. Evidence from Zambia suggests that the organization of work, and possibly even the technology itself, may be quite consciously adopted for purposes of coercively controlling and disciplining the labor force.[7]

For illustrative purposes, I will summarize a study conducted in 1971, five years after independence, of one particular job known as "lashing."[8] All Zambians entering the mining industry in a productive capacity had to spend an initial period lashing. This involved shoveling ore, blasted on the previous shift from the ore face, into a wheelbarrow and carrying it to a tip. It is one of the toughest and most exhausting jobs in the industry. It received the minimum pay grade, even though the job-evaluation scheme placed it at a higher pay grade. Apart from removing ore, hand lashing serves two other functions. First, as an internal labor reservoir, it provides workers for vacancies that open up elsewhere in the organization. Second, as an initiation ceremony, it prepares and disciplines the labor force, weeding out the "weak" and "irresolute" and preparing the remainder for the harsh realities of a colonial labor process. That it was seen in these terms became apparent to me from the comments of management and from the fact that expatriate (white) shift bosses were not subjected to lashing but black shift bosses were. However, it is more difficult to uncover evidence that would suggest that the mining operation was deliberately organized to create ore faces, inaccessible to mechanical ore-removers and therefore requiring hand lashing. Nevertheless, following independence, one of the two mining companies successfully abandoned hand lashing, but the other company did not. Even if it is not clear whether the choice of mining technology and the manner of excavation were shaped by the colonial political order, there is little doubt that, once technology had been chosen, it was then harnessed to a colonial organization of work.

Response to Political Change

What happens when the external relations in which an organization is created, and to which it has adapted, are transformed, as when colonialism gives way to a "democratic" political order? Arthur

Stinchcombe has examined the tendencies of organizational forms to persist despite changes in the environment in which they were originally shaped. Although he does not actually discuss it, one condition for such persistence is the capacity of the organization to insulate itself from changes in the environment.[9] But this is not always possible, particularly when the change is as dramatic as a political revolution. I noted, above, the elimination of hand lashing in some mines, and this may have reflected changes in the political order.

A more significant change concerns the patterns of mobility within industry and the resulting organizational changes and conflicts. Again, I can only briefly summarize what I have discussed in greater detail elsewhere.[10] As long as Africans had few if any rights, either within industry or in the political system, and white workers possessed both economic and political rights, the dual wage structure, together with the color bar, was impregnable. When African trade unions emerged and gained strength in the fifties and the importance of migrant labor diminished, the color bar came under continuous attack, and white workers were forced to relinquish their monopoly over certain jobs. But the principle of the color bar—that no White should ever have to take instructions from a black worker—was never itself undermined, even after independence; instead, it was displaced into higher reaches of the organizational hierarchy.

The evolution from slow "African advancement" before independence to the more rapid government-surveyed "Zambianization" after independence has posed serious organizational problems. Here I will confine myself to three. First, discriminatory pay scales (associated with the dual wage structure) and the heritage of colonial industrial relations could no longer be sustained. Africans performing jobs hitherto monopolized by Whites would have to receive similar levels of pay. This in turn led to demands for general wage increases among the entire mine labor force—increases that cut into profits and forced up wages in other sectors of the Zambian economy. Second, the continued vesting of power and authority in expatriate personnel led to organizational distortions designed to accommodate Zambianization programs, the preservation of a color bar, and the creation of new jobs for some of the displaced white employees. Third, Zambians promoted into supervisory positions did not command the same unquestioned authority as their white predecessors, nor could they draw on the same support from their supervisors. Furthermore, the arbitrary, coercive sanctions, characteristic of the colonial era, could no longer be imposed by either white or black supervisors. As a result, the coercive apparatus and total subordination of the labor force so necessary for the bureaucratic organization of mining were no longer feasible. Changes in work behavior reflected changes in the political order mediated by the organization of industry. Inefficiencies and conflicts within the organization, stemming from the incongruity of organizational form and the demands of the prevailing political order, were concealed by the ideological castigation and exhortation of the black mineworker. It is to the changing response of miners themselves that I now wish to turn.

The Myth of the Traditional Worker

I have explained the characteristic features of mining in southern Africa in terms of a reaction to colonialism. Management and colonial ideology justified the tyranny to which African workers were subjected by reference to their "traditional," "tribal," etc., background. The African worker is "lazy," "has to be taught industrial discipline," "has to be coerced into work," is a "target" worker, not interested in providing more than a bare minimum (the backward-bending labor-supply curve), etc., because of his "premodern" attachments. The resemblance to early British entrepreneurial ideology is clear.[11]

Much of the development literature, dominated by a Weberian tradition, is concerned with the impact of "traditional" values on economic behavior. Ideology and reality are only too frequently confused. Studies such as Bendix's *Work and Authority in Industry* provide little evidence for what they assume to be true, namely, that industrial behavior is modified by external social relations such as village kinship ties and work patterns.[12] Migration and the target worker (who is largely a mythical figure anyway) are usually explained as hangovers from tribal commitments, which lead workers back to their rural habitat ("natural environment"). African workers supposedly have higher absenteeism records than "modern" workers because they have not developed a "work ethic" or are unable to free themselves from "primordial loyalties." The reality is more austere. Colonial governments, and the South African government to this day, created a coercive state apparatus to drive laborers back and forth between rural and urban areas. Moreover, with the relaxation of such extraeconomic compulsion, turnover in the Zambian mining industry has fallen rapidly and is now very low by any standard.

Even before the myths of development theory had gained widespread currency, there was ample evidence for a more realistic assessment. As Max Gluckman wrote:

> An African townsman is a townsman, an African miner is a miner.... The urbanized African is outside the tribe but not beyond the influence of the tribe. Correspondingly when a man returns from the town into the political area of his tribe he is tribalized again—de-urbanized—though not beyond the influence of the towns.[13]

Gluckman's insistence on a "situational" analysis laid the basis for the seminal work of the Manchester School of social anthropology. Thus, Epstein's study of African mineworkers shows that "tribe" becomes irrelevant when laborers organize on the basis of their common interest as miners.[14] It is as miners, not as tribesmen, that Africans strike against the company. Where "tribalism" is significant—namely, in the compounds—it is so only as the result of management's deliberate reconstruction of "tribalism" as a mode of social control. Moreover, as Clyde Mitchell demonstrates, "tribalism" in towns is a very different phenomenon from "tribalism" in the village.[15] In other words, Africans, like machine operators at Geer Company and Allied Corporation, respond to the structures in which they are immediately enmeshed and in which they carry out particular sets of activities. "But the switch of action patterns from rural to urban set of objectives is as rapid as the migrant's journey to town."[16] The impact of different and "irrelevant" structures is of only secondary importance. Workers' actions do not spring from cultural lags between one system of relations and another. The

values and norms of the village derive from the organization of life
in the village and are not the basis for activities on the shop floor,
though these activities may be couched in the *idiom* of village life.

The myth of the "traditional" and "indolent" worker continues
into the era of Zambian independence. This is not surprising, since
the class structure, upon which managerial ideology is founded, has
remained largely unchanged, despite the transformation of the
political system.[17] Moreover, management is no longer alone in
justifying the imposition of punitive sanctions and harsh discipline.
The Zambian government, in the pursuit of development and its
class objectives, has taken over the ideological whip, admonishing
the labor force for its "absenteeism," "lack of patriotism," and so
on; it has also outlawed strikes and has coopted and, where necessary, forced the compliance of once-militant union leaders. The
transformation from a colonial state, based on white supremacy, to
a "nation" state, based on universal suffrage, represents a consolidation of the apparatus subordinating the worker to the dominant
class. In the fifteen years before independence, union-led strikes
occurred with some frequency in the copper mines; since independence, they have become increasingly rare. Those that have occurred
have tended to be wildcat strikes, easily ended by the intervention of
the ruling party.

Writing in the tradition of development theory, Robert Bates
presents a different view.[18] He argues that the Zambian government
failed to exact subservience from Zambian miners after independence. Elsewhere I have shown in detail that Bates adopts government ideology as a definition of reality; that he fails to critically
examine the publicly available statistics he uses to document the
"failure" thesis; and that other statistics, collected by the mining
companies, do not uphold his conclusions.[19] A careful analysis of
the available information shows that the government and the ruling
party have been able to exercise even greater control than the
colonial government and that Zambian mineworkers are more
"disciplined," have better attendance records, lower turnover, fewer
strikes, etc., than miners in other parts of the world. As the result of
confusing ideology with reality, Bates gives uncritical credence to
the myth of the "indolent" black worker—a myth that the government has created (or, rather has borrowed from its colonial

predecessors) and used as an ideological weapon to justify its authoritarian regulation and ritual punishment of Zambian mineworkers.

This does not mean that mining is now more efficient than it was before independence. For reasons outlined in the previous section, greater friction and conflict at the workplace have been created by the incongruities between the work organization and the political system: the expansion of the organizational structure and increased pay for workers to accommodate the repercussions of Zambianization. Workers are caught between the contradictory demands of an organization that requires a coercive bureaucracy but, for political reasons, can no longer exercise that coercion. What creates inefficiency is not the "primordial" commitments of African mineworkers but the structural dilemmas facing a colonial organization in a postcolonial era.

What can we say about the importance of ethnic, racial, and other external allegiances within the structure of work? I have already suggested that a racially divided labor market shaped an organization of work based on the color-bar principle. Once allocated to a position within the labor process, relations and activities are governed by the structure of that labor process. It was not a worker's race that shaped the relations in production; rather, these relations recreated and reproduced racism at the point of production. My own study of four work situations in the mines and Bruce Kapferer's study of a garment factory in Kabwe both suggest that relations among Zambian workers, though frequently couched in the idiom of other allegiances, such as ethnicity, are dictated by the organization of work.[20] Kapferer was mainly concerned with the basis of group formation and the ability of leaders to mobilize support on the shop floor. His conclusions suggest that seniority and position in the process of production are the most important factors determining the outcome of factionalism among workers and conflict between workers and management.

Conclusion

Managerial ideology, political exhortation, and development theory all converge to create distorted portraits of the Zambian mineworker

as unable or unwilling to adapt to the industrial order because of his
primordial attachments and traditional values. In fact, mineworkers
demonstrated their absorption into capitalism as long ago as 1935,
when they successfully organized the first major peaceful strike on
the copperbelt. No less than the machine operators at Geer and
Allied, lashers were adept at goldbricking and quota restriction.
Instead of being less disciplined, Zambian mineworkers prove to be
more disciplined than their comrades in other parts of the world,
but again only as a consequence of the organization of the mining
industry. In short, activities of Zambian workers on the shop floor,
in the mines, and in the office were determined within narrow limits
by the relations in production. As we discovered at Allied Corporation, ethnic and racial categories are usually important only when
reproduced by the labor process itself. Otherwise, they live on as
prejudices, attitudes, and, above all, as an idiom in which to couch
production relations. At the same time, these relations in production
were the product of a colonial order. By recreating within its own
structure conditions reflecting the existing political and market
arrangements, the mining industry managed to preserve the relative
autonomy of the labor process. With the transformation of the
political order, changes did occur, but only through the mediation
of existing relations in production.

Notes

Preface

1. See Michael Burawoy, *The Politics of Production* (London: New Left Books, forthcoming).

Chapter One

1. Arthur Ross and Paul Hartman, *Changing Patterns of Industrial Conflict* (New York: John Wiley, 1960); Clark Kerr and Abraham Siegal, "The Interindustry Propensity to Strike—An International Comparison," in *Industrial Conflict,* ed. Arthur Kornhauser, Robert Dubin, and Arthur M. Ross (New York: McGraw-Hill, 1954).

2. Seymour Martin Lipset, *Political Man* (New York: Doubleday, 1959), chap. 4; Daniel Bell, *The End of Ideology* (New York: Free Press, 1960), chap. 10.

3. Interest in the blue-collar worker has been revived to some degree in the seventies. See, for example, Richard Sennett and Jonathan Cobb, *The Hidden Injuries of Class* (New York: Random House, 1972); Harold Sheppard and Neal Herrick, *Where Have All the Robots Gone?* (New York: Free Press, 1972); and William Kornblum, *Blue Collar Community* (Chicago: University of Chicago Press, 1974).

4. See, for example, Leon Baritz, *The Servants of Power: A History of the Use of Social Science in American Industry* (New York: John Wiley, 1965); Alex Carey, "The Hawthorne Studies: A Radical Criticism," *American Sociological Review* 32 (1967): 403–16; John Goldthorpe et al., *The Affluent Worker: Industrial Attitudes and Behaviour* (New York: Cambridge University Press, 1968); Clark Kerr and Lloyd Fisher, "Plant Sociology: The Elite and the Aborigines," in *Common Frontiers of the Social Sciences,* ed. Mirra Komarovsky (Glencoe: Free Press, 1957); Henry Landsberger, *Hawthorne Revisited* (Ithaca, N.Y.: Cornell University Press, 1958); Donald Roy, "Efficiency and the Fix: Informal Intergroup Relations in a Piecework Machine Shop," *American Journal of Sociology* 60 (1954): 255–66; Harold Wilensky, "Human Relations in the Work Place: An Appraisal of Some Recent Research," in *Research in Industrial Human Relations,* ed. Conrad Arensberg (New York: Harper & Row, 1957), pp. 25–59.

5. See, for example, Robert Merton, *Social Theory and Social Structure* (New York: Free Press, 1968), chap. 8; Alvin Gouldner, *Patterns of Industrial Bureaucracy* (New York: Free Press, 1954); Peter Blau, *The Dynamics of Bureaucracy* (Chicago: University of Chicago Press, 1955); and, more recently, Michel Crozier, *The Bureaucratic Phenomenon* (Chicago: University of Chicago Press, 1964).

6. James March and Herbert Simon, *Organizations* (New York: Wiley, 1958), is typical of this approach.

7. See, for example, Goldthorpe et al., *The Affluent Worker;* James Thompson, *Organizations in Action* (New York: McGraw-Hill, 1967); and Clark Kerr et al., *Industrialism and Industrial Man* (Cambridge, Mass.: Harvard University Press, 1960). In addition, there is, of course, the classic by Reinhard Bendix, *Work and Authority in Industry: Ideologies of Management in the Course of Industrialization* (New York: John Wiley, 1956).

8. Many of these studies are heavily influenced by Max Weber and Robert Michels. See, for example, Philip Selznick, *Law, Society, and Industrial Justice* (New York: Russell Sage Foundation, 1969).

9. Thus, for example, Morris Janowitz compiles a series of factors contributing to changes in the military over a period of fifty years but never comes to grips with the problem of explaining those changes. He vacillates between a form of technological determinism and claims of the following nature: "Popular demand for equality of treatment grows with industrialization. As the standard of living rises, tolerance for the discomforts of military life decreases. The skepticism of urban life carries over into the military to a greater degree than in previous generations, so that men will no longer act blindly, but demand some sort of explanation from their commanders" (*The Professional Soldier* [New York: Free Press, 1960], p. 40).

10. Arthur Stinchcombe, "Social Structure and Organizations," in *Handbook of Organizations,* ed. James March (Chicago: Rand McNally, 1965); Robert Blauner, *Alienation and Freedom* (Chicago: University of Chicago Press, 1964).

11. Arnold Tannenbaum, *Control in Organizations* (New York: McGraw-Hill, 1967), p. 3.

12. Ibid., p. 46.

13. Amitai Etzioni, *A Comparative Analysis of Complex Organizations* (New York: Free Press, 1961).

14. Elton Mayo, *The Human Problems of an Industrial Civilization* (New York: Macmillan, 1933), p. 116.

15. Rensis Likert, *New Patterns of Management* (New York: McGraw-Hill, 1961); Chris Argyris, *Integrating the Individual and the Organization* (New York: John Wiley, 1964).

16. Blauner, *Alienation and Freedom.* But see also Theo Nichols and Huw Beynon, *Living with Capitalism: Class Relations and the Modern Factory* (London: Routledge & Kegan Paul, 1977) for a convincing refutation of Blauner's thesis.

17. See, for example, E. L. Trist, G. W. Higgin, H. Murray, and A. B. Pollock, *Organizational Choice* (London: Tavistock Institute of Human Relations, 1963).

18. Roy, "Efficiency and the Fix." Tom Lupton, *On the Shop Floor* (Oxford: Pergamon Press, 1963), makes the same point forcefully, although not from the perspective of any harmony theory.

19. See, particularly, Crozier, *The Bureaucratic Phenomenon.*

20. See, for example, Alan Fox, *Beyond Contract: Work, Power, and Trust Relations* (London: Faber & Faber, 1974); but see also Clark Kerr, *Labor and Management in Industrial Society* (New York: Doubleday, 1964).

21. William Baldamus, *Efficiency and Effort* (London: Tavistock Institute of Human Relations, 1961), p. 1.

22. Ibid., p. 8.

23. Ibid., chap. 8. See also, Hilda Behrend, "A Fair Day's Work," *Scottish Journal of Political Economy* 8 (1961): 102–18.

Chapter Two

1. The formulations in this chapter are heavily influenced by the writings of a group of French Marxists: Louis Althusser, *For Marx* (London: Allen Lane, 1969); Nicos Poulantzas, *Political Power and Social Classes* (London: New Left Books, 1973); and, above all, Etienne Balibar, "The Basic Concepts of Historical Materialism," in Louis Althusser and Etienne Balibar,

Reading Capital (New York: Pantheon, 1970) pp. 201–308. Like many contemporary Marxists, these French theorists try to move away from a teleological view of history, in which the succession of modes of production follow a fixed and inevitable pattern in accordance with the expansion of the "forces of production." The indeterminacy which they introduce is developed in an extreme form by Barry Hindess and Paul Hirst, *Pre-Capitalist Modes of Production* (London: Routledge & Kegan Paul, 1975).

2. Karl Marx, *The German Ideology* (New York: International Publishers, 1970), p. 48.

3. A mode of production is more usually seen as a combination of relations of production and forces of production. I have avoided using the concept of forces of production for two reasons. First, it is often presented as a set of things—raw materials, machinery, technique, etc.—that are themselves neutral with respect to exploitation and domination. Here I want to suggest the way in which the relations of production indelibly imprint themselves on the mode of appropriating nature. Second, the notion of forces of production is usually associated with a teleological view of history, in which the expansion of the productive forces makes necessary the overthrow of capitalism and also lays the basis for socialism. In this study I try to dispel such historically unwarranted optimism. For a more detailed critique of the concept of forces of production see Michael Burawoy, "The Politics of Production and the Production of Politics: A Comparative Analysis of Machine Shops in the United States and Hungary," *Political Power and Social Theory* 1 (1979).

4. The distinction between relations and activities is at the basis of the concept of social structure used here. The social structure is a pattern of relations among "empty places" that individuals occupy as they engage in activities, that is, as they transform something into something else. Social relations are viewed as existing prior to individuals who "support" them and who act within constraints determined by those relations. Just as social relations shape practices, so practices set limits on social relations. Sociology, by contrast, collapses the distinction between relations and activities into such notions as "role expectations." Social structure becomes the relationships among *concrete* individuals executing values they have internalized. In part 4 I examine the relative merits of these two views of social structure.

5. This implies that there are two essential forms of politics: that linked to the relations *in* production—the politics of production—and that linked to the relations *of* production—global politics.

6. Karl Marx, *Capital*, 3 vols. (New York: International Publishers, 1967), 3:791.

7. Althusser, *For Marx,* p. 233.

8. Karl Marx, *Capital,* 1:72.

9. Ibid., p. 74. "For Marx, a determined mode of *appearance* corresponds to each determined structure of the real, and this mode of appearance is the starting-point for a kind of *spontaneous* consciousness of the structure for which neither consciousness nor the individual is responsible. It follows that the scientific understanding of a structure does not abolish the spontaneous consciousness of that structure. It modifies its role and its effects, but it does not suppress it" (Maurice Godelier, "Structure and Contradiction in *Capital,*" in *Ideology in Social Science,* ed. Robin Blackburn [New York: Vintage Books, 1973], p. 338).

10. On the one hand, Marx's analysis of commodity fetishism sees ideology as inscribed in the very production of commodities. On the other hand, Marx accords the dominant class the capacity to manipulate and impress ideas on the dominated classes through its monopoly of the means of disseminating ideas. See Karl Marx, *The German Ideology,* p. 64. At the same time, he insists on the limits of such manipulations and in his discussion of bourgeois political economy shows how it corresponds to the perspectives of the capitalist. Naturally, the range of ideologies that mesh with a given lived experience will vary according to the context. In his stimulating discussion of ideology, Alvin Gouldner formulates the problem in similar terms by drawing on Basil Bernstein's concepts of restricted and elaborated linguistic codes (*The Dialectic of Ideology and Technology* [New York: Seabury Press, 1976]).

11. Nicos Poulantzas expresses this position well:

In referring to ideological apparatuses, we must recognize that these apparatuses neither create ideology, nor are they even the sole or primary factors in reproducing relations of ideological domination and subordination. Ideological apparatuses only serve to fashion and inculcate (materialize) the dominant ideology. Thus Max Weber was wrong in claiming that the Church creates and perpetuates religion: rather it is religion which creates and perpetuates the Church. In the case of capitalist ideological relations, when Marx analyses the fetishism of commodities as relating directly to the process of valorization of capital, he offers us an excellent example of the reproduction of a dominant ideology which goes beyond the apparatuses; this was noted by Marx himself in his frequent references to a "correspondence" between "institutions" and "forms of social consciousness," in which he implied the distinction. [*Classes in Contemporary Capitalism* (London: New Left Books, 1975), p. 31]

12. Louis Althusser, *Lenin and Philosophy and Other Essays* (London: New Left Books, 1971), p. 168.

13. Karl Marx, *Early Writings* (New York: Vintage Books, 1975), p. 251.

14. Antonio Gramsci, *Selections from Prison Notebooks* (New York: International Publishers, 1971), p. 126.

15. Karl Marx, "Preface to *A Contribution to the Critique of Political Economy,*" in *The Marx-Engels Reader,* ed. Robert Tucker (New York: W. W. Norton, 1972), p. 5.

16. Eugene Genovese, *Roll, Jordan, Roll* (New York: Vintage Books, 1976).

17. For an exposition of these two views, see Clifford Geertz, *The Interpretation of Cultures* (New York: Basic Books, 1973), chap. 8.

18. Maurice Godelier, *Rationality and Irrationality in Economics* (New York: Monthly Review Press, 1972), p. 45.

19. Agnes Heller, *The Theory of Need in Marx* (London: Allison & Busby, 1976), p. 60.

20. See, for example, Rodney Hilton, ed., *The Transition from Feudalism to Capitalism* (London: New Left Books, 1976); Perry Anderson, *Lineages of the Absolutist State* (London: New Left Books, 1974); Hindess and Hirst, *Pre-Capitalist Modes of Production;* Robert Brenner, "The Origins of Capitalist Development: A Critique of Neo-Smithian Marxism," *New Left Review* no. 104 (July–August, 1977): 25–92.

21. "Modes of Production in a Materialist Conception of History," *Capital and Class* no. 3 (Autumn 1977): 19.

22. Hindess and Hirst add the following important qualifying remarks to this conventional interpretation:

Although he [the tenant/laborer] may *own* the instruments of production, have tenant-right to the land, and be able to organise the production of his subsistence, he does not control the *reproduction* of means and conditions of production. It is primarily through the control of the reproduction of the means of production that the landlord/exploiter separates the tenant/laborer from the means of production. It should be noted, nevertheless, that the control of the production of the *surplus-product* under demesne production, and the ownership and operation of certain important means of production (mills, dykes, etc.), are important means of control of the conditions of reproduction for the feudal lord. [*Pre-Capitalist Modes of Production,* p. 238]

23. George Homans, in his analysis of thirteenth-century England, writes:

Anyone who has studied manorial custumals must have been struck by the extreme detail into which they go. For instance, they often do not say simply that a man must plow, sow, and harrow one acre of the lord's land. They say that he must plow it with as many oxen as he has in his plow, harrow with his own horse and harrow, and sow it with seed he must fetch from the lord's granary with his own horse and sack. Services were remembered in a minute detail, and when further details, even the most obvious and the most necessary, were not nominated in the custumal or attested by a long history of past performances, they were not custom and were not done. [*English Villagers of the Thirteenth Century* (New York: W. W. Norton, 1975), p. 272]

The very static imagery that Homans adopts is partly a reflection of his own bias but also a reflection of the particular period he chose to study, which was one of the most settled in the history of feudal England. For more variegated and dynamic pictures involving struggles over the commutation of labor rent, see Rodney Hilton, *A Medieval Society* (London: Weidenfeld & Nicolson, 1966), chap. 5; E. A. Kosminsky, *Studies in the Agrarian History of England in the Thirteenth Century* (Oxford: Basil Blackwell, 1956), chap. 3; and M. M. Postan, *The Medieval Economy and Society* (Harmondsworth, Eng.: Penguin Books, 1975), chap. 9.

24. The fusion of control and coordination allows sociologists to ignore the specifically capitalist nature of industrial work. Thus, Marx wrote of the political economist: "When considering the capitalist mode of production, he, on the contrary, treats the work of control made necessary by the cooperative character of the labour-process as identical with the different work of control, necessitated by the capitalist character of that process and the antagonism of interests between capitalist and labourer" (*Capital,* 1:332).

25. See, for example, Rodney Hilton, "Freedom and Villeinage in England," *Past and Present* no. 31 (July 1965): 3–19.

26. Or, as Louis Althusser puts it, "The individual is interpellated as a (free) subject in order that he shall (freely) accept his subjection, i.e., in order that he shall make the gestures and actions of his subjection 'all by himself.' There are no subjects except by and for their subjection. That is why 'they work all by themselves.'" (*Lenin and Philosophy and Other Essays,* p. 182). The creation of an apparent freedom—freedom within limits—and the expression of consent on the shop floor is illustrated by the responses I received from fellow workers when I asked them why they worked so hard. A common reaction was a look of bewilderment and a statement like "You think I work hard?" They would walk off chuckling to themselves. In other words, many workers not only did not think they were working hard but even thought they were getting back at management by goofing off as much as they did. Others would respond, "You've got to make a living." Such an answer denied the distinction between coming to work and the application of effort once at work—a distinction suggested by the comment, "The hardest part of working is coming to work." Alternatively, operators might say, "What else am I going to do here?" or "It makes the time pass more quickly. You'd get bored if you didn't work."

Hard work was an adaptation to the deprivation inherent in routine, monotonous tasks. Some would claim, "If we don't work so hard, then the company will go broke and we'll be out of a job"—a recognition of a common interest between worker and management. Yet others, like my day man, Bill, clearly enjoyed working hard more than "goofing off." I suspect this was true of a number of people, but few would ever admit it. What is interesting about all these responses is the absence of fear or coercion as a motivating factor and the assumption that there is a real choice open to workers as to how hard they are going to work. Moreover, in evaluating the choice and in deciding whether they were working hard or not, they unquestioningly measured their behavior against managerial norms. Thus they recognized that it was possible to be dismissed for consistently "goofing off," but such disciplinary action was viewed as legitimate, natural, and inevitable.

27. Marx discusses the mystifying effects of competition and capital on the source of profit in volume 3 of *Capital,* particularly chapters 2, 10, 48, and 50.

28. Even in France and Italy, where many workers do believe that their labor is the source of profit and Marxist theories are widely accepted, there is no evidence to suggest that these beliefs directly determine how hard a French or Italian laborer works; for Marxist theories like these cannot become a material force—an ideology—until they are embodied in the lived experience of the shop floor.

29. Marx also recognized this possibility:

The actual difference of magnitude between profit and surplus value— not merely between the rate of profit and rate of surplus value—in the various spheres of production now completely conceals the true nature and origin of profit not only from the capitalist, who has a special interest in deceiving himself on this score, but also from the labourer. The transformation of values into prices of production serves to obscure the basis for determining value itself. [*Capital* 3:168]

30. See, for example, Harry Braverman, *Labor and Monopoly Capital* (New York: Monthly Review Press, 1974); André Gorz, ed., *The Division of Labor* (Atlantic Highlands, N.J.: Humanities Press, 1976); Richard Edwards, "The Social Relations of Production in the Firm and Labor Market Structure," *Politics and Society* 5 (1): 83–108.

Chapter Three

1. Donald Roy, "Restriction of Output in a Piecework Machine Shop" (Ph.D. diss., University of Chicago, 1952); "Quota Restriction and Gold-

bricking in a Machine Shop," *American Journal of Sociology* 57 (1952): 427–42; "Work Satisfaction and Social Reward in Quota Achievement," *American Sociological Review* 18 (1953): 507–14; "Efficiency and the Fix," *American Journal of Sociology* 60 (1954): 255–66.

2. Roy, "Restriction of Output," chap. 9.

3. Ibid., p. 543.

4. There have since been a number of reinterpretations of the Western Electric studies. See, for example, Alex Carey, "The Hawthorne Studies: A Radical Criticism," *American Sociological Review* 32 (1967): 403–16; Henry Landsberger, *Hawthorne Revisited* (Ithaca, N.Y.: Cornell University Press, 1958); Richard Franke and James Kaul, "The Hawthorne Experiments: First Statistical Interpretation," *American Sociological Review* 43 (1978): 623–43.

5. A notable exception is, of course, William Lloyd Warner and J. Low, *The Social System of a Modern Factory* (New Haven: Yale University Press, 1947).

6. Roy, "Restriction of Output," p. 51. According to Roy, this extract was the major portion of volume 1, no. 3, of *Geer News,* the only issue he ever received. Roy makes no other reference to the nature of the company.

7. Joel Seidman, *American Labor from Defense to Reconversion* (Chicago: University of Chicago Press, 1953), p. 129.

8. Roy, "Restriction of Output," chap. 16.

9. Roy does note that, toward the end of his employment at Geer, the union did begin to show some militancy (ibid., p. 440).

10. Seidman, *American Labor,* p. 130.

11. Ibid., chap. 7.

12. Ibid., chap. 9.

13. Roy, "Restriction of Output," p. 311.

14. Ibid., p. 339.

15. See Seidman, *American Labor,* chaps. 5 and 8; Nelson Lichtenstein, "Defending the No-Strike Pledge: CIO Politics during World War II," *Radical America* 9, nos. 4–5 (1975): 49–76.

16. James Green, "Fighting on Two Fronts: Working Class Militancy in the 1940's," *Radical America* 9, nos. 4–5 (1975): 7–48; Lichtenstein, "Defending the No-Strike Pledge."

17. Seidman, *American Labor,* pp. 123, 129.

18. Lichtenstein, "Defending the No-Strike Pledge," p. 56.

19. Seidman, *American Labor,* chap. 8; Green, "Fighting on Two Fronts"; Edward Jennings, "Wildcat! The Wartime Strike Wave in Auto," *Radical America* 9, nos. 4–5 (1975): 77–105.

20. Roy, "Restriction of Output," pp. 208, 224–27.

21. This widespread change is documented by Alfred Chandler in

Strategy and Structure: Chapters in the History of the American Industrial Enterprise (Cambridge: M.I.T. Press, 1962).

22. According to Wilson, whom I had the opportunity to interview, pricing policies have become increasingly liberal over the years because of changes in the organization of the corporation, in particular the distribution of divisions to vice-presidents.

Chapter Four

1. David Noble, "Before the Fact: Social Choice in Machine Design," paper presented at the National Convention of the Organization of American Historians, April 1978. For a more general history of the role of science in the development of capitalism, see his *America by Design: Science, Technology, and the Rise of Corporate Capitalism* (New York: Alfred A. Knopf, 1977).

2. William Friedland, Amy Barton, and Robert Thomas, "Manufacturing Green Gold: The Conditions and Social Consequences of Lettuce Harvest Mechanization" (unpublished ms., University of California, Santa Cruz, 1978), and William Friedland and Amy Barton, *Destalking the Wily Tomato* (Davis, Calif.: Department of Applied Behavioral Sciences, College of Agriculture and Environmental Sciences, University of California, 1975).

3. See, for example, Taylor's *Shop Management* (New York: American Society of Mechanical Engineers, 1903).

4. Donald Roy, "Restriction of Output in a Piecework Machine Shop," (Ph.D. diss., University of Chicago, 1952), p. 76.

5. Ibid., pp. 419–23.

6. Roy refers to hot jobs on two occasions (ibid., pp. 405, 504).

7. When a job was really "hot," the scheduling man might appeal to the foreman or even to the superintendent for support if the operator appeared recalcitrant.

8. I have not been able to discover the nature or existence of equivalent penalties during the war.

9. Roy, "Restriction of Output," p. 307.

10. The change is one of degree, since Roy was also expected to check his pieces from time to time (ibid., pp. 267, 338).

11. Indeed, the general manager expected managers of quality control to make consistent efforts to cut the numbers of inspectors.

12. Roy, "Restriction of Output," p. 388.

13. From conversations with various management officials and reading between the lines of Roy's dissertation, I am left with the impression that

Geer Company tended to be more concerned with shipping the goods out than with quality control, particularly in view of the demand. (Managers of Geer have, of course, tended to deny this.) The problem of quality control has been endemic in the engine division since Allied took over. As long as quality control is subordinated to production, it is impossible to find good quality-control managers. What conscientious quality-control manager could possibly countenance subjugation to the imperatives of shipping? It is not surprising, therefore, to learn that there is a considerable turnover of quality-control managers.

14. My day man, Bill, never penciled in the time but always got his cards punched in on the clock at the time office. This restricted his room for manipulation; but since he was very experienced on the miscellaneous job, this did not reduce his earnings by very much. When I filled in for him on first shift, I did in fact pencil in the times, and no one complained. This may have been a reflection of my power, since, with Bill away, hardly anyone knew how to do the various jobs or where the fixtures were. By penciling in the times, I reckoned I could earn the same amount of money as Bill but with less effort.

15. Roy, "Restriction of Output," p. 240.

16. Ibid., table 4, p. 94.

17. During the week 17 November 1975 to 23 November 1975, there were sixteen radial-drill operators in the small-parts department. Their average "measured performances" for the entire year (or for the period of the year since they had begun to operate a radial drill) were as follows (all figures are percentages): 92, 108, 109, 110, 110, 111, 112, 115, 116, 119, 125, 133, 137, 139, 141, 142. The average was 120 percent, which turns out to be precisely Roy's average in his second period. Moreover, the average period spent on a radial drill in the *first eleven months of 1975* among these sixteen operators was of the order of six months, though a number of these operators had probably been operating radial drills for years. The data do not suggest significant differences between the rates on radial drills in Geer's Jack Shop and on radial drills in Allied's small-parts department.

18. Roy, "Restriction of Output," p. 102.

19. Ibid., p. 290.

20. Reinhard Bendix, *Work and Authority in Industry: Ideologies of Management in the Course of Industrialization* (New York: John Wiley, 1956); Frederick Taylor, *Shop Management;* Richard Edwards, "The Social Relations of Production in the Firm and Labor Market Structure," *Politics and Society* 5 (1975): 83–108.

21. Donald Roy, "Work Satisfaction and Social Reward in Quota Achievement," *American Journal of Sociology* 57 (1953): 509–10.

22. Karl Marx, *Capital,* 1:555.

23. I vividly recall being bawled out by a manager who came into the time office long after he should have gone home. He found me going through the books to see how many pieces had been handed in on a particular operation. Second-shift shop-floor management allowed and even encouraged operators to look these sorts of things up for themselves rather than bother the time clerks, but senior management regarded this as a criminal act.

24. Stuart Klein, *Workers under Stress: The Impact of Work Pressure on Group Cohesion* (Lexington, Ky.: University of Kentucky Press, 1971), p. 100.

25. This enhanced power was one of the attractions of the miscellaneous job, which no one wanted because it was rough, dirty, and dangerous as well as low-paying. Since the other operators on second shift knew virtually nothing about the jobs I did, I was able to develop a certain bargaining power, although by no means as great as Bill's.

26. Personal communication, July 1975.

27. Roy, "Restriction of Output," chap. 11.

28. A similar argument, made by Lupton, is worth citing in full:

> In Jay's, I would also say that the "fiddle" [chiseling] was an effective form of worker control over the job environment. The strength and solidarity of the workers, and the flexibility of the management system of control, made a form of adjustment possible in which different values about fair day's work, and about "proper" worker behaviour, could exist side by side. I have no doubt that, if management controls had been made less flexible, and management planning more effective, the "fiddle" would have been made more difficult to operate and probably output could have been slightly increased. But this might have destroyed the balance of social adjustment between management and the workers, and the outcome might have been loss in work satisfaction. The shop would no longer have been a "comfortable," may be not even a "happy," shop. And, in turn, this might have produced higher labor turnover, absenteeism and the like. One can only guess about these things, since there are so many other considerations involved: the existence of alternative employment, the ability of existing management-worker relationships to withstand the impact of radical change, for example, but it seems to be that when relationships are adjusted in a way similar to that I have described, which resembles the indulgency pattern noted by Gouldner, then any attempt to "tighten up" might lead to resentment and resistance. In the circumstances, management might prefer to live with the "fiddle" at the cost of what they believe to be some slight loss of output, and regard this as the price they pay for a good relationship. [Tom Lupton, *On the Shop Floor* (Oxford: Pergamon Press, 1963), pp. 182–83]

Though Lupton fails to see the organization of work as the consequence and object of struggles between workers and managers, among workers and among managers, his characterization of the *functions* of the "fiddle" are illuminating.

29. In interpreting these changes we will repeatedly come up against a difficult problem, namely, the degree to which Roy's observations reflect the exigencies of wartime conditions. For example, during the war, government contracts encouraged the overmanning of industry, since profits were fixed as a percentage of costs. Boosting costs did not change the rate of profit. As a consequence, we should not be surprised to discover cutbacks in personnel after the war. Thus, Roy informs us that after V-J Day, just before he left Geer, there was a reorganization in which foremen were demoted and the setup function was eliminated (Roy, "Restriction of Output," pp. 60, 219). Hostility of workers to the company must have been, at least in part, engendered by wartime restraints on union militancy and by the choking-off of the grievance machinery.

30. Paul Cardan (alias Cornelius Castoriadis), *Redefining Revolution* (London: Solidarity Pamphlet 44, n.d.), p. 11.

31. Cornelius Castoriadis, "On the History of the Workers' Movement," *Telos* no. 30 (Winter 1976–77): 35.

32. See, for example, Herbert Marcuse, *One Dimensional Man* (Boston: Beacon Press, 1964), chap. 1; *An Essay on Liberation* (Boston: Beacon Press, 1969); *Eros and Civilization* (Boston: Beacon Press, 1955), chap. 10.

Chapter Five

1. This is as true of "scientific Marxism" and of French structuralists such as Louis Althusser, Etienne Balibar, and Maurice Godelier as it is of so-called "Western Marxism," exemplified in the work of Georg Lukács, Max Horkheimer, and Theodor Adorno. However, Marxism has more recently rediscovered "spontaneous subjectivity" in the writings of Henri Lefebvre, Cornelius Castoriadis, Jürgen Habermas, Maurice Merleau-Ponty, and others, although Herbert Marcuse has long since recognized this as "false subjectivity," or what Paul Piccone recently referred to as "artificial negativity."

2. Michael Mann, "The Social Cohesion of Liberal Democracy," *American Sociological Review* 35 (1970): 423–39.

3. Henri De Man, *The Psychology of Socialism* (New York: Henry Holt, 1927), pp. 80–81, cited in Donald Roy, "'Banana Time': Job Satisfaction and Informal Interaction," *Human Organization* 18 (1958): 160.

4. William Baldamus, *Efficiency and Effort* (London: Tavistock Publications, 1961), p. 53.

5. Ibid., chaps. 5–7.

6. William Foot Whyte, *Money and Motivation* (New York: Harper, 1955), p. 37.

7. Ibid., p. 38.

8. F. J. Roethlisberger and William Dickson, *Management and the Worker* (Cambridge: Harvard University Press, 1939), p. 457.

9. Ibid., p. 445.

10. George Homans, *The Human Group* (New York: Harcourt, Brace, 1955), p. 155.

11. Elton Mayo, *The Human Problems of an Industrial Civilization* (New York: Macmillan, 1933), pp. 119–20.

12. Michel Crozier, "Comparing Structures and Comparing Games," in *European Contributions to Organization Theory,* ed. G. Hofstede and M. Kassem (Amsterdam: Van Gorcum, 1976), pp. 193–207. See also Michel Crozier's *The Bureaucratic Phenomenon* (Chicago: University of Chicago Press, 1964).

13. Roethlisberger and Dickson, *Management and the Worker,* chap. 19.

14. Jason Ditton, "Perks, Pilferage, and the Fiddle," *Theory and Society* 4 (1977): 39–71, and "Moral Horror versus Folk Terror: Output Restriction, Class, and the Social Organization of Exploitation," *Sociological Review* 24 (1976): 519–44.

15. Stanley Mathewson, *Restriction of Output among Unorganized Workers* (New York: Viking Press, 1931), chap. 2.

16. Stanley Aronowitz, *False Promises: The Shaping of American Working Class Consciousness* (New York: McGraw-Hill, 1973), p. 38; Emma Rothschild, *Paradise Lost: The Decline of the Auto-Industrial Age* (New York: Vintage Books, 1974), chap. 4.

17. Crozier, *The Bureaucratic Phenomenon,* p. 163.

18. Ronald Dore notes a similar conflict between foreman and time-study men in the English factory. See his *British Factory—Japanese Factory* (Berkeley and Los Angeles: University of California Press, 1973), p. 93. In a personal communication, Bill Friedland indicates that the opposition between foremen and methods departments assumed a similar form in the United States auto industry.

19. Herbert Marcuse, *One Dimensional Man* (Boston: Beacon Press, 1964), p. 5.

20. Donald Roy, "Restriction of Output in a Piecework Machine Shop," (Ph.D. diss., University of Chicago, 1952), pp. 499–500.

21. Ibid., p. 511.

22. Further insight into the dominance of the values inherent in making out is to be found in the infrequency with which operators complained about the level of maximum pay or the 140 percent ceiling as compared with

the persistent grudge that some rates were impossible or difficult to make. As Roy puts it: "No dissatisfaction was expressed concerning quota levels; there was apparent acceptance of earning limits. No one ever complained to the writer that $1.25 an hour wasn't enough; the complaint was that such an earning rate could be achieved only intermittently, with quota earning days few and far between" (ibid., p. 136). In this way, constituting work as a game of making out had the effect of drawing attention to variations within specified limits and deflecting attention away from the limits themselves.

23. Karl Marx, *Capital,* vol. 1, chap. xxi.

24. Peter Blau, *The Dynamics of Bureaucracy* (Chicago: University of Chicago Press, 1963), p. 81.

25. See, for example, James March and Herbert Simon, *Organizations* (New York: John Wiley, 1958), chap. 6; Michel Crozier, *The Bureaucratic Phenomenon,* chap. 6; James Thompson, *Organizations in Action* (New York: McGraw-Hill, 1967), chap. 1; Harry Braverman, *Labor and Monopoly Capital* (New York: Monthly Review Press, 1974).

26. Roy, "Restriction of Output," pp. 511–12.

27. One might conclude that the greater the variation among jobs, as regards the ease with which one makes out, the more divisions, that is, the stronger the hierarchy, established on the shop floor. In 1945 the variation among machines as regards easy rates was not widely known, but it appears to have been less than in 1975, which would be a further factor contributing to the greater solidarity among workers thirty years ago.

28. Roy, "Restriction of Output," pp. 517–18.

29. For the origin of these terms see Jürgen Habermas, *Legitimation Crisis* (Boston: Beacon Press, 1975), pt. II, chap. 3.

30. Clustering around these points could also indicate effective cross-booking (chiseling).

31. Baldamus, *Efficiency and Effort;* Donald Roy, "Banana Time"; Harvey Swados, *On the Line* (Boston: Little, Brown, 1957).

32. My use of the notion of game here is the *opposite* of "play" as commonly used in critical theory, where it refers to "a set of principles for organizing experience, constituted by an activity that is voluntary and open-ended (i.e., free from both external and internal compulsions), non-instrumental (in the sense that it is pursued for its sake and has at its center of interest process rather than goal), and transcendent of ordinary states of being and consciousness" (Francis Hearn, "Toward a Critical Theory of Play," *Telos* no. 30 [Winter 1976–77]: 145). For Herbert Marcuse, play is counterposed to work: "play expresses objectless autoeroticism and gratifies those component instincts which are already directed toward the objective world. Work, on the other hand, serves ends outside itself—namely the ends

of self-preservation" (*Eros and Civilization* [Boston: Beacon Press, 1955], p. 196). In my usage of the word, game is assimilated to work rather than play.

33. I am referring here to Habermas's notions of the political formation of consensus, the public sphere, and undistorted communication. See, for example, his *Theory and Practice* (Boston: Beacon Press, 1973).

34. Many Marxists, following Marx, have tended to assume that in a postrevolutionary society or in an emancipated society there would be no politics. This is emminently false. See Karl Korsch, "What Is Socialization?" *New German Critique* no. 6 (Fall 1975): 60–81; Cornelius Castoriadis, "The Hungarian Source," *Telos* no. 29 (Fall 1976): 4–22; Claude Lefort, "The Age of Novelty," *Telos* no. 29 (Fall 1976): 23–38.

Chapter Six

1. Peter Doeringer and Michael Piore, *Internal Labor Markets and Manpower Analysis* (Lexington, Mass.: D. C. Heath, 1971); Bennett Harrison, "Public Employment and the Theory of the Dual Economy," in *The Political Economy of Public Service Employment,* ed. H. L. Sheppard, B. Harrison, and W. J. Spring (Lexington, Mass.: Heath-Lexington, 1972), pp. 41–76; Richard Edwards, "The Social Relations of Production in the Firm and Labor Market Structure," *Politics and Society* 5 (1975): 83–108.

2. Doeringer and Piore, *Internal Labor Markets,* pp. 1–2.

3. Edwards, "The Social Relations of Production," p. 86.

4. See, for example, Doeringer and Piore, *Internal Labor Markets,* chaps. 2–4; Koji Taira, "Internal Labor Markets, Human Resource Utilization, and Economic Growth," paper presented at the Urban Labor Market Research Conference, 1974.

5. Karl Polanyi, *The Great Transformation* (New York: Rinehart, 1944), p. 134.

6. This may not be true for all "internal labor markets." It is possible—for example, in Japan—for internal labor markets to operate through a managerial distribution of employees to jobs on the basis of seniority, that is, without the organization of a full-fledged bidding system. This would explain part of the variation among enterprises in the degree of individuality expressed on the shop floor.

7. Ronald Dore, *British Factory—Japanese Factory* (Berkeley and Los Angeles: University of California Press, 1973); Koji Taira, *Economic Development and the Labor Market in Japan* (New York: Columbia University Press, 1970).

8. A cautionary note: the low levels of mobility within the firm in 1944–45

can in part be explained by the wartime freeze on labor mobility between firms.

9. Donald Roy, "Restriction of Output in a Piecework Machine Shop," (Ph.D. diss., University of Chicago, 1952), p. 104.

10. Ibid., pp. 134–35.

11. Ibid., p. 134.

12. Ibid., p. 416, pp. 134–35.

13. Ibid., pp. 211, 311, 312, 488, 489.

14. Ibid., p. 101.

15. In an interview, Wilson (the general manager, who took over the engine division in 1957) told me that expanded application of plant-wide seniority could work against the interests of labor. He maintained that after the introduction of plant-wide bumping for all those with more than one year's service, management tended to lay off employees in much larger batches so as to avoid some of the complicated reshuffling processes that would take place if layoffs took place gradually.

16. The effective operation of an internal labor market therefore depends on the existence of strong union protection for the labor force and on nonarbitrary firing.

17. Edwards, "The Social Relations of Production," pp. 96–97.

Chapter Seven

1. James Weinstein, *The Corporate Ideal in the Liberal State: 1900–1918* (Boston: Beacon Press, 1968).

2. Jürgen Habermas, *Legitimation Crisis* (Boston: Beacon Press, 1975), pt. II.

3. Philip Selznick, *Law, Society, and Industrial Justice* (New York: Russell Sage Foundation, 1969), p. 154.

4. Donald Roy, "Restriction of Output in a Piecework Machine Shop (Ph.D. diss., University of Chicago, 1952), p. 434.

5. Roy, "Restriction of Output," pp. 438–39.

6. Walter Reuther, "Individualism vs. Unionism," in *Source Book on Labor,* ed. Neil Chamberlain (New York: McGraw-Hill, 1958), p. 144.

7. Unfortunately, Roy never attended any union meetings in 1944–45. It is therefore difficult to assess whether the union leadership has assumed a more or less aggressive role in its relationship with management. Certainly, one finds it difficult to imagine a president in the early days of the union presenting absenteeism as a "union" problem.

8. Adam Przeworski has conceptualized this situation as "capitalist profit equals worker savings," by which he means that workers ensure their

employment in future months or years by "consenting" to a restricted growth in wages. That is to say, wage restraint today allows accumulation of profit and therefore increased wages tomorrow. In this way the interests of capitalists and workers are concretely coordinated (Przeworski, "Capitalist Democracy and the Transition to Socialism," unpublished ms., University of Chicago, 1978).

9. See ibid. for further details on the material basis of consent and the conditions under which it will break down.

10. Selznick, *Law, Society, and Industrial Justice,* chap. 4.

11. Ibid., p. 215.

12. Ibid., p. 229. This is naturally an outgrowth of laissez faire, in which the strong unions manage to protect their membership, while the weak unions and unorganized workers can achieve little.

13. Thus, the two-party system described by Seymour Martin Lipset, Martin Trow, and James Coleman in their study of the International Typographical Union is the counterpart of the two-party system in the organization of politics in the wider society. In some respects it fosters consent in the same way that party systems foster consent in global politics. At the same time, studies of miners, longshoremen, and also the ITU indicate the importance of local autonomy in the emergence and maintenance of "democratic" practices in the government of industry. The two-party trade-union system, instead of being the cause of such forms of democracy at the point of production, tends, on the contrary, to be a consequence (Seymour Martin Lipset et al., *Union Democracy* [Glencoe: Free Press, 1956]).

14. It may be objected that these views of industrial government are tainted with euphoria. I have repeatedly pointed out, however, that my conclusions apply to only certain sectors of the economy, namely, those where strong unions prevail and where the product market is dominated by a few large firms. In other sectors, such as agribusiness and the public sector, the internal state and the internal labor market may be rudimentary or nonexistent. Moreover, even in the so-called monopoly sector, it may be argued that the internal state and the internal labor market do not operate in the frictionless, formally neutral fashion suggested here. But, as I indicated earlier, the existence of bias (as long as it is not too substantial or too persistent) in the administration of "justice" and in the allocation of personnel has the paradoxical effect of increasing rather than decreasing the effectiveness of the internal labor market and the internal state in the production of consent. In normal times, bias directs attention to the imperfections of the system rather than to the underlying relations upon which the system rests.

15. The emphasis in this chapter has been on the implications of bureaucracy as a form of domination. Traditionally, industrial sociology has

tended to take off from the view, perhaps more prevalent in Weber's work, of bureaucracy as "technically superior to any other form of organization" (Max Weber, *Economy and Society,* 3 vols. [New York: Bedminster Press, 1968], 3:973). Thus, industrial bureaucracies have been regarded as more or less efficient ways of organizing production. (See, for example, Robert Merton, *Social Theory and Social Structure* [New York: Free Press, 1968], chap. 8; Peter Blau, *The Dynamics of Bureaucracy* [Chicago: University of Chicago Press, 1955]; Philip Selznick, *TVA and the Grass Roots* [Berkeley: University of California Press, 1949].) By contrast, Alvin Gouldner and Michel Crozier have recognized the other strand in Weber's view of bureaucracy, showing how rules diffuse tensions between worker and management (Alvin Gouldner, *Patterns of Industrial Bureaucracy* [New York: Free Press, 1954]; Michel Crozier, *The Bureaucratic Phenomenon* [Chicago: University of Chicago Press, 1964]). Crozier regards domination as an inevitable feature of industrial work, and Gouldner argues against such inevitability; both views differ from the formulation implicit in the internal state, that domination is a product of capitalist relations of production.

16. The dual perspective of force and consent runs throughout Antonio Gramsci's work in such forms as domination vs. hegemony; violence vs. civilization; political society vs. civil society. His view of the relationship between the two perspectives is suggestive if underdeveloped: "In actual fact, it often happens that the more the first 'perspective' is 'immediate' and elementary, the more the second has to be 'distant' (not in time, but as a dialectical relation), complex and ambitious." In another passage he writes:

> The "normal" exercise of hegemony on the now classical terrain of the parliamentary regime is characterized by the combination of force and consent, which balance each other reciprocally, without force predominating excessively over consent. Indeed, the attempt is always made to ensure that force will appear to be based on the consent of the majority, expressed by the so-called organs of public opinion—newspapers and associations—which, therefore, in certain situations, are artificially multiplied. [*Selections from Prison Notebooks* (New York: International Publishers, 1971), pp. 170, 80]

Chapter Eight

1. R. H. Franke and J. D. Kaul, "The Hawthorne Experiments: First Statistical Interpretation," *American Sociological Review* 43 (1978): 623–43.

2. James Thompson, *Organizations in Action* (New York: McGraw-Hill, 1967), chap. 2.

3. See, for example, Paul Lawrence and Jay Lorsch, *Organizations and Environment* (Boston: Harvard University Press for the Graduate School of

Business Administration, 1967); F. E. Emery and E. L. Trist, "The Causal Texture of Organizational Environments," *Human Relations* 18 (1963): 20–26. Thompson himself writes: "My focus is on the behavior of organizations; behavior within organizations is considered only to the extent that it helps us understand organization in the round" (*Organizations in Action,* p. ix).

4. So far in this study, I have tried to explain the organization of consent, the obscuring and securing of surplus value, without recourse to an explicit psychology. Such an omission is justified to the extent that the translation of relations into activities is invariant or, as in Marx, rests on survival. If capitalists are to survive as capitalists, they must compete and accumulate; if workers are to survive as workers, they must sell their labor power to a capitalist. Presenting individuals as carriers or agents of social relations and activities as the effects (within limits) of those social relations captures the essential quality of existence under capitalism. Within such a context, psychology can be reduced to a theory of needs: how capitalism generates needs, what these needs are in the different phases of capitalist development, and whether capitalism can satisfy the needs it produces. The Budapest School, and, in particular, Agnes Heller's *The Theory of Need in Marx* (London: Allison & Busby, 1976), has probably moved the farthest in developing such a theory. The Budapest School, however, ignores unconscious feelings and drives, while one of the most notable contributions of the Frankfurt School has been the critical appropriation of Freudian psychology (see, for example, Herbert Marcuse, *Eros and Civilization* [Boston: Beacon Press, 1955]; Wilhelm Reich, *Sex-Pol* [New York: Vintage Books, 1972]; Max Horkheimer, "Authority and the Family," in *Critical Theory: Selected Essays* [New York: Seabury Press, 1972], pp. 47–128; Theodor Adorno, "Sociology and Psychology," *New Left Review* no. 46 [November–December 1967]: 67–80, and no. 47 [January–February 1968]: 79–99; for two recent but divergent formulations in the critical-theory tradition see Russell Jacoby, *Social Amnesia* [Boston: Beacon Press, 1975], and Jessica Benjamin, "The End of Internalization: Adorno's Social Psychology," *Telos* no. 32 [Summer 1977]: 42–64). The unmediated way in which individuals under capitalism carry out the dictates embodied in social relations becomes a problem and a point of critique. For Adorno, therefore, monopoly capitalism so strips the individual of defenses that psychoanalysis, conceived of in terms of a dynamic *tension* among ego, id, and superego, becomes irrelevant. Russell Jacoby, following in Adorno's shadow, calls for a "negative psychoanalysis"—a theory of the subjectless subject. Thus the central figures of the Frankfurt School maintain that the institutions of advanced capitalism penetrate and shape individual instincts and drives in accordance with the reproduction of capitalist rationality. Wilhelm Reich, however,

insists on the impermeability and emancipatory potential of individual instincts; capitalism represses but does not destroy the instinctual impetus to liberation. From all these writings it becomes clear that no Marxism can be complete as long as it does not clarify its assumptions about human nature, whether in terms of needs or psychoanalytic categories.

In looking upon the labor process as a game, I am not only showing how capitalism mobilizes adaptation to alienation for its own ends but am pointing to the empirical existence of a human potential for emancipation, to an instinctive compulsion of workers to collectively control the labor process—a compulsion that under capitalism expresses itself in the distorted form of a game.

5. It is relatively easy to increase the strength of direct labor but very difficult to get additional auxiliary workers, or indirect labor. Every addition to indirect costs is carefully scrutinized by all levels of management, up to and including the general manager. It is much more difficult to recruit a chip-handler than a drill-press operator. This is because management regards the ratio of indirect to direct labor costs as a measure of efficiency.

6. Difficult as it is to believe, until January 1975 no records were kept of the production performance of individual departments. No one appeared to know how well each department was doing from week to week. Of course, each department had its own budget, but this did not pinpoint the source of changes.

7. Personnel management attributed the decline in absenteeism to a publicity campaign and a new human-relations program, which sought to help the absentee "rectify his behavior." Absenteeism was not recorded systematically by the company until January 1975.

8. Maurice Zeitlin has suggested to me that the nature of the interdependence among operators and auxiliary workers provides the basis for regarding absenteeism as illegitimate. This is certainly an interesting idea, but it could be assessed only through comparisons among labor processes.

Chapter Nine

1. John Goldthorpe, David Lockwood, Frank Bechhofer, and Jennifer Platt, *The Affluent Worker: Industrial Attitudes and Behaviour* (New York: Cambridge University Press, 1968). An important earlier paper, which, on the basis of an attitude survey, claims that work is a means to fulfilling central life-interests outside the factory, is Robert Dubin's "Industrial Workers' Worlds: A Study of the Central Life Interests of Industrial Workers," *Social Problems* 3 (1956): 131–42. Dubin's conclusions can be subjected to the same criticism as the work of Goldthorpe et al.

2. Goldthorpe et al., p. 185.

3. Ibid., p. 179.

4. See tables 73 and 74, ibid., pp. 164–65.

5. *Workers' Attitudes and Technology* (Cambridge, Eng.: At the University Press, 1972).

6. For a discussion of the existence of the traditional worker see David Lockwood, "In Search of the Traditional Worker," in *Working Class Images of Society,* ed. Martin Bulmer (London: Routledge & Kegan Paul, 1976), pp. 239–51.

7. See Edward H. Carr, *The New Society* (London: Macmillan, 1951).

8. "The Social Cohesion of Liberal Democracy," *American Sociological Review* 35 (1970): 423–39.

9. John Westergaard, "The Rediscovery of the Cash Nexus," in *The Socialist Register 1970,* ed. Ralph Miliband and John Saville (London: Merlin Press, 1970), pp. 111–38.

10. Ibid., p. 120.

11. Ibid.

12. Everett Hughes, "The Knitting of Racial Groups in Industry," *American Sociological Review* 11 (1946): 512–19.

13. William Kornblum, *Blue Collar Community* (Chicago: University of Chicago Press, 1974), p. 36.

14. A. R. Radcliffe-Brown, *Structure and Function in Primitive Society* (London: Cohen & West, 1952), p. 92.

15. There was one young white worker who spent most of his time with the younger Blacks, both on the shop floor and in outside work. He was the only White on second shift to sit with the group of Blacks at lunch. He would also invite them to his house for parties and so forth. His black friends held him up as an exemplary case of the unprejudiced White.

16. Although it is difficult to prove that racial discrimination took place, it was widely assumed (both by management and by the rank and file) that the union leadership was discriminatory in the way it pursued grievances. Blacks were certainly convinced of this and responded by attending union meetings in disproportionate numbers. Frequently these meetings would erupt into a heated exchange between the black membership and the white president of the local.

17. Donald Roy did not collect any data on the relationship of output to social background because he did not have access to output data for any worker but himself.

18. Melville Dalton, "The Industrial Rate Buster," *Applied Anthropology* 7 (1948): 5–18.

19. Dalton does not give the average age of his sample. It is possible that the average age was boosted during the war.

20. Hughes, "The Knitting of Racial Groups," p. 517.

21. In using the notions of "intervention" and "mediation," I am following the meaning given to them by Erik Olin Wright in his *Class, Crisis, and the State* (London: New Left Books, 1978), chap. 1.

22. It might be argued that seniority, therefore, largely measures a characteristic of piece rates; that senior operators will manage to place themselves on the jobs with the easiest rates that also happen to be the highest in prestige. Two comments are relevant. First, just because a rate is easy does not mean that operators will attempt to maximize output. It could be argued, for example, that external factors would determine whether operators would try to make out on gravy jobs. Second, piece rates are themselves nothing but an expression of social relations between time-study men, operators, and foremen. That piece rates are associated with seniority therefore only strengthens seniority as a measure of relations in production.

23. The 185 machine operators in the small-parts department at Allied's engine division constitute a discrete and distinctive population. I am not suggesting that the results of my statistical analysis are generalizable to workers in all industries, although, as in any case study, the conclusions are suggestive as well as illustrative. Since I am not dealing with a true sample but with a population, the statistical significance of the results has little meaning. However, I have decided to include the results of significance tests as a polemical device: if this were a sample, we could have a certain confidence in generalizing to the population as a whole. Thus, in this first regression, the coefficients for seniority and experience are significant at the 0.001 level, while coefficients for the other variables are not significant even at the 0.05 level.

24. When average output for the first eleven months of 1975 is regressed on the external variables alone, 21.5 percent of the variance is explained as compared with the 37.5 percent explained by the work variables. Most of the variance explained by the external variables is due to age (20 percent), and this is due to the high correlation between age and log seniority (0.69). Since these are the only two independent variables that have a correlation coefficient greater than 0.5, multicolinearity does not pose a problem. It is worth noting that these results also cast serious doubt on the view that behavior on the shop floor can be understood in terms of the "cash nexus." Had money been an important influence, one would have expected operators with large families to work harder. The regression shows no significant independent effect of marital status or age on output.

25. Of the regression coefficients, only one, log seniority, was significant at the 0.01 level; the rest, including experience, were not significant at the 0.05 level.

26. Although some of the discrepancies between the coefficients appear to be quite considerable, none of them is statistically significant even at

the 0.1 level, which suggests that they cannot be taken too seriously.

27. Again, relatively little variance in output is explained by the external variables; in the one case, it is 7.1 percent, and in the other it is 6.1 percent. The only external variable to have a statistically significant effect on output is marital status, and then only for the subpopulation with three years or less of seniority. One might note that, although its impact is slight, race has opposite effects for the two subpopulations: for the more-senior group, being black rather than white enhances output; for the less-senior group, being black rather than white reduces output.

28. Indeed, many theorists do claim that such a common experience of domination and discipline is produced in all areas of society. See, for example, Max Horkheimer and Theodor Adorno, *The Dialectic of Enlightenment* (New York: Seabury Press, 1972) and Michel Foucault, *Discipline and Punish* (New York: Pantheon, 1977). Of particular relevance is the work of Samuel Bowles and Herbert Gintis, *Schooling in Capitalist America* (New York: Basic Books, 1976). They argue that there is a correspondence between the social relations of the classroom and those of the workplace and that this is no accident but the result of the deliberate attempts by the dominant class to use schools as an instrument to

> depoliticize the potentially explosive class relations, . . . perpetuate the social relationships of economic life through which these patterns are set, by facilitating a smooth integration of youth into the labor force, . . . legitimate inequality through the ostensibly meritocratic manner by which they reward and promote students, . . . create and reinforce patterns of social class, racial and sexual identification among students, [and] foster types of personal development compatible with the relationships of dominance and subordinacy in the economic sphere. [P. 11]

All this—in addition to imparting technical and social skills and appropriate motivations for participation in the labor force. They conclude:

> The economic system is stable only if the consciousness of the strata and classes which compose it remains compatible with the social relations which characterize it as a mode of production. The perpetuation of the class structure requires that the hierarchical division of labor be reproduced in the consciousness of its participants. The educational system is one of several reproduction mechanisms through which dominant elites seek to achieve this objective. . . . The educational system reproduces the capitalist social division of labor, in part, through a correspondence between its own internal social relationships and those of the workplace. [P. 147]

At the same time, Bowles and Gintis do recognize that "work must be organized so as to make authority relationships in the firm appear at best just, or at least inevitable. That is, relationships among superiors, subordinates and peers must not violate the norms of society" (p. 82). The inversion of race, age, or gender relations at the workplace can lead only to conflict and instability. They come to this conclusion because they have little sense of the relative autonomy of the labor process and its capacity to reproduce and "legitimate" its own relations. The totality seen by Bowles and Gintis is one in which each part is an expression of, and therefore has to be compatible with, capitalist relations. For them the important point is not merely that a different system of schooling or a different family life would produce a consciousness incompatible with relations at work and thereby promote instability but that such schools and families could never realistically appear without first transforming the labor process. "Patterns of inequality, repression, and forms of class domination cannot be restricted to a single sphere of life, but reappear in substantially altered, yet structurally comparable, form in all spheres" (p. 148). Although Bowles' and Gintis' view of the correspondence between work relations and schooling would anticipate the results of this chapter, they would probably attach greater importance to the contribution of schooling to the production of able and willing workers and would more narrowly restrict the range of educational systems compatible with capitalist relations. At the same time, I am obviously not denying the importance of education and the family in the allocation of people to places in the class structure and in the learning of such basic skills as literacy and numeracy. Yet, even at this level, as my studies of the Zambian copper industry indicate, a distinctive work language is created at the point of production when workers and supervisors come from a variety of linguistic backgrounds. Finally, as I shall argue in chapter 12, labor processes do vary in their independence of imported consciousness and external changes. These factors may be more important in the competitive sector of the economy, where the labor process is less protected by the elaborate buffering of internal labor markets and the internal state.

Chapter Ten

1. Donald Roy, "Restriction of Output in a Piecework Machine Shop," (Ph.D. diss., University of Chicago, 1952), p. 238.

2. Ibid., pp. 252–53.

3. Ibid., pp. 239–40.

4. The time-study men worked only between 8 A.M. and 5 P.M. Since Roy was on second shift, he overlapped with them for only about an hour and a half.

5. Roy, "Restriction of Output," p. 113.

6. Geer Company Contract 1945, Article IX, section 4.

7. Roy, "Restriction of Output," p. 111.

8. Ibid., p. 242.

9. Ibid., p. 245.

10. Ibid., pp. 322–23.

11. Frederick Winslow Taylor, *Scientific Management* (New York: Harper & Bros., 1947), pp. 79–85.

12. Donald Roy, "Efficiency and the Fix: Informal Intergroup Relations in a Piecework Machine Shop," *American Journal of Sociology* 60 (1954): 255–66.

13. Roy offers no explanation for the introduction of the new rules. The nearest he comes to an explanation is the comment of the setup man: "The next day Johnny 'interpreted' the new ruling as an attempt by management to find out 'what is holding up production,' following a complaint that the former 'help yourself' policy slowed production rather than expediting it" (Roy, "Restriction of Output," p. 416). Why the new rules were introduced at that particular time is not discussed.

14. Roy, "Restriction of Output," p. 415.

15. Ibid.

16. Ibid., pp. 373–75.

17. Ibid., p. 374.

18. Ibid., p. 432.

19. On one occasion I was searching through the methods books for a rate on a particular operation when a senior manager walked into the office and bawled me out. He lectured me on why operators should never come into the office, yet the practice was customary for second-shift operators and was endorsed by shop-floor management. In view of the confrontation, the scheduling man suggested that in future I wait until seven o'clock before looking through the books. By that time all senior management would have gone home.

20. See, for example, Alvin Gouldner, *Patterns of Industrial Bureaucracy* (New York: Free Press, 1954).

Chapter Eleven

1. I am making the assumption that the changes described in part 3 evolved gradually in a unilinear fashion. All the evidence from the content of management-union contracts points in that direction, although, as we shall see, changes under Geer were of a different kind from those under Allied.

2. There are, in fact, two types of political class struggles, namely, those whose object is the relations in production and those whose object is the

relations of production. At the level of the enterprise, the latter tend to merge with ideological struggles, whereas, at the level of the economy as a whole, they concern the various forms of state intervention.

3. Such activities were associated with the National Civic Federation during the Progressive Era and supposedly provided the basis of "welfare capitalism" in the twenties. See William Appleman Williams, *The Contours of American History* (Cleveland: World Publishing Co., 1961); James Weinstein, *The Corporate Ideal in the Liberal State, 1900-1918* (Boston: Beacon Press, 1968); Gabriel Kolko, *The Triumph of Conservatism* (New York: Free Press, 1963); Stephen Scheinberg, "The Development of Corporation Labor Policy, 1900-1940" (Ph.D. diss., University of Wisconsin, 1966).

4. In a personal communication to me (16 August 1976), Mitchell Fein, an eminent professional engineer, wrote:

> In general, I'd guess there are not fewer time study men on the floor today than there were in 1944; rather it depends on company policies, the type of production, the operations performed, whether incentives are used or not, and other such questions. Also, by the use of standard data which is developed through detailed time studies, engineers can, after awhile, set standards from a desk without venturing out on the floor, if they have sufficient details on how the operation will be performed. Most companies have gone this route and, by now, have sufficient data available so that less time is needed on the floor to set standards.... The tough manager has not deliberately withdrawn the time study man as a way of reducing industrial conflict. On the contrary, he doesn't give a damn and if injecting more time study men would attain his objective of raising productivity, he wouldn't care whether conflict was lowered or raised.

5. "Changing Patterns of Organizational Authority: The Military Establishment," *Administrative Science Quarterly* 3 (1959): 473-93.

6. Although I did get some insight into the various struggles and alliances among the departments from different managers and from what I saw from the shop floor, it is too fragmentary to warrant analysis. Unfortunately, there have been all too few studies of politics within management. See, however, Melville Dalton, *Men Who Manage* (New York: John Wiley, 1966), and Tom Burns and G. M. Stalker, *The Management of Innovation* (London: Tavistock Publications, 1961).

7. The new general manager arrived in January 1975 and immediately set about reorganizing the division, with some of the effects I described in chapter 8. During the following two years the division consistently made profits every quarter—an almost unprecedented achievement. However, toward the end of 1976, problems of quality control were becoming an

increasing headache, and, as a result, the division was being threatened with the loss of a large customer from within the corporation. Even though it has been transformed since 1953, the engine division is still faced with many of the problems that plagued Geer Company. The plant is too small, and the engines too diversified, for it to be able to sell its product competitively. These are structural problems that no manager can solve except through expansion or through reduction in the number of different engines being manufactured.

8. For one interesting view of bargaining between the largest corporations and the largest unions, see William Serrin, *The Company and the Union* (New York: Vintage Books, 1974).

9. From the various accounts I have heard, the organization of the steel workers local at Geer followed the pattern described by Peter Friedlander in his *The Emergence of a UAW Local, 1936–1939* (Pittsburgh: University of Pittsburgh Press, 1975).

10. Obviously, other factors cannot be ignored. The arrival of a generation of workers who had not experienced the great depression and who had no sense of the preunion days and the recruitment of black workers coming out of a more politically militant background necessarily affected the conduct of union leadership.

11. See, for example, Huw Beynon's description of a Ford assembly plant at Liverpool (*Working for Ford* [London: Allen Lane, 1973]) and the description of machine shops to be found in Ronald Dore, *British Factory—Japanese Factory* (Berkeley and Los Angeles: University of California Press, 1973), chaps. 5 and 6; and in Tom Lupton, *On the Shop Floor* (Oxford: Pergamon Press, 1963).

12. See Theo Nichols and Huw Beynon, *Living with Capitalism* (London: Routledge & Kegan Paul, 1977).

13. David Noble, "Before the Fact: Social Choice in Machine Design," paper presented at the National Convention of the Organization of American Historians, April 1978.

14. Growing recognition of the importance of the concrete experience of the working class is also to be found in recent contributions to United States labor history, influenced by the work of two British historians: Eric Hobsbawm, *Labouring Men* (London: Weidenfeld & Nicolson, 1964), and Edward Thompson, *The Making of the English Working Class* (London: Victor Gollancz, 1963). See, for example, David Montgomery, "Workers' Control of Machine Production in the Nineteenth Century," *Labor History* 17 (Fall 1976): 485–509; idem, "The 'New Unionism' and the Transformation in Workers' Consciousness," *Journal of Social History* 7 (Summer 1974): 509–29; Herbert Gutman, *Work, Culture, and Society in Industrializing America* (New York: Vintage Books, 1977).

Chapter Twelve

1. Cornelius Castoriadis, "On the History of the Workers' Movement," *Telos* no. 30 (Winter 1976-77): 35-36.

2. Thus, in 1880, Engels writes:

> In the trusts, freedom of competition changes into its very opposite—into monopoly; and the production without any definite plan of capitalistic society capitulates to the production upon a definite plan of the invading socialistic society. Certainly this is so far still to the benefit and advantage of the capitalists. But in this case the exploitation is so palpable that it must break down. No nation will put up with production conducted by trusts, with so barefaced an exploitation of the community by a small band of dividend-mongers... the transformation of the great establishments for production and distribution into joint-stock companies, trusts and state property shows how unnecessary the bourgeoisie are for that purpose.... The more it [the state] proceeds by taking over productive forces, the more does it actually become the national capitalist, the more citizens does it exploit. The workers remain wage-workers—proletarians. The capitalist relation is not done away with. It is rather brought to a head. But, brought to a head, it topples over. State ownership of the productive forces is not the solution of the conflict, but concealed within it are the technical conditions that form the elements of that solution. ["Socialism: Utopian and Scientific," in *The Marx-Engels Reader,* ed. Robert Tucker (New York: W. W. Norton, 1972), pp. 632-34]

3. There are, of course, numerous accounts of this period, but see, particularly, Charles Maier, *Recasting Bourgeois Europe* (Princeton: Princeton University Press, 1975); Nicos Poulantzas, *Fascism and Dictatorship* (London: New Left Books, 1974). For the United States, see James Weinstein, *The Corporate Ideal in the Liberal State, 1900-1918* (Boston: Beacon Press, 1968); Gabriel Kolko, *The Triumph of Conservatism* (New York: Free Press, 1963); and William Appleman Williams, *The Contours of American History* (Cleveland: World Publishing Co., 1961).

4. It cannot be repeated too often that twentieth-century Marxism is not a simple regurgitation of Marx's writings but a response to the inadequacy of those writings for understanding the historical trajectory of capitalism and the transition to socialism. That Marxists are like other people and can learn from history is still not widely recognized by American sociologists, who continue to ignore *Marxism* because *Marx's* "predictions about the course of the socioeconomic system have been deeply invalidated by the course of events in the most advanced industrial societies," and his "doctrines, however important in their time, have been rendered obsolete by technical developments in theoretical economics." Accordingly, Marxism is reduced to a dogma of "certain categories of intellectuals, who have

professed to speak for the masses of the underprivileged in their respective societies and, in their latest phase, for the underprivileged society as a whole" (Talcott Parsons, "Some Comments on the Sociology of Karl Marx," in *Sociological Theory and Modern Society* [New York: Free Press, 1967], pp. 127, 109–10, 128). These comments, coming as they do from the high priest of American sociological theory, are remarkable for their ignorance of what either unites or divides Marx from Marxism. It was Lukács who wrote that, if research showed all Marx's "predictions" to be false, "every serious 'orthodox' Marxist would still be able to accept all such modern findings without reservation and hence dismiss all of Marx's theses *in toto*—without having to renounce his orthodoxy for a single moment" (*History and Class Consciousness* [Cambridge, Mass.: M.I.T. Press, 1968], p. 1).

5. For contemporary theories of the interventionist state see James O'Connor, *The Fiscal Crisis of the State* (New York: St. Martin's Press, 1973); Jürgen Habermas, *Legitimation Crisis* (Boston: Beacon Press, 1975); and Claus Offe, "The Theory of the Capitalist State and the Problem of Policy Formation," in *Stress and Contradiction in Modern Capitalism,* ed. Leon Lidberg, Robert Alford, Colin Crouch, and Claus Offe (Lexington, Mass.: Lexington Books, D. C. Heath, 1975), pp. 125–44.

6. For Marxist theories of the state that emphasize the repression or organization of class struggles, see Antonio Gramsci, *Selections from Prison Notebooks* (New York: International Publishers, 1971); Ralph Miliband, *The State in Capitalist Society* (New York: Basic Books, 1969); and Nicos Poulantzas, *Political Power and Social Classes* (London: New Left Books, 1973). All these works are inspired by Marx's political works, in particular *The Eighteenth Brumaire of Louis Bonaparte* and *Class Struggles in France.*

7. There are, of course, notable exceptions, such as Paul Baran and Paul Sweezy, *Monopoly Capital* (New York: Monthly Review, 1966).

8. For early attempts to regulate relations between labor and capital in the United States, see James Weinstein, *The Corporate Ideal in the Liberal State,* and Stuart Brandes, *American Welfare Capitalism, 1880–1940* (Chicago: University of Chicago Press, 1976). David Brody makes the interesting argument that welfare capitalism, which reached its height in the 1920s, would have survived and American industrial relations would have continued on its paternalistic course had it not been for the depression ("The Rise and Decline of Welfare Capitalism" in *Change and Continuity in Twentieth Century America: The 1920's,* ed. John Braeman, Robert Brenner, and David Brody [Columbus, Ohio: Ohio State University Press, 1968], pp. 147–78). It was only after World War II that the internal labor

market and the internal state resumed their ascendancy, this time aided and abetted by organized labor.

9. It is difficult to determine the extent to which relations in production are shaped by the technical imperatives of machines and how much by relations of production, that is, by the need to obscure and secure surplus labor. It does appear that these technical aspects of the relations in production will vary with the machine; they are different for the automated (numerically controlled) machine tool and the assembly line. Nor is it easy to draw any firm conclusions about the nature of the change in technical relations in production as one moves from competitive to monopoly capitalism unless one confuses competitive capitalism with the era of the craft worker.

10. As usual, Alvin Gouldner puts his finger on the trigger when he writes:

> For Weber, therefore, authority was given consent because it was legitimate, rather than being legitimate because it evoked consent. For Weber, therefore, consent is always a datum to be taken for granted, rather than being a problem whose sources had to be traced. In consequence, he never systematically analyzed the actual social processes which either generated or thwarted the emergence of consent. [*Patterns of Industrial Bureaucracy* (New York: Free Press, 1954), p. 223]

Unfortunately, Gouldner gets cold feet and does not pull the trigger.

11. See Ronald Dore, *British Factory—Japanese Factory* (Berkeley and Los Angeles: University of California Press, 1973).

12. See note 4, chapter 8.

13. This is not to suggest that capitalism has in any way solved all of its major problems—as was presumed by the emminent political sociologists of the fifties—but only that theorists such as O'Connor and Habermas fail to demonstrate that the problems they highlight necessarily become worse and crises deepen as advanced capitalism develops. In addition, while they do recognize the distinctions between economic and political crises, between system and social crises, they do not show how the one leads to the other—how people become conscious of the postulated crises as crises of capitalism.

14. Antonio Gramsci was probably the first major Marxist to recognize the significance of the absence of precapitalist modes of production for the relatively smooth reproduction of capitalism in the United States. (He seems to have ignored slavery as a distinct precapitalist mode of production.) Capitalism, he argued, could develop only unevenly in a country such as Italy, handicapped by the parasitic residues of feudalism. In a similar line of argument, Michael Mann has recently tried to link the appearance of more

revolutionary working classes to the continued existence or recent destruction of precapitalist modes of production. Samir Amin's theories of accumulation on a world scale and unequal development are probably the most comprehensive to incorporate as their central tenet the inception of socialism as occurring in the underdeveloped world. See Antonio Gramsci, *Selections from Prison Notebooks;* Michael Mann, *Consciousness and Action among the Western Working Class* (Cambridge, Eng.: At the University Press, 1973); Samir Amin, *Unequal Development* (New York: Monthly Review Press, 1976).

Appendix

1. By far the most outstanding comparative study is Ronald Dore's *British Factory—Japanese Factory* (Berkeley and Los Angeles: University of California Press, 1973). The weight of his argument seems to favor understanding variations in industrial behavior in terms of the historical emergence of different patterns of industrial relations. His perspective is therefore very similar to my own. By contrast, Michel Crozier (*The Bureaucratic Phenomenon* [Chicago: University of Chicago Press, 1964]) argues that culture directly affects both the organization of work and patterns of work behavior. He does not disentangle the two forms of cultural determination, and his conclusions are less than convincing, since he has no comparative data from other countries.

2. Michael Burawoy, "The Politics of Production and the Production of Politics: A Comparative Analysis of Machine Shops in the United States and Hungary," *Political Power and Social Theory* 1 (1979).

3. See, for example, Alvin Gouldner, *Patterns of Industrial Bureaucracy* (New York: Free Press, 1954), and Norman Dennis, F. Henriques, and C. Slaughter, *Coal is Our Life* (London: Eyre & Spottiswoode, 1956), chap. 2.

4. The problem of uncertainty that confronts the organization of work in mining and the two modal types of adaptation have their parallel in the organization of a combat unit. See Morris Janowitz, "Changing Patterns of Organizational Authority: The Military Establishment," *Administrative Science Quarterly* 3 (1959): 473–93.

5. Eric Trist, G. W. Higgin, H. Murray, and A. B. Pollock, *Organizational Choice* (London: Tavistock Publications, 1963), pp. 66–67.

6. For further details, see Frederick Johnstone, *Class, Race and Gold* (London: Routledge & Kegan Paul, 1976); H. J. Simons and R. E. Simons, *Class and Colour in South Africa, 1850–1950* (Harmondsworth, Eng.: Penguin Books, 1969), particularly chaps. 2 and 3; Charles van Onselen,

Chibaro (London: Pluto Press, 1976); and Harold Wolpe, "Capitalism and Cheap Labor Power in South Africa: From Segregation to Apartheid," *Economy and Society* 1 (1972): 425–56.

7. This, of course, is not peculiar to southern Africa. See André Gorz, ed., *The Division of Labor* (Atlantic Highlands, N.J.: Humanities Press, 1976); Katherine Stone, "The Origins of Job Structures in the Steel Industry," *Review of Radical Political Economics* 6 (1974): 113–73; and Harry Braverman, *Labor and Monopoly Capital* (New York: Monthly Review Press, 1974).

8. Michael Burawoy, *Constraint and Manipulation in Industrial Conflict* (Lusaka: Institute for African Studies, Communication no. 10, 1974), chaps. 2 and 3. The lashing job seems to have originated in the South African gold mines and was later adopted in the Zambian copper mines.

9. Arthur Stinchcombe, "Social Structure and Organizations," in *Handbook of Organizations*, ed. James March (Chicago: Rand McNally, 1965), pp. 142–69. Interestingly, Stinchcombe does write that "the main exceptions to the generalizations are in 'machine building' industries. These industries, whether building ships, locomotives and railroad cars, machine tools, automobiles, aircraft, electrical machinery, all have modern forms of organization, whatever their age" (p. 159)—as opposed to the more normal correlation between age and organizational form of industry. Paradoxically, however, the technology and work organization of machine shops have remained essentially the same since the Industrial Revolution. Yet, according to Stinchcombe, the "structural characteristics" of these industries have always been modern. Clearly, Stinchcombe is measuring something very different from the structure of work. (In fact, he measures "structure" by the proportion of unpaid family members, proportion of self-employed and family workers, clerical workers as a proportion of administrative workers, and professionals as a proportion of people occupying positions of authority.) It appears that he is is measuring the size of certain "buffering" elements of an organization that insulate the productive process from the environment. Accordingly, when the buffering elements are weak, as in agriculture, the production process is most vulnerable to influence from external factors and is therefore also subject to transformation. On the other hand, where the buffering elements are relatively strong, as in the machine industry, the structure of work is protected from environmental contingencies and will therefore tend to persist. External change is absorbed by a bureaucratic apparatus. Only in this way can we explain the growth of bureaucratic elements, on the one hand, and the persistence of the structure of work, on the other. In other words, the positive correlation between Stinchcombe's organizational characteristics and age of the industry tends

to obscure the absence of a correlation between the structure of work and the age of the industry. The alternative hypothesis I am suggesting is that certain organizations develop auxiliary institutions (possibly measured by Stinchcombe's organizational characteristics) that obstruct the transformation of the work process. Moreover, the older the industry, the less well developed are these institutions (according to Stinchcombe's data) and the more likely it is that the work process will undergo transformation. Further, the more modern the organization—that is, the more developed the buffer institutions—the more difficult it is to transform the technology and the work process.

10. Michael Burawoy, *The Colour of Class on the Copper Mines: From African Advancement to Zambianization* (Manchester: Manchester University Press for the Institute of African Studies, Zambian Papers no. 7, 1972).

11. See, for example, Reinhard Bendix, *Work and Authority in Industry* (New York: Wiley, 1956), pp. 34–73.

12. Morris Janowitz adequately describes the endeavors of such development scholars:

> In particular, in *Old Societies and New States,* edited by Clifford Geertz, they have sought to identify those patterns of social and cultural stratification that offer the strongest barrier to "modernization." They have probed the consequences of different types of primordial sentiments— ethnic, descent group, language, race, and religion—on the development of "civil" or secular politics. [*Political Conflict* (Chicago: Quadrangle Books, 1970), p. 24]

This approach to development has deservedly come under attack from writers like Gundar Frank (*Latin America: Underdevelopment or Revolution* [New York: Monthly Review Press, 1969], chap. 2).

13. "Anthropological Problems Arising from the African Industrial Revolution," in *Social Change in Modern Africa,* ed. Aidan Southall (London: Oxford University Press for Internal African Institute, 1961), pp. 69–70.

14. A. L. Epstein, *Politics in an Urban African Community* (Manchester: Manchester University Press, 1958).

15. Clyde Mitchell, *The Kalela Dance* (Manchester: Manchester University Press for the Rhodes-Livingstone Institute, Rhodes-Livingstone Paper no. 27, 1956).

16. Southall, *Social Change in Modern Africa,* p. 19.

17. Burawoy, *The Colour of Class,* chap. 9.

18. Robert Bates, *Unions, Parties, and Political Development* (New Haven: Yale University Press, 1971).

19. Burawoy, "Another Look at the Mineworker," *African Social Research* no. 14 (1972): 239-87.

20. Burawoy, *Constraint and Manipulation in Industrial Conflict;* idem, *The Colour of Class;* and Bruce Kapferer, *Strategy and Transaction in an African Factory* (Manchester: Manchester University Press, 1972).

Bibliography

Adorno, Theodor. "Sociology and Psychology." *New Left Review* 46 (November-December 1967): 67-80; 47 (January-February 1968): 79-99.

Althusser, Louis. *For Marx.* London: Allen Lane, 1969.

————. *Lenin and Philosophy and Other Essays.* London: New Left Books, 1971.

Amin, Samir. *Unequal Development.* New York: Monthly Review Press, 1976.

Anderson, Perry. *Lineages of the Abolutist State.* London: New Left Books, 1974.

Argyris, Chris. *Integrating the Individual and the Organization.* New York: John Wiley, 1964.

Aronowitz, Stanley. *False Promises: The Shaping of American Working Class Consciousness.* New York: McGraw-Hill Book Co., 1973.

Bachrach, Peter, and Baratz, Morton. *Power and Poverty: Theory and Practice.* New York: Oxford University Press, 1970.

Baldamus, William. *Efficiency and Effort.* London: Tavistock Institute of Human Relations, 1961.

Balibar, Etienne. "The Basic Concepts of Historical Materialism." Pp. 201-308 in Louis Althusser and Etienne Balibar, *Reading Capital.* New York: Pantheon, 1970.

Banaji, Jairus. "Modes of Production in a Materialist Conception of History." *Capital and Class* 3 (Autumn 1977): 1–44.

Baran, Paul, and Sweezy, Paul. *Monopoly Capital.* New York: Monthly Review Press, 1966.

Baritz, Leon. *The Servants of Power: A History of the Use of Social Science in American Industry.* New York: John Wiley, 1965.

Bates, Robert. *Unions, Parties and Political Development.* New Haven: Yale University Press, 1971.

Behrend, Hilda. "A Fair Day's Work." *Scottish Journal of Political Economy* 8 (1961): 102–18.

Bell, Daniel. *The End of Ideology.* New York: Free Press, 1960.

Bendix, Reinhard. *Work and Authority in Industry: Ideologies of Management in the Course of Industrialization.* New York: John Wiley, 1956.

Benjamin, Jessica. "The End of Internalization: Adorno's Social Psychology." *Telos* 32 (Summer 1977): 42–64.

Beynon, Huw. *Working for Ford.* London: Allen Lane, 1973.

Blau, Peter. *The Dynamics of Bureaucracy.* Chicago: University of Chicago Press, 1955.

Blauner, Robert. *Alienation and Freedom.* Chicago: University of Chicago Press, 1964.

Bowles, Samuel, and Gintis, Herbert. *Schooling in Capitalist America.* New York: Basic Books, 1976.

Brandes, Stuart. *American Welfare Capitalism, 1880–1940.* Chicago: University of Chicago Press, 1976.

Braverman, Harry. *Labor and Monopoly Capital.* New York: Monthly Review Press, 1974.

Brenner, Robert. "The Origins of Capitalist Development: A Critique of Neo-Smithian Marxism." *New Left Review* 104 (July–August 1977): 25–92.

Brody, David. "The Rise and Decline of Welfare Capitalism." Pp. 147–78 in *Change and Continuity in Twentieth Century America: The 1920's,* edited by John Braeman, Robert Brenner, and David Brody. Columbus, Ohio: Ohio State University Press, 1968.

Burawoy, Michael. "Another Look at the Mineworker." *African Social Research* 14 (1972): 239–87.

———. *The Colour of Class in the Copper Mines: From African Advancement to Zambianization.* Manchester: Manchester University Press for the Institute of African Studies, Zambian Papers no. 7, 1972.

———. *Constraint and Manipulation in Industrial Conflict.* Lusaka: Institute for African Studies, Communication 10, 1974.

———. "The Politics of Production and the Production of Politics: A Comparative Analysis of Piecework Machine Shops in the United

States and Hungary." *Political Power and Social Theory* 1 (1979).

―――. *The Politics of Production.* London: New Left Books, forthcoming.

Burns, Tom, and Stalker, G. M. *The Management of Innovation.* London: Tavistock Publications, 1961.

Cardan, Paul. *See* Cornelius Castoriadis.

Carey, Alex. "The Hawthorne Studies: A Radical Criticism." *American Sociological Review* 32 (1967): 403-16.

Carr, Edward H. *The New Society.* London: Macmillan, 1951.

Castoriadis, Cornelius. "The Hungarian Source." *Telos* 29 (Fall 1976): 4-22.

―――. "On the History of the Workers' Movement." *Telos* 30 (Winter 1976-77): 3-42.

―――. *Redefining Revolution.* London: Solidarity Pamphlet 44, n.d.

Chandler, Alfred. *Strategy and Structure: Chapters in the History of the American Industrial Enterprise.* Cambridge, Mass.: M.I.T. Press, 1962.

Crozier, Michel. *The Bureaucratic Phenomenon.* Chicago: University of Chicago Press, 1964.

―――. "Comparing Structures and Comparing Games." Pp. 197-207 in *European Contributions to Organization Theory,* edited by G. Hofstede and M. Kassem. Amsterdam: Van Gorcum, 1976.

Dalton, Melville. "The Industrial Rate Buster." *Applied Anthropology* 7 (1948): 5-18.

―――. *Men Who Manage.* New York: John Wiley, 1966.

De Man, Henri. *The Psychology of Socialism.* New York: Henry Holt, 1927.

Dennis, Norman; Henriques, F.; and Slaughter, C. *Coal Is Our Life.* London: Eyre & Spottiswoode, 1956.

Ditton, Jason. "Moral Horror versus Folk Terror: Output Restriction, Class and the Social Organization of Exploitation." *Sociological Review* 24 (1976): 519-44.

―――. "Perks, Pilferage, and the Fiddle." *Theory and Society* 4 (1977): 39-71.

Doeringer, Peter, and Piore, Michael. *Internal Labor Markets and Manpower Analysis.* Lexington, Mass.: D. C. Heath, 1971.

Dore, Ronald. *British Factory—Japanese Factory.* Berkeley and Los Angeles: University of California Press, 1973.

Dubin, Robert. "Industrial Workers' Worlds: A Study of the Central Life Interests of Industrial Workers." *Social Problems* 3 (1956): 131-42.

Edwards, Richard. "The Social Relations of Production in the Firm and Labor Market Structure." *Politics and Society* 5 (1975): 83-108.

Emery, F. E., and Trist, E. L. "The Causal Texture of Organizational Environments." *Human Relations* 18 (1963): 20-26.

Engels, Frederick. "Socialism: Utopian and Scientific." Pp. 605-39 in *The*

Marx-Engels Reader, edited by Robert Tucker. New York: W. W. Norton, 1972.

Epstein, A. L. *Politics in an Urban African Community.* Manchester: Manchester University Press, 1958.

Etzioni, Amitai. *A Comparative Analysis of Complex Organizations.* New York: Free Press, 1961.

Foucault, Michel. *Discipline and Punish.* New York: Pantheon, 1977.

Fox, Alan. *Beyond Contract: Work, Power and Trust Relations.* London: Faber & Faber, 1974.

Frank, Gundar. *Latin America: Underdevelopment or Revolution?* New York: Monthly Review Press, 1969.

Franke, R. H., and Kaul, J. D. "The Hawthorne Experiments: First Statistical Interpretation." *American Sociological Review* 43 (1978): 623–43.

Friedland, William, and Barton, Amy. *Destalking the Wily Tomato.* Manuscript. Department of Applied Behavioral Sciences, College of Agriculture and Environmental Sciences, University of California, Davis, 1975.

———; Barton, Amy; and Thomas, Robert. "Manufacturing Green Gold: The Conditions and Social Consequences of Lettuce Harvest Mechanization." Manuscript. University of California, Santa Cruz, 1978.

Friedlander, Peter. *The Emergence of a UAW Local, 1936–1939.* Pittsburgh: University of Pittsburgh Press, 1975.

Geertz, Clifford. *The Interpretation of Cultures.* New York: Basic Books, 1973.

Genovese, Eugene. *Roll, Jordan, Roll.* New York: Vintage Books, 1976.

Gluckman, Max. "Anthropological Problems Arising from the African Industrial Revolution." Pp. 67–82 in *Social Change in Modern Africa,* edited by Aidan Southall. London: Oxford University Press for Internal African Institute, 1961.

Godelier, Maurice. *Rationality and Irrationality in Economics.* New York: Monthly Review Press, 1972.

———. "Structure and Contradiction in *Capital.*" Pp. 334–68 in *Ideology in Social Science,* edited by Robin Blackburn. New York: Vintage Books, 1973.

Goldthorpe, John; Lockwood, David; Bechhofer, Frank; and Platt, Jennifer. *The Affluent Worker: Industrial Attitudes and Behaviour.* New York: Cambridge University Press, 1968.

Gorz, André, ed. *The Division of Labor.* Atlantic Highlands, N.J.: Humanities Press, 1976.

Gouldner, Alvin. *The Dialectic of Ideology and Technology.* New York: Seabury Press, 1976.

————. *Patterns of Industrial Bureaucracy.* New York: Free Press, 1954.

Gramsci, Antonio. *Selections from Prison Notebooks.* New York: International Publishers, 1971.

Green, James. "Fighting on Two Fronts: Working Class Militancy in the 1940's." *Radical America* 9, nos. 4-5 (1975): 7-48.

Gutman, Herbert. *Work, Culture and Society in Industrializing America.* New York: Vintage Books, 1977.

Habermas, Jürgen. *Legitimation Crisis.* Boston: Beacon Press, 1975.

————. *Theory and Practice.* Boston: Beacon Press, 1973.

Harrison, Bennett. "Public Employment and the Theory of the Dual Economy." Pp. 41-76 in *The Political Economy of Public Service Employment,* edited by H. L. Sheppard, B. Harrison, and W. J. Spring. Lexington, Mass.: Heath-Lexington, 1972.

Hearn, Francis. "Toward a Critical Theory of Play." *Telos* 30 (Winter 1976-77): 145-60.

Heller, Agnes. *The Theory of Need in Marx.* London: Allison & Busby, 1976.

Hilton, Rodney. "Freedom and Villeinage in England." *Past and Present* 31 (July 1965): 3-19.

————. *A Medieval Society.* London: Weidenfeld & Nicolson, 1966.

————, ed. *The Transition from Feudalism to Capitalism.* London: New Left Books, 1976.

Hindess, Barry, and Hirst, Paul. *Pre-Capitalist Modes of Production.* London: Routledge & Kegan Paul, 1975.

Hobsbawm, Eric. *Labouring Men.* London: Weidenfeld & Nicolson, 1964.

Homans, George. *English Villagers of the Thirteenth Century.* New York: W. W. Norton, 1975.

————. *The Human Group.* New York: Harcourt, Brace & Co., 1955.

Horkheimer, Max. *Critical Theory: Selected Essays.* New York: Seabury Press, 1972.

———— and Adorno, Theodor. *The Dialectic of Enlightenment.* New York: Seabury Press, 1972.

Hughes, Everett. "The Knitting of Racial Groups in Industry." *American Sociological Review* 11 (1946): 512-19.

Jacoby, Russell. *Social Amnesia.* Boston: Beacon Press, 1975.

Janowitz, Morris. "Changing Patterns of Organizational Authority: The Military Establishment." *Administrative Science Quarterly* 3 (1959): 473-93.

————. *Political Conflict.* Chicago: Quadrangle Books, 1970.

————. *The Professional Soldier.* New York: Free Press, 1960.

Jennings, Edward. "Wildcat! The Wartime Strike Wave in Auto." *Radical America* 9, nos. 4-5 (1975): 77-105.

Johnstone, Frederick. *Class, Race and Gold.* London: Routledge & Kegan Paul, 1976.

Kapferer, Bruce. *Strategy and Transaction in an African Factory.* Manchester: Manchester University Press, 1972.

Kerr, Clark. *Labor and Management in Industrial Society.* New York: Doubleday, 1964.

———; Dunlop, J. T.; Harrison, F. H.; and Myers, C. A. *Industrialism and Industrial Man.* Cambridge, Mass.: Harvard University Press, 1960.

——— and Fisher, Lloyd. "Plant Sociology: The Elite and the Aborigines." Pp. 281–309 in *Common Frontiers of the Social Sciences,* edited by Mirra Komarovsky. Glencoe: Free Press, 1957.

——— and Siegal, Abraham. "The Interindustry Propensity to Strike—An International Comparison." Pp. 189–212 in *Industrial Conflict,* edited by Arthur Kornhauser, Robert Dubin, and Arthur M. Ross. New York: McGraw-Hill, 1954.

Klein, Stuart. *Workers under Stress: The Impact of Work Pressure on Group Cohesion.* Lexington, Ky.: University of Kentucky Press, 1971.

Kolko, Gabriel. *The Triumph of Conservatism.* New York: Free Press, 1963.

Kornblum, William. *Blue Collar Community.* Chicago: University of Chicago Press, 1974.

Korsch, Karl. "What Is Socialization?" *New German Critique* 6 (Fall 1975): 60–81.

Kosminsky, E. A. *Studies in the Agrarian History of England in the Thirteenth Century.* Oxford: Basil Blackwell, 1956.

Landsberger, Henry. *Hawthorne Revisited.* Ithaca, N.Y.: Cornell University Press, 1958.

Lawrence, Paul, and Lorsch, Jay. *Organizations and Environment.* Boston: Graduate School of Business Administration, Harvard University Press, 1967.

Lefort, Claude. "The Age of Novelty." *Telos* 29 (Fall 1976): 23–38.

Lichtenstein, Nelson. "Defending the No-Strike Pledge: CIO Politics during World War II." *Radical America* 9, nos. 4–5 (1975): 49–76.

Likert, Rensis. *New Patterns of Management.* New York: McGraw-Hill, 1961.

Lipset, Seymour Martin. *Political Man.* New York: Doubleday, 1959.

———; Trow, Martin; and Coleman, James. *Union Democracy.* Glencoe, Ill.: Free Press, 1956.

Lockwood, David. "In Search of the Traditional Worker." Pp. 239–51 in *Working Class Images of Society,* edited by Martin Bulmer. London: Routledge & Kegan Paul, 1976.

Lukács, Georg. *History and Class Consciousness.* Cambridge, Mass.: M.I.T. Press, 1968.

Lupton, Tom. *On the Shop Floor.* Oxford: Pergamon Press, 1963.

Maier, Charles. *Recasting Bourgeois Europe.* Princeton: Princeton University Press, 1975.

Mann, Michael. "The Social Cohesion of Liberal Democracy." *American Sociological Review* 35 (1970): 423–39.

————. *Consciousness and Action among the Western Working Class.* Cambridge, Eng.: At the University Press, 1973.

March, James, and Simon, Herbert. *Organizations.* New York: John Wiley, 1958.

Marcuse, Herbert. *Eros and Civilization.* Boston: Beacon Press, 1955.

————. *An Essay on Liberation.* Boston: Beacon Press, 1969.

————. *One Dimensional Man.* Boston: Beacon Press, 1964.

Marx, Karl. *Capital.* 3 vols. New York: International Publishers, 1967.

————. *Early Writings.* New York: Vintage Books, 1975.

————. "Preface to *A Contribution to the Critique of Political Economy.*" In *The Marx-Engels Reader,* edited by Robert Tucker. New York: W. W. Norton, 1972.

———— and Engels, Frederick. *The German Ideology.* New York: International Publishers, 1970.

Mathewson, Stanley. *Restriction of Output among Unorganized Workers.* New York: Viking Press, 1931.

Mayo, Elton. *The Human Problems of an Industrial Civilization.* New York: Macmillan, 1933.

Merton, Robert. *Social Theory and Social Structure.* New York: Free Press, 1968.

Miliband, Ralph. *The State in Capitalist Society.* New York: Basic Books, 1969.

Mitchell, Clyde. *The Kalela Dance.* Manchester: Manchester University Press for the Rhodes-Livingston Institute, Rhodes-Livingstone Papers 27, 1956.

Montgomery, David. "The 'New Unionism' and the Transformation in Workers' Consciousness." *Journal of Social History* 7 (Summer 1974): 509–29.

————. "Workers' Control of Machine Production in the Nineteenth Century." *Labor History* 17 (Fall 1976): 485–509.

Nichols, Theo, and Beynon, Huw. *Living with Capitalism: Class Relations and the Modern Factory.* London: Routledge & Kegan Paul, 1977.

Noble, David. "Before the Fact: Social Choice in Machine Design." Paper presented at the National Convention of the Organization of American Historians, April 1978.

———. *America by Design: Science, Technology, and the Rise of Corporate Capitalism.* New York: Alfred A. Knopf, 1977.

O'Connor, James. *The Fiscal Crisis of the State.* New York: St. Martin's Press, 1973.

Offe, Claus. "The Theory of the Capitalist State and the Problem of Policy Formation." Pp. 125–44 in *Stress and Contradiction in Modern Capitalism,* edited by Leon Lindberg, Robert Alford, Colin Crouch, and Claus Offe. Lexington, Mass.: Lexington Books–D. C. Heath, 1975.

Parsons, Talcott. *Sociological Theory and Modern Society.* New York: Free Press, 1967.

Polanyi, Karl. *The Great Transformation.* New York: Reinhart, 1944.

Postan, M. M. *The Medieval Economy and Society.* Harmondsworth, Eng.: Penguin Books, 1975.

Poulantzas, Nicos. *Classes in Contemporary Capitalism.* London: New Left Books, 1975.

———. *Political Power and Social Classes.* London: New Left Books, 1973.

———. *Fascism and Dictatorship.* London: New Left Books, 1974.

Przeworski, Adam. "Capitalist Democracy and the Transition to Socialism." Manuscript, University of Chicago, 1978.

Radcliffe-Brown, A. R. *Structure and Function in Primitive Society.* London: Cohen & West, 1952.

Reich, Wilhelm. *Sex-Pol.* New York: Vintage Books, 1972.

Reuther, Walter. "Individualism vs. Unionism." Pp. 144–49 in *Source Book on Labor,* edited by Neil Chamberlain. New York: McGraw Hill, 1958.

Roethlisberger, F. J., and Dickson, William. *Management and the Worker.* Cambridge, Mass.: Harvard University Press, 1939.

Ross, Arthur, and Hartman, Paul. *Changing Patterns of Industrial Conflict.* New York: John Wiley, 1960.

Rothschild, Emma. *Paradise Lost: The Decline of the Auto-Industrial Age.* New York: Vintage Books, 1974.

Roy, Donald. "'Banana Time': Job Satisfaction and Informal Interaction." *Human Organization* 18 (1958): 158–68.

———. "Efficiency and the Fix: Informal Intergroup Relations in a Piecework Machine Shop." *American Journal of Sociology* 60 (1954): 255–66.

———. "Quota Restriction and Goldbricking in a Machine Shop." *American Journal of Sociology* 57 (1952): 427–42.

———. "Restriction of Output in a Piecework Machine Shop." Ph.D. dissertation, University of Chicago, 1952.

————. "Work Satisfaction and Social Reward in Quota Achievement." *American Sociological Review* 18 (1953): 507–14.

Scheinberg, Stephen. "The Development of Corporation Labor Policy, 1900–1940." Ph.D. dissertation, University of Wisconsin, 1966.

Seidman, Joel. *American Labor from Defense to Reconversion.* Chicago: University of Chicago Press, 1953.

Selznick, Philip. *Law, Society, and Industrial Justice.* New York: Russell Sage Foundation, 1969.

————. *TVA and the Grass Roots.* Berkeley: University of California Press, 1949.

Sennett, Richard, and Cobb, Jonathan. *The Hidden Injuries of Class.* New York: Random House, 1972.

Serrin, William. *The Company and the Union.* New York: Vintage Books, 1974.

Sheppard, Harold, and Herrick, Neal. *Where Have All the Robots Gone?* New York: Free Press, 1972.

Simons, H. J., and Simons, R. E. *Class and Colour in South Africa 1850–1950.* Harmondsworth, Eng.: Penguin Books, 1969.

Stinchcombe, Arthur. "Social Structure and Organizations." Pp. 142–69 in *Handbook of Organizations,* edited by James March. Chicago: Rand McNally, 1965.

Stone, Katherine. "The Origins of Job Structures in the Steel Industry." *Review of Radical Political Economics* 6 (1974): 113–73.

Swados, Harvey. *On the Line.* Boston: Little, Brown, 1957.

Taira, Koji. *Economic Development and the Labor Market in Japan.* New York: Columbia University Press, 1970.

————. "Internal Labor Markets, Human Resource Utilization, and Economic Growth." Paper presented at the Urban Labor Market Research Conference, 1974.

Tannenbaum, Arnold. *Control in Organizations.* New York: McGraw-Hill, 1967.

Taylor, Frederick Winslow. *Scientific Management.* New York: Harper & Bros., 1947.

————. *Shop Management.* New York: American Society of Mechanical Engineers, 1903.

Thompson, E. P. *The Making of the English Working Class.* London: Victor Gollancz, 1963.

Thompson, James. *Organizations in Action.* New York: McGraw-Hill, 1967.

Trist, E. L.; Higgin, G. W.; Murray, H.; and Pollock, A. B. *Organizational Choice.* London: Tavistock Publications, 1963.

Van Onselen, Charles. *Chibaro.* London: Pluto Press, 1976.

Warner, William Lloyd, and Low, J. *The Social System of a Modern Factory.* New Haven: Yale University Press, 1947.

Weber, Max. *Economy and Society.* 3 vols. New York: Bedminster Press, 1968.

Wedderburn, Dorothy, and Crompton, Rosemary. *Workers' Attitudes and Technology.* Cambridge, Eng.: At the University Press, 1972.

Weinstein, James. *The Corporate Ideal in the Liberal State: 1900-1918.* Boston: Beacon Press, 1968.

Westergaard, John. "The Rediscovery of the Cash Nexus." Pp. 111-38 in *The Socialist Register 1970,* edited by Ralph Miliband and John Saville. London: Merlin Press, 1970.

Whyte, William Foot. *Money and Motivation.* New York: Harper, 1955.

Wilensky, Harold. "Human Relations in the Work Place: An Appraisal of Some Recent Research." Pp. 25-59 in *Research in Industrial Human Relations,* edited by Conrad Arensberg. New York: Harper & Row, 1957.

Williams, William Appleman. *The Contours of American History.* Cleveland: World Publishing Co., 1961.

Wolpe, Harold. "Capitalism and Cheap Labor Power in South Africa: From Segregation to Apartheid." *Economy and Society* 1 (1972): 425-56.

Wright, Erik Olin. *Class, Crisis and the State.* London: New Left Books, 1978.

Index